CORPORATE MAN TO CORPORATE SKUNK

That's a brilliant idea. But how could it possibly work in my organization?

How often do you think as you read a business book that if only you could ask the author a simple question you could transform your organization?

Capstone is creating a unique partnership between authors and readers, delivering for the first time in business book publishing a genuine after-sales service for book buyers. Simply visit Capstone's home page on **http://www.book-shop.co.uk/capstone/** to leave your question (with details of date and place of purchase of a copy of *Corporate Man to Corporate Skunk*) and Stuart Crainer will try to answer it.

Capstone authors travel and consult extensively so we do not promise 24-hour turnaround. But that one question answered might just jump-start your company and your career.

Capstone is more than a publisher. It is an electronic clearing house for pioneering business thinking, putting the creators of new business ideas in touch with the people who use them.

CORPORATE MAN TO CORPORATE SKUNK

The
TOM PETERS
Phenomenon
A Biography

Stuart Crainer

CAPSTONE

For Ro

Corporate Man: A managerial worker whose career is characterized by security; grey suits; unwavering support for the status quo; an ability to pass the buck; and loyalty to the organization. Regularly and wrongly reported as being extinct.

Corporate Skunk: Someone who is part of a Skunk Works, an innovative, fast-moving, and sometimes eccentric activity operating on the fringes of a corporation. First used at Lockheed in the 1940s.

*"No one rises so high
as he who knows not whither he is going"*
Oliver Cromwell

First published 1997 by
Capstone Publishing Limited
Oxford Centre for Innovation
Mill Street
Oxford OX2 0JX
United Kingdom

British Library Cataloguing in Publication Data
A CIP catalogue record for this book is available from the British Library

ISBN 1-900961-01-6

Typeset in 11/14 pt Plantin by
Archetype, Stow-on-the-Wold
http://ourworld/compuserve.com/homepages/Archetype
Printed and bound in Great Britain by
T.J. International Ltd, Padstow, Cornwall

This book is printed on acid-free paper

Contents

Nine: Uncle Tom's Cabin

Acknowledgments

As you will discover in the story of Tom Peters, books always have a history. I first approached Tom Peters over five years ago about the idea of writing a biography. He declined to take part. The time, he said, was not right. The idea hung around – in my mind at least. In 1996, having secured agreement from a publisher, Tom Peters agreed to cooperate in my research. He made himself available for extensive interviews on his work and career. He also provided numerous of his publications. While Tom Peters has generously supported the writing of this book in these ways, he has had no control over its content. Any inaccuracies and ommissions are my responsibility.

I am also grateful to the many other people who agreed to be interviewed. Lennart Arvedson, a friend of Peters' since their time at Stanford, provided a wealth of insights; Bill Matassoni of McKinsey & Co. talked about the genesis of the initial research which led to *In Search of Excellence*; Richard Pascale explained his involvement in the development of the Seven S framework; and Bob Le Duc was highly informative on the development of the Tom Peters Group.

Former McKinsey consultants provided an abundance of information. I am grateful to Jim Balloun, Michael Lanning, George Binney, and Andrew Campbell. Those who have been on the receiving end of a Peters' case study also shed a great deal of light on his approach and personality. In particular, Robert Buckman of Buckman Laboratories; Hilary Cropper, chief executive of FI Group, and Ralph Ardill, marketing director of Imagination, gave their time and insights generously.

Colleagues of Tom Peters, past and present, were a useful source of anecdotes and opinion. Paul Cohen, managing editor of *Leader to Leader,* was extremely helpful, as was Jayne Pearl.

I would also like to thank others I interviewed during the course of my research: Sven Atterhed of the Foresight Group; Bo Burlingham of *Inc.* magazine; Colin Carnell and Ray Wild of Henley Management College; Donna Carpenter of Word Works; Daniel T. Carroll; Ben Cole; Gay Haskins of London Business School; Art Kleiner, author of *The Age of Heretics*; Joel Kurtzman, editor of *Strategy & Business*; Jan Lapidoth of the Customer Focus Institute in Stockholm; Don Laurie of Laurie International; Henry Mintzberg; Michael Pieschewski; Philip Sadler; Blair Sheppard of Duke University; Wickham Skinner; Albert Vicere of Penn State; Randy White; and Max Worcester of *Frankfurter Allgemeine Zeitung.*

I am grateful to the many other people I have corresponded with in the course of my research. These include Percy Barnevik of Asea Brown Boveri; Warren Bennis of the University of Southern California; James Brian Quinn of Dartmouth College's Amos Tuck School; James March of Stanford University; Herbert Simon of Carnegie-Mellon University; Bill Davis, CEO of Holland Mark Martin; Tom Horton; Herb Kelleher of Southwest Airlines; Mimi Webb, widow of the late Gene Webb; Harold Leavitt; Fons Trompenaars; and Lars Kolind of Oticon.

Gerry Griffin of London Business School and Liza Jones of Henley Management College were also helpful in giving me the opportunity to use their library resources. Robert Sharrock kindly read through the manuscript.

I am grateful to the *Harvard Business Review* for permission to use extracts from Robert Hayes and William Abernathy's "Managing our way to economic decline," *Harvard Business Review,* July/August 1980 © 1980 by the President and Fellows of Harvard College. All rights reserved. And to Simon & Schuster for permission to use the table from *Grow to be Great* by Dwight Gertz & Joao Baptista, Free Press, New York, 1995.

Paul Stringer dragged the book to the printers. Finally, Mark Allin and Richard Burton of Capstone Publishing were enthusiasts from the start and thoroughly skunkish.

ONE

THE BIRTH OF EXCELLENCE

" *Excellence came from a series of coincidences* "

Tom Peters

April 1978, San Francisco

"Tom, Larson wants to see you."

The messenger disappeared. The recipient laid back in his chair and looked out of the office window. Dressed in regulation office suit with white shirt and painfully drab tie, Thomas J. Peters looked faintly disheveled, as if he had been up all night working. In fact, he had – and his tiredness was made worse by a headache which seemed to have arrived with the job. In four years it had never really gone away. Too many late nights working, too many trips. He was thirty-six and it would be a year or two before he made partner. Perhaps it would end then.

From the pile of books and papers on his desk, Peters extricated a pad of paper and pen and headed off to find his boss. "I've gone to see Larson if anyone wants me," he said to no-one in particular as he walked through the sparsely populated office.

Arriving at Larson's office, Peters found it empty and sat down. He noticed his last report sitting on the filing cabinet. It looked pristine. Larson was OK but a real quant-jock, Peters thought, as he waited. "Too many words, not enough charts and figures," was Larson's perennial complaint. That's why Larson never read them. Then, Larson returned.

"Ah, Tom, good to see you. I've got a problem."

Peters reclined in the chair. Larson's problems usually led to him being dispatched to some far-flung location at a moment's notice. He was ready for the worst. In the past year he had traveled the world at the company's expense. It sounded exciting, and it would've been once, but it wasn't. The novelty had worn off long ago. Where this time? Nebraska, Alaska or Dakota?

"You know we're doing this quantitative stuff for Dart?"

Peters had heard the name but knew nothing about the work. Yet more figures and charts with a tidy conclusion and an even tidier invoice at the end of it.

"I know of it," he replied, congratulating himself on his tact. Larson seemed to have forgotten that he had just spent eight weeks away and was now deep into another project that was keeping him up all night.

"Well, the computer program's crashed and we can't make it," said Larson.

"Can't make what?"

"Next week's presentation. So, I've got a big problem. We've spent months getting all that stuff and it's great, and there's no way I can cancel. They'll be there expecting answers to the shit they're in."

Dart, Peters now remembered, was headquartered in LA, not Dakota anyway.

"Where do I come in? I know nothing about the project or the company. Remember I've been away, John."

"You've been running around the world and now it's time to earn your pay," said Larson, laughing. "I'll come to LA with you. Just get the stuff from your research, give it a sexy title and give the presentation. Then they're off my back, we'll sort out the program, and everyone's happy.'

"But I haven't got a presentation. I've just talked to people, got a stack of interview notes, and a pile of tapes waiting to be transcribed."

"Well, all you have to do is talk some more next week. It's Good Friday so it screws up Easter if you were going anywhere," said Larson.

"No, I wasn't," admitted Peters, surrendering to the inevitable.

"Just be there Tom," concluded Larson as the telephone rang.

Looking more disheveled and feeling the pounding of his headache, Tom headed back to his office. A sexy title? Not a chance.

The Charismatic Chameleon

One week later, on Good Friday 1978, Tom Peters gave his presentation to the Dart Corporation in Los Angeles. It was the birth of a management phenomenon which swept the business world and also elevated one of its parents into the pantheon of management gurus. Thomas J. Peters has since been transformed into the folksy and approachable Tom. The staid suits have been left behind, as have the do or die presentations. The older Peters, now in his fifties, is a multimillionaire, the best-known – and best-paid – management commentator and thinker the world has ever known.

Peters fills auditoriums in countries as far apart as New Zealand and Belgium. He travels the globe with startling regularity – he even named his horse "Frequent Flyer." His syndicated column appeared throughout the world until he brought it to a halt and his new books – "charismatic shockers" according to one reviewer – continue to sell in unprecedented quantities. The *Guinness Book of Business Records* cites Peters as "the highest paid management consultant" calculating that his income is $6.4 million per year from consultancy, lectures and book royalties.[1] Along the way he has been compared by *The Economist* to Ronald Reagan ("a great communicator"[2]); by himself to Bill Clinton, and, by occasional interviewers, to Harrison Ford.

As the comparisons suggest, Tom Peters is a chameleon. In person I have found him to be charming and humorous. He is charismatic – something that those who have encountered him all observe. He holds people in his sway by force of personality, energy, and intellect. Yet, he wants to be liked (hence the comparison with the political-chameleon, Bill Clinton). "Everyone wants to be liked but Tom *needs* to be liked. It comes with the profile. He wouldn't do what he does unless being liked was a major craving," says Jan Lapidoth, who first encountered Peters in the 1980s when Lapidoth was with the Swedish airline SAS. For all his wealth and bestsellers, Tom Peters wants to be liked. He wants to be accepted – as a writer, as an academic, as a serious thinker.

Peters the communicator-chameleon is forceful and vital, spreading his managerial gospel far and wide in a flood of passionate hyperbole. He describes himself in characteristic fashion as a "gadfly, curmudgeon, champion of bold failures, prince of disorder, maestro of zest, corporate cheerleader, lover of markets, capitalist pig, and card-carrying member of the American Civil Liberties Union." More bluntly, *BusinessWeek* has described him as business' "best friend and worst nightmare."[3]

Then there is Peters the recluse. "He is a very down-to-earth guy, very easy to talk to. But he is also a hermit who keeps his private life to himself," says consultant Don Laurie. The hermit-Peters spends his time in the country reading his way through the great works of literature – and anything else that comes his way. Peters is hungry for knowledge. He is curious and driven by a feeling that he knows so little. The arrogant strider of platforms is continually humbled by his ignorance. The public loudmouth is, privately, the keenest pupil in the class.

The worldly Peters has served in Vietnam, worked for the most prestigious consulting firm of them all, traveled the globe many times and sold millions of books. Yet, he retains a childlike air. "I've worked with a lot of successful people and most are a little bit crazy," reflects Michael Pieschewski who worked for the European arm of Peters' business. "Tom is not a very confident man. I've seen him disturbed when he doesn't feel safe or secure. He can degenerate into a child." The trained engineer is an *ingénue*. "He is a fabulous catalyst. When he talks of organizational revolution it is compelling and populist but, in part, he is as naive as hell," says Blair Sheppard, associate dean of Duke University's Fuqua School of Business.

Chameleons change color or simply slip away. They are as elusive as they are beautiful. When I talked to another of Peters' former employees, I could sense his discomfort in trying to pin down the essence of the man. He liked him. He was impressed by him. He enjoyed working with him. And yet, there was something else. "He can *be* a regular guy but I am not sure he *is* a regular guy," is how he eventually put it.

It is difficult to be a regular guy when you become a brand – ask Yves St. Laurent or Calvin Klein. Regularity breeds contempt, suspicion, and pure jealousy. And, Tom Peters is a brand. Peters *is* a business. His company, the Tom Peters Group generates revenues of millions of dollars from its Palo Alto headquarters. Its success is such that Peters is no longer the company's only star name commanding big bucks in the clamoring marketplace. But, its success is Tom Peters. No more and no less.

Tom Peters has spawned an industry – the management guru business – populated by an array of top academics, consultants, a sprinkling of former executives, and a fair share of charlatans. Competition is fierce and the pace fast. The world's managers demand a constant stream of books, seminars, conferences, and videos. And they want more. Ideas are packaged and repackaged. Names become brands and every grain of innovative thinking is exploited for all its worth. The bitchiness of academia is combined with the ruthlessness of the world of management consultancy.

In the middle of an interview with me, one star name asked for the tape recorder to be turned off. He then spent ten minutes outlining the inadequacies of the respected co-author of his bestseller – "I wrote it, the whole thing," he said. I was mystified that someone so bright and intellectually brilliant, should be so desperately childish and stupid.

I shouldn't have been so surprised. These people aren't playing for peanuts. The rewards are lucrative – ten thousand dollars does not buy you much of Peters' time. "Getting Mercedes- rather than Daihatsu-sized checks is a fair measure of competitive strength in my niche," he reflects.[4] And cynicism is rife. "Why suffer the hassles and indignities of running a business when you can earn more advising others how to do their job?" the cynics routinely ask.

And, amid the bucks, bullshit, and ballyhoo, there is Thomas J. Peters. It is a strange world for the renowned management guru, a world Peters was the first to inhabit. Fame and fortune are his. (Research showed American executives in 1996 ranked Peters as number one on "awareness and credibility of business leaders" – his credibility index score of 50 was more than twice that of the runner-up, a Seattle-based businessman called Bill Gates.)[5] Yet, they come with few of the usual caveats of fame and fortune. The paparazzi do not camp out on Peters lawn to find out what he is going to say or wear. (His lawn is big enough and he is always quotable but, given his dress sense, this is probably just as well.) Paparazzi or not, Peters has been quoted in virtually every newspaper on earth. Magazines and newspapers have featured profiles of Peters. He is rich, opinionated, working in an area which touches the lives of virtually everyone on earth. And yet, little is known about his roots, the genesis of his ideas or his influences. The man remains aloof.

There have, of course, been many interviews and profiles of Peters over the past few years. Like anyone who has been interviewed frequently, he plays the game. He gives a little away, a few titbits of information, and the journalists retreat, content with their story, their piece of the man. "With Tom you get a lot of his take on the world but little of him personally," says *Inc.*'s Bo Burlingham. Apocryphal stories gather momentum as each journalist pillages the cuttings file and adds another twist to a well-worn tale.

Throughout all this, Peters' private life has remained carefully under wraps. The only intrusion I found was a piece *People* magazine once ran on him. This in itself is surprising – he is a multimillionaire who has been married four times – but Peters guards his privacy. "It's interesting that someone who gives so much has managed to keep his private life so private," reflected one manager I interviewed. He has not become public property living his life out under a million flash bulbs. He is no Lee Iacocca, and for that the world can perhaps be thankful. And this is not a book about the private life of Tom Peters; it is one which seeks to examine the public growth of a private man and the evolution of his ideas which have, for better or worse, influenced executives the world over.

The Roots of
Excellence

For Peters, the presentation in Los Angeles during Easter 1978 was the turning point of his career and his life. In his search for a sexy title, Peters came up with excellence – a seemingly innocuous word. "The Dart presentation was called 'Excellence' – I've no idea why I called it that. It was about ideas that worked. It got a great response. That's the actual birth of excellence."

Excellence undoubtedly had a difficult birth and uncovering its roots is a tortuous and tangled process. The 1982 bestseller which Peters co-authored with his McKinsey colleague Robert Waterman, *In Search of Excellence*, proclaimed that excellence was born on July 4th, 1979 in The Hague in the Netherlands at a presentation to the board of Royal Dutch Shell. "If this research has a birthday, that was it," they write.[6] This discards the project's extensive pre-history.

History always starts somewhere. In this case the obvious starting point is December 1974 when Tom Peters joined the consultancy firm McKinsey & Company. For the next two years, until January 1976, Peters worked on the company's usual brand of high charging, senior level, strategic projects. Then he developed a kidney problem and took a "medical sabbatical" – in any other business he would have been called "sick," but not in the jargon-infested world of consultancy. Contemplating life from his sick-bed, Peters took the unconventional decision to extend his leave of absence. If McKinsey could do without him for a few months, why not extend it to a full year? He decided to spend his time completing his PhD at Stanford. "Half way through my Stanford MBA, I transferred to the PhD course and half finished it, but had no idea what to do my thesis on. I always assumed I would go back and complete it," says Peters. He decided to write his thesis on organizational behavior, and eventually received his PhD from Stanford in March 1977.

Returning to the cut-and-thrust of reality early in 1977, Peters found that McKinsey was in an unprecedented situation. The doyen of consultancy firms was facing intense competition. "Basically, McKinsey was getting beaten up by BCG [Boston Consulting Group] and BCG was beating up McKinsey not because it was better at client relations but because it had bright ideas," says Peters.

While McKinsey was selling its own innate brilliance, BCG was selling products and selling lots of them. Set up in 1964 by Bruce Henderson, BCG invented the BCG Matrix (which measures market growth and relative market share for all the businesses within a particular industry) and the Experience Curve (when the accumulated production of any goods or service doubles, unit costs in real terms have the potential to fall by 20 percent). Put like this, BCG's products don't exactly sound earth-shattering but, in the mid-1970s, big corporations were queuing at BCG's doors and at those of another relative upstart, Bain and Co.

With its offices filled with some of the world's smartest intellects, McKinsey decided to move into the ideas business. The feeling was that the company had become too process-oriented and its value to clients needed more input from that elusive consultancy ingredient, knowledge. To maintain its exalted position McKinsey needed to know more – and, perhaps more to the point, to demonstrate to the business world that it knew more. In 1976 it appointed (or elected in the unusual world of McKinsey) a new managing director, Ron Daniel, who had made his name in the sixties by championing decentralization. Daniel was charged with shifting the company's emphasis. Over the next 12 years, Daniel revived McKinsey. He later reflected that the job was "like trying to herd cats."

To start the process, Daniel took Fred Gluck (later to become managing director himself) and launched what Peters recalls as "a big game strategy project headed in New York. Daniel thought if ours died it made no difference." Eminently sensible and thoroughly conservative, McKinsey wanted to change but wasn't prepared to risk the company to do so.

In fact, McKinsey launched three "practices" (calling them "projects" or "initiatives" would have demeaned McKinsey's grand intent). Their aim was to consider the nature of the relationship between strategy, structure, and management effectiveness. Sexy it wasn't. One group was to review thinking on strategy, while another was to go back to the drawing board on organizational effectiveness. From McKinsey's perspective the work on strategy was crucial. Strategy was, after all, the cornerstone of its business. The organization practice, while not unimportant, was a catch-all showcase of what was worthwhile out there in the real world. Its brief was to figure out what McKinsey knew and what it needed to learn. Finally, there was the operations practice. This went nowhere. McKinsey couldn't convince itself, let alone others, that it belonged on the shop floor talking to factory workers.

At the time, Ron Daniel's number two was Warren Cannon, something of an *éminence grise* in the cloistered world of McKinsey. One of Cannon's portfolios was business schools. Cannon knew Peters had finished his PhD and asked if he would like to join the organization practice. After spending time recuperating and studying, Peters was more than willing, especially when he was told that he had to spend eight weeks traveling around the world gathering information. "It was a free plane ticket and interesting people," says Peters.

During the spring of 1977 he left his base at McKinsey's San Francisco office and traveled the world, visiting 12 business schools and a number of companies in the US and Europe. Somewhat surprisingly, given that Japan was the emerging industrial powerhouse, his first port of call was Scandinavia. "Tom called me and asked who should he see in Scandinavia," recalls Lennart Arvedson, a long-time Swedish friend of Peters who was then based in Stockholm working with the Business and Social Research Institute. "He arrived in Sweden after seeing Herb

Simon at Carnegie-Mellon, and I set up a few meetings in Norway and Sweden."

Among the meetings organized by Lennart Arvedson was one with Einar Thorsrud, a former war-time resistance leader and friend of Eric Trist, the British champion of industrial democracy. Thorsrud was founder of the Arbeidspsykologisk Institut in Oslo which had become the focal point for Scandinavian experiments in industrial democracy. At the time of Peters' visit, Thorsrud was applying the ideas of self-government to work teams on Norwegian oil tankers. This was about as far removed as you could get from the American corporate giants Peters was used to dealing with. McKinsey was more in tune with luxury liners than oil tankers. In Scandinavia, Peters also visited Volvo's factory floor, where technicians were taking over the flow of work, and the Saab-Scania factory outside Stockholm which was following a new socio-technical design. It was big industry, but not as Peters knew it.

"Tom was fascinated with what was going on in work-organization in Scandinavia – it was a concerted movement to find new ways of organizing work which tapped into human talent and made organizations more human and more effective. It really interested him," says Peters' Scandinavian guide, Lennart Arvedson. The visit had a profound and long-lasting effect on Peters' fledgling thinking on organizational effectiveness (when he came to give a copy of *In Search of Excellence* to Arvedson, Peters wrote inside: "These themes are your themes").

While Peters was doing the work, or what passed for work, he was not actually in charge of the project. McKinsey's hierarchical etiquette did not allow for someone relatively junior, such as Peters, to run a major project. At the time, Peters was an associate in the San Francisco office – the McKinsey hierarchy runs associate, principal, director. And so, a principal, Jim Bennett (then in McKinsey's Toronto office and now manager of Cleveland) got the job.

The starting point of the project was to look at the entire literature and current thinking on organizational effectiveness. Peters and Bennett concluded that obsessive concentration on the demonic twins, strategy and structure, was now outdated and unlikely to yield the expected corporate miracles. Instead, they suggested that other factors were also critically important and deserved more explicit attention. The only problem was identifying and codifying the exact nature of these mysterious "other factors."

Taking a stab at decoding these mysteries, Bennett and Peters argued that the impact of management style, systems and, importantly, management's guiding concepts, were little understood and often overlooked by academics. Peters pointed out that successful companies managed a greater number of variables than their less successful competitors. The innovative companies he had visited in Scandinavia and beyond weren't solely driven by the rigors of the bottom-line. They acknowledged that people mattered and that a committed and involved workforce was vital to corporate success.

Peters and Bennett were basically saying that strategy and structure were only part of the corporate puzzle. As McKinsey had built its business on its expertise in the fields of strategy and structure, it was not an easy message. And certainly not a message liable to accelerate Peters' movement up the hierarchy. A senior partner took Peters aside and gave him some advice: "You're going to be saying some things that people around here don't want to hear. So make sure you are always beyond reproach on the 'little stuff' – getting to client meetings early, dressing conservatively, etc."[7] The message was simple: if you're going to cause trouble make sure you play by the rules or you'll be on your way.

After concluding his round-the-world jaunt in the summer of 1977, Peters returned to be speedily dispatched to Copenhagen to present his findings to the McKinsey powers that be. (His presentation anticipated some of what became the Seven S model featured in *In Search of Excellence*.)

And that appeared to be that. Peters' conclusions remained vague and inconclusive. His eyes had been opened but he did not know where to focus next. Indeed, he was arguing that companies were more complex, vague and inconclusive than traditional theorists and practices had led executives to believe. But, following his Copenhagen presentation, they were obviously convincing enough for the project to continue. At the same time, there was little enthusiasm to suggest that it was likely to herald a significant change in McKinsey's thinking. The anticipated end-result would, following the age-old tradition of consultants, be a thick and largely unreadable report circulated to interested parties inside the tightknit web of McKinsey and its clients. McKinsey could show that it knew the latest thinking and that, in the war of ideas, it was up there fighting – or, at least, preparing a report on the possibility.

For the remainder of 1977 Peters carried on with his normal assignments. His filing cabinet bulged with the material he had collected on his travels, but it remained gathering dust. Excellence did not exist.

At this point, Jim Bennett was promoted and moved off the project. "We were then hunting for someone to take charge," recalls Peters. "Bob Waterman was the number two choice behind a guy in the London office, but Bob had a taste for this stuff. He was chosen early in 1978 because he was an American and based in San Francisco." On such prejudices are important decisions made – even in somewhere like McKinsey.

Robert H. Waterman Junior was a McKinsey director who had joined the company in 1963.[8] During the late sixties and early seventies, he had worked extensively with companies which were restructuring and decentralizing. A safe pair of hands, he was then dispatched to Australia where he had been charged with turning round the fortunes of McKinsey's Australian operation. After accomplishing his managerial task, Waterman (somewhat unusually for a McKinsey partner) spent a year teaching at IMEDE in Lausanne, Switzerland, before returning to McKinsey's San Francisco office. He first met Peters late in 1975 when Waterman moved into the corner office on the same floor as Peters.

Though he had been with McKinsey for 15 years, 12 months' absence had, to some extent, opened Waterman's eyes. His management experience in Australia had also given him a new perspective. In McKinsey there is precious little opportunity to actually manage. Consultants shuttle from assignment to assignment, fighting hard to manage their own time and sanity rather than managing others.

The two were an unlikely combination, though Peters later

referred to Waterman as "a kindred spirit."[9] Peters was opinion-ated and operated with his foot flat to the floor all of the time; Waterman was more contemplative and cautious. "[We] were both engineers by training (and disposition – or we wouldn't have been at McKinsey in the first place)," says Peters. "But Bob enjoyed painting as much as consulting. And I thought curling up with good, circular fiction was far more pleasurable than perusing the wooden analyses in the latest management journals."[10]

One of the duo's colleagues in the San Francisco office was McKinsey veteran, Jim Balloun. "Bob was always one of the most thoughtful people you could ever imagine. He was one of the most gifted consultants, not only in McKinsey. Bob was always a guy who took a fresh approach," Balloun recalls. Stanford Business School's Harold Leavitt provides a similar view of Waterman. "I didn't meet Bob Waterman until late in the game, after their book I think. Bob is much more soft spoken and careful, but, like Tom, he is also a man of high integrity and decency."[11]

Waterman was the father figure, though only six years older; while Peters was the bright but reckless junior half of the partnership. "Waterman is quiet, engaging and affable. You could imagine him being a senior partner in a consulting firm. You would go to him if you had a problem and then he'd be behind you all the way," says the writer Art Kleiner, author of *The Age of Heretics*. A photograph of the duo (later used for the promotion of *In Search of Excellence*) showed a seated Peters looking engagingly up at Waterman in a book-lined office. It is the classic master–pupil pose. "Waterman was a natural foil for Peters; he had a gift for speaking plainly, in a subdued and reasonable way that raised controversies without raising hackles. He was a cracker-jack networker and an avid reader, who kept pumping Peters for all the source material he'd gathered," concludes Art Kleiner.[12]

Under Waterman's quiet but sure direction, the organization practice began to gain momentum. The team expanded. One of the interested observers of its development was Bill Matassoni. After finishing an MBA at Harvard, Matassoni worked as a consultant in the not-for-profit sector. "I wasn't sure I wanted to be in business, but then I was approached by McKinsey. I said if you're looking for a PR guy I don't know a single reporter. But I had some ideas about what they could do and took the job," he says. Matassoni headed up McKinsey's communications.

Initially, Bill Matassoni was drawn to the strategy practice, which was, after all, natural McKinsey territory. "Basically, BCG and Bain were eating our lunch. We thought of ourselves as strategy athletes. Strategy was what management was all about at the top. Then there was the organization practice. This was the soft, fuzzy side of our work which we weren't really proud of or confident about."

Matassoni found his interest in the strategy practice short-lived. "I was involved in the strategy group for four or five months. I read through a lot of the stuff. It was good and proved useful later on, but after a while I was bored. I wanted to read something real. Then I received an internal staff paper 'Structure is not organization.' It basically said we paid too much attention to structure and didn't look at the other variables. I read it and thought I understand it and thought what it would do for our clients. I thought it was our territory, a breath of fresh air."

Soon after, he met Peters. It was not an auspicious meeting, though it was memorable. "So I had read this paper and walked into the men's room in our New York office. I found a guy there who looked as if he had slept in his suit. He looked like shit and was taking a bath in the sink. He turned round and said, 'Hi, I'm Tom Peters I've just flown in from Dusseldorf.' I was relatively new and impressed by someone just flying in from Dusseldorf. I didn't realize that I was never going to see him looking any better."

Matassoni jibes at the notion that the hyper-energetic Peters was simply reined in by Waterman. "Waterman was protecting Peters from McKinsey a little. He was a kind of godfather but he contributed intellectually and made the thinking more rigorous. Underneath Bob's placid exterior, he is as fiercesomely competitive as Tom. He sets high standards and pushes himself, he just doesn't show it."

The Peters and Waterman combination was, it seems, a twinning of chameleons. On one side was the talkative, opinionated, and energetic Peters, with his reclusive, heavy reading alter ego. On the other side was the calm, softly spoken, Waterman, who had not spent over a decade in the most competitive of environments without mastering a few hard-headed tricks of his own.

The Waterman/Peters partnership was only beginning to establish itself by Easter 1978, when along came the Dart presentation. Despite Peters' success in extricating John Larson from a difficult situation, and the fact that the material was well received, nothing happened. Excellence was relegated to the back-burner. It was, it seemed, another false start. "Excellence came from a series of coincidences," Peters now reflects. "After the Dart presentation, it laid fallow for a year. Bob [Waterman] got interested but I wasn't particularly interested."

Waterman liked the material. He liked the idea that there was more to life than strategy and structure. After 15 years in the business this fitted what he had seen. The trouble was that actually trying to communicate the ideas seemed to lead down blind alleys. Weaned on a steady diet of strategic management and the importance of structure, executives were unwilling, or plain unable, to come to terms with what Peters and Waterman were telling them.

The Magnificent
Seven

Interest in Peters and Waterman's work was to some extent maintained through internal seminars at McKinsey during the spring of 1978. The duo sketched out their, as yet, rudimentary observations and then the audience dispersed to get on with the work of billing clients.

The organization practice team had taken to escaping for meetings to the unlikely setting of Cody, Wyoming. It also roamed further afield to Gidleigh Park in the UK among other places. "By then the organization practice was a quasi-religious group which held these meetings in Cody," says Bill Matassoni. "Someone had decided it was a neat place to have meetings so we went to this ranch outside Cody. We'd talk about organizations and then go for a walk or ride and then we'd talk some more. It was a great time in the firm. There was a sense of purpose."

Peters only recalls paying a brief visit to Cody. "I went to Cody for one and a half days of a five-day meeting. I had a million other things I had to do and remember being driven to Billings, Montana to catch a plane. I remember at the ranch there were a lot of cottonwood trees and it was like it had been snowing. My other memory of Cody is that I was there when I rang Larson and found out I was now a partner. It was like I had joined the priesthood though we didn't have to wear cassocks."

The strategy practice, which was still running, chose slightly more traditional McKinsey methods. "There was some rivalry when the practices got underway. The organization practice were

zealots. They thought they had a mission to get McKinsey back
to its roots. The strategy practice had meetings in Switzerland and
everyone got up and talked about the work they had been doing.
In the strategy practice everyone was actually doing the work,"
says Bill Matassoni. "The organization practice was less inclusive.
There was less turnover of people and they were absolutely
determined. Then there was this crazy guy, Tom Peters, who had
a different sort of background. He was the intellectual horsepower
behind it. He was the driving force, the intellectual leader, and
really believed in what he was developing. He was messianic and
great fun."

Though it was an enjoyable talking shop for highly intelligent
consultants no doubt keen for a rural break from the urban sweat
of corporate clients, Cody didn't provide the code to make sense
of the ideas. Cody didn't codify. And, in the world of management
thinking, ideas without clear codes usually get nowhere. The ideas
were there. The big question was becoming more pressing: how to
communicate them.

Later, in the summer of 1978, the project gained much needed
resuscitation. Waterman asked Anthony Athos and Richard Pascale to join the team as consultants. Athos and Pascale had known
each other for a number of years. Athos was a long-time teacher
at Harvard Business School, an early investigator of corporate
culture and a close friend of McKinsey chief, Ron Daniel. At the
time, Athos was on sabbatical in California and Pascale was
teaching at Stanford.

While Peters hadn't met Athos, his path had fleetingly crossed
with Pascale's while at Stanford. "I knew Peters when he was an
MBA student. He was energetic, a live wire," Pascale recalls. He
also knew Ron Daniel and Waterman, and had done work for
McKinsey previously.

In their 1981 bestseller, *The Art of Japanese Management,* Athos
and Pascale explained the common ground between themselves
and Peters and Waterman: "Athos had long been interested in the
source and impact of higher-order meanings generated within
some organizations, and intrigued by the relationship of top
executive values and style with those meanings. Pascale had been
for years conducting comparative research of American and

Japanese companies, which led him increasingly to focus his attention upon the kind of additional variables Peters and Athos were exploring."[13]

The aim of the combination was, as Athos and Pascale later explained, "to help develop the McKinsey team's thinking in such a way that the resulting idea would be not only more conceptually advanced but also more effectively communicable."[14] Some cynics might suggest that behind Pascale and Athos's diplomatic mission there is the suggestion that Peters and Waterman's ideas were sketchy and impossible to explain convincingly. In this case, the cynics are probably right.

Athos and Pascale discussed the possibilities of working together in the Bank of America building office of McKinsey where it was agreed that the gang of four would spend five days in a small room discovering what they knew and didn't know about organizations. The theory was neat and tidy, though, to put it delicately, Athos and Pascale had reservations about the human dynamics. "Athos and I had breakfast and we walked around a few blocks," Pascale remembers. "Athos said we needed an agenda for the five days or we'd be driven round the bend by Peters – he's so energetic, such a scatter shot. Otherwise we wouldn't survive the five days."

Under pressure to figure out a means of surviving five days in the company of Peters, Athos sought inspiration. "He said he had given it some thought and said there was a guy at Harvard, Cyrus (Chuck) Gibson, who had a scheme – strategy, structure and systems," recalls Richard Pascale. "Gibson had developed these three Ss for Harvard's PMD [Program for Management Development] which he and Tony were in charge of. So, he said why didn't we start with strategy on Monday, then move on to structure on Tuesday, and systems on Wednesday? Tony said he had a couple of his own to add – guiding concepts and shared values. I was working on *The Art of Japanese Management* so was interested in the idea of shared values, though it was Tony who really started the entire visioning industry in the US. Back in the seventies no one had really thought about it. So Tony insisted on guiding concepts which he renamed super-ordinate goals, and I contributed style, and we walked in with five of what became the Seven Ss. It was nothing more than a tool to control Tom Peters."

Management tools come and go with ever increasing rapidity. This one worked – at least when the quartet were ensconced in their discussions. "That's what we did. It was very productive. We had a lot to say. Athos and I persuaded Peters and Waterman to use the alliterative labeling, arguing that its advantages outweighed its lack of sophistication. We then discussed the sequence of them and added skills," says Richard Pascale. Peters was the member of the quartet who suggested adding "skill" to the framework as this encapsulated the idea of "organizational capability" which Waterman had championed.

Peters and Waterman gave Athos credit for the alliteration – "Anthony Athos at the Harvard Business School gave us the courage to do it that way, urging that without the memory hooks provided by alliteration, our stuff was just too hard to explain, too easily forgettable" – while admitting that it took "a bit of stretching, cutting."[15]

So, armed with six words beginning with S which appeared to make sense of something, Peters and Waterman acquainted interested parties in McKinsey with their developing model. A few weeks later, they introduced the six Ss at an internal meeting. In preparing for the meeting, Peters and Waterman, still aided by Athos and Pascale, labored over how to make their message more accessible and understandable. "Tom had a stroke of genius," says Pascale. "He got one of his researchers, Nancy Kaible, to take an article on Tupperware and make it into a case study. I rewrote it. He had the idea of getting the people in the meeting to read the case from the vantage point of the six Ss. So it moved from a way of organizing a meeting to a screen for sifting through the organization. We understood they were levers which managers used, but the idea of applying them to a case was a brilliant move on Tom's part. It gave the framework some legitimacy as a diagnostic tool." Not content with six variables, Peters and Pascale suggested another was needed, one that had to do with timing and implementation. Athos and Pascale proposed calling it "sequencing."

This version of the magnificent seven proved short-lived. Julien Phillips, an associate in McKinsey's San Francisco office who had known Peters at Stanford, then joined the team. He argued that sequencing should be replaced by staff. The other four quickly agreed as sequencing was proving troublesome to fit in. Peters had suggested "people" should be included and, in his teaching at Harvard, Athos was using the awkward and decidedly unallitera-tive "aggregates of people." Peters also weighed in with the possibility of adding "power" somewhere. This didn't happen. So, the group were left with seven: systems, strategy, structure, style, skills, shared values and staff.

Tom Peters provides a slightly different version of events. "During the summer of 1978, Bob Waterman, Richard Pascale, Tony Athos, and I worked up the McKinsey Seven Ss which became the centerpiece of internal teaching. I think I know the straight story about the Seven Ss. Tony and Richard got involved before I started teaching it at McKinsey. I had a model I had developed at internal presentations. They didn't all have Ss. I had five. Tony had been on the cover of *Time* in the sixties as one of the great college teachers in the US and he took my thing and transformed in into something like the Six Ss model. Richard Pascale is also a fabulous teacher and he was involved. I had given them a mass of material and they transformed it into the alliterative diamond. Tony, who is a keen epistomolgist, came up with super-ordinate goals. Waterman got excited, though I thought it a little corny, especially for McKinsey. Waterman took a shine to it and I worked on it. Waterman was the chief salesman and I was the chief writer."

However they came about, the quartet agreed on seven Ss. These were then passed on to McKinsey's graphics department which created an image of a molecule. The Seven S model was born. It was neatly alliterative, accessible, understandable, and (with its logo, later named "the happy atom") highly marketable. (Indeed, for one of the organization practice meetings, at Pocara Dunes near Monterey, Peters and Waterman had T-shirts printed with the model. "The great bet was whether we would get the rather stiff managing director of the London office, Hugh Parker, into one of these T-shirts. We succeeded on the last day," recalls Peters.)

The next step was to take the model to a wider audience. The first target was McKinsey's consultants, where the skeptics, somewhat ironically, included John Larson. The company launched a series of workshops for its consultants and clients, in which Pascale continued to be involved both as a teacher and participant. Athos and Pascale began using the framework in their classes at Harvard and Stanford, and in their own consulting work, with some success. It seemed to get the message across and, what's more, people liked and remembered it.

Michael Lanning, then a McKinsey consultant, recalls one of Peters' presentations. "I saw a talk by Peters in New York, some time in 1980 or 1981, when he was finishing *In Search of Excellence*. At the time we didn't know he was writing a book. This was just the internal findings from the research. I thought it made common sense and had an intuitive ring, but I thought that it was a bit arbitrary and the definitions of excellence were pretty shaky." Peters and Waterman's San Francisco colleague, Jim Balloun, provides a more positive perspective: "I went to some of the early seminars and it was very exciting. We'd always done organization work and people were beginning to understand that boxes and lines didn't work. There was more to it. This took a whole new, fresh look at what makes them work."

The decision was then made to take the model to the real world. Managers liked it. The Seven S model was a business theory to fit all occasions encapsulated on a single page or on the front of a T-shirt. "We started running workshops around the world with McKinsey. People would come to a one-week meeting and would apply the Seven Ss to their own situation," says Richard Pascale.

The Seven S model first saw the light of the day in published form in June 1980. Encouraged by a visit to San Francisco by Roland Mann, then publisher of the *McKinsey Quarterly*, Waterman, Peters, and Phillips (now established as the third part of the San Francisco troika) put together an article: "Structure is not organization." This was published in *Business Horizons*, the journal of Indiana University's Graduate School of Business. Sandwiched between articles titled "No-name products: a step towards no-name retailing" and "Low productivity? Try improving the social environment," this was not exactly a grand entrance into the world of publishing (though it was the article which ignited Bill Matassoni's interest).

After three years of effort and distillation, Peters and Waterman were far from confident as to the worth of their tidy framework. The *Business Horizons* article is almost apologetic. "As yet the Seven S framework is admittedly no more than a rough conceptual tool for helping managers to understand the complexity of effective organization change – and to design change programs that are rich in concept and humble in expectations. The Framework's virtues – realism and relative simplicity – are likely to have a good deal more appeal to practicing managers than the academic researchers."[16] Hardly a ringing endorsement.

Meanwhile Pascale and Athos were working on what was to become *The Art of Japanese Management,* published in 1981. Athos had been invited by the McKinsey team to be a co-author on the *Business Horizons* article. Athos declined, saying he would rather write about it separately. "The deal was we would all be able to use it," says Pascale. In fact, *The Art of Japanese Management* was the first book to feature the Seven Ss. It appeared Peters and Waterman had been pipped at the post.

There was, Peters recalls, some ill-feeling. "Athos and Pascale dropped out and then came out with *The Art of Japanese Management*, which involved the Seven S model. Waterman thought they had taken more credit than they deserved.

Whatever the machinations involved in the genesis of the Seven Ss, it proved highly popular. "The Seven S Framework is probably the one lasting thing Peters has been involved in. I still use it because managers respond to it immediately," says Philip Sadler, former chief executive of Ashridge Management College. The Dutch thinker Fons Trompenaars says: "With the Seven S model, Peters proved that management is beyond simple rationalization."[17]

The Seven Ss are brilliantly memorable. "The model represents a simple but powerful insight into what makes enterprise succeed," said McKinsey's managing director, Ron Daniel.[18] The model's usefulness, however, is more debatable. There is the temptation to believe that the model's chief advantage is that it sounds alluringly simple. The trouble is you then have to bring in consultants to complicate it.

Harvard Business School's Quinn Mills is one of the critics of the Seven S model. "The basic notion is that any organization can be shaped to carry through a chosen strategy successfully. In this thinking, strategy is clearly the senior partner, with organizational matters merely secondary and derivative considerations. Although this approach may make sense in establishing a new company where nothing is already in place, it is close to absurd when applied to an established organization with years of history and methods of doing business that are already firmly set. An existing organization, especially a large one, cannot be altered easily to fit a shifting business strategy."[19]

Inevitably a model which simplifies something as complex as organizational behavior is open to abuse and misinterpretation. It is hostage to its own simplicity. It is no surprise then that the Seven S framework has been overplayed. The idea of creating an accessible model was hardly original – Peters and Waterman later acknowledged their debt to Harold Leavitt's "Diamond" model which boiled the facts of managerial life down to task, structure, people, information, control, and environment. Leavitt's model is obviously not a million miles away from the Seven S model. Though the Seven Ss are a pithy summation of the major issues which bedevil managerial life, the question must be whether they actually help managerial life. What do organizations actually do with them? This remains open to debate.

Nevertheless, from Peters and Waterman's point of view, the Seven S model was a foundation, something tangible to show for their efforts – even if it barely covered a sheet of paper.

Mastering the Model

It is, of course, one thing coming up with a neat and under-standable model; it's quite another to persuade people that it makes sense. During 1979 and 1980, Peters and Waterman took the Seven S framework to a number of high-level corporate presentations. They presented their findings and assembled more material about excellent organizations.

Responses to the presentations were decidedly mixed – even at the supposed "birth" of excellence. "This deal came up in 1979. Shell had been McKinsey's first European client. There was a tradition that every summer the partner in charge would get three or four interesting McKinsey people to spend a day with the managing board of Shell. In 1979 it was decided that Gluck would talk about strategy, Ken Ohmae about life, and Waterman and Peters on whatever we were up to," says Peters. "Bob went back to the files and said let's do something with excellence. Literally, we threw together a 15 to 20 page presentation. We worked on the presentation in April and did it on July 4th, 1979."

To prepare for the Shell presentation, Peters and Waterman interviewed the Hewlett-Packard president, John Young. "What do you do to promote excellence at your company?" they asked. It was one of those generic ice-breaking questions interviewers are wont to use. Young, however, had an answer. He told them and sent them to interview others in the company.

Armed with this material, Peters and Waterman headed to Europe aware, no doubt, that Shell was important to McKinsey, very important. They knew they had to be good. Shell had first hired McKinsey in 1957 to examine the company's structure.

McKinsey labored long and hard – taking a year to create Shell's "matrix." The company had remained a client ever since.

For all the preparation, the Shell presentation was an unmitigated disaster. "We got an awful response. Gluck was long-winded and Ohmae was talking about the Japanese taking over the world. We had prepared the shit out of this stuff and finished up with 20 minutes. Shell didn't want to hear it," says Peters.

There was a silver lining to spending July 4th in The Hague. The Shell presentation had one admirer, a senior partner in McKinsey's Munich office, Herbert Henzler. He sold the idea of a research project on excellent companies to the German giant, Siemens soon after in the summer of 1979. This was good news, because, as Bill Matassoni says, "The organization practice was a major investment by McKinsey." Somewhere along the line it needed to start bringing in money. During the fall of 1979 up to February 1980, Peters, Waterman, and a colleague, David G. Anderson, carried out the research which was to form the core of *In Search of Excellence*.

Siemens basically wanted to know what it needed to do to emulate its American role models. "The Siemens questions were wrong. They were asking: How do we become successful like you Americans? They should have been asking how do we become successful?" says Max Worcester of *Frankfurter Allgemeine Zeitung*. Under pressure, Peters and Waterman weren't really in a position to question their brief.

With a working definition of excellent organizations as "continually innovative big companies,"[20] Peters and Waterman surveyed McKinsey partners asking who they thought met the criteria. Eventually, 75 "highly regarded companies" were selected and Peters and Waterman set off to find out more. (As research methods go, this is about as arbitrary and as basic as you can get.) During the winter of 1979–1980 they carried out "intense, structured interviews" in about half the companies.

The experience opened their eyes still further. And, slowly, they were beginning to focus. "When Waterman and I went out in the dead of winter in 1979 and began looking at 3M and Dana, at Wal-Mart and Disney, and McDonald's, we stumbled across 'new' words: people, involvement, trust, customers, listening, service, quality, wandering (as in MBWA, or Managing By Wandering Around)," Peters recalled.[21]

Fired with new enthusiasm, the duo made their presentation to Siemens in the spring of 1980. It was a good presentation, but it flopped. McKinsey also had a tradition of speaking in Lyford Cay in the Bahamas to PepsiCo's top 100 managers. Peters presented their findings to PepsiCo in May 1980. Again, it flopped.

At this point, Peters and Waterman had carried out extensive research over three years covering companies and organizations throughout the world. They had come up with a neat framework which went down well with some audiences. It seemed a great combination. But, in reality, it appeared destined to sink without trace. The great white hopes kept hitting the canvas.

"All the reactions were poor. The thing wasn't shaped when I talked to Dart. The really big presentation to Siemens was professionally great but the response stunk. Shell and Siemens were totally self-confident about what they knew and what they needed and didn't want. Then I did PepsiCo and that was a disaster. There was a positive response but I screwed up the presentation. In baseball parlance it was 0 for 4," says Peters. "We then went back to Hewlett-Packard and went through it. They were turned on."

Hewlett-Packard president, John Young, was highly receptive to Peters and Waterman's message. He was intent on creating a more entrepreneurial culture within the company. Peters and Waterman got lucky: they found a corporate enthusiast who was helpfully based in their own Californian backyard. Young espoused his belief that managers should become involved instead of sitting on the sidelines composing decorative plans. "I don't care if they come from Stanford Business School, for a few years they get their hands dirty, or we are not interested," Young told Peters and Waterman – forgetting perhaps that he was talking to a Stanford graduate and that he was one as well.[22] (Despite his involvement at this turning point of Peters and Waterman's research, John Young admits: "It has been a very long time since I first met Peters and Waterman, and subsequently *In Search of Excellence* was published. My recollection of surrounding events is nil."[23] Young, it seems, was too busy practicing excellence to take much notice of its theoretical genesis.)

Young wasn't the only one showing an interest. Peters and Waterman's basic presentation was now available – and circulating among colleagues and clients – in a bound 125-page version. This became known as the "Orange Book" and was basically a collection of Peters and Waterman's overheads from their presentation. This was the usual end of the line: a neat looking report. Unusually, people were actually asking for copies and, even more unusually, were reading them. The Canadian academic, Henry Mintzberg was one of the recipients of this draft version – "Tom sent me an unbound copy of what became *In Search of Excellence* and I met him about that time. What I read was consistent with my own prejudices."

Buoyed by the interest from Hewlett-Packard, Peters and Waterman then had another change of fortune. "I saw a summary of the key ideas of excellence and pressed Tom to meet Lew Young, editor of *Business Week*," says Bill Matassoni. "I remember we met at about six in the evening in New York. Tom had his slides and his presentation ready to go. Lew stopped him and said he didn't need it – he'd read the stuff. He rewrote it and, a week later, we were on the cover of *Business Week*." On July 21st, 1980, the world was made aware of McKinsey's research.

The magazine's cover featured an unflattering picture of Commerce Secretary, Philip M. Klutznick. (These were duller days in the magazine world.) On the right-hand side was a simple headline: "Putting excellence into management. The eight basics." Inside, Peters asked "What makes for excellence in the management of a company?" pointing out that his conclusions were based on studies of 37 companies, and ten in particular, identified as being "well-managed" – IBM, Texas Instruments, Hewlett-Packard, 3M, Digital Equipment, Procter & Gamble, Johnson & Johnson, McDonald's, Dana, and Emerson Electric. "Far too many managers have lost sight of the basics – service to customers, low-cost manufacturing, productivity improvement, innovation, and risk-taking," wrote Peters. "In many cases, they have been seduced by the availability of MBAs, armed with the 'latest' in strategic planning techniques. MBAs who specialize in strategy

are bright, but they often cannot implement their ideas, and their
companies wind up losing the capacity to act."[24]

Of course, Peters had an MBA and McKinsey's ranks were
brimfull of strategy specialists. "It made us a little uncomfortable
as he criticized MBAs," admits McKinsey's Bill Matassoni. But,
despite such misgivings, the four-page article buried on page 196
was a watershed. "That was a huge break. The phone started
ringing. It was the last day of peace I ever had," says Peters. During
the next 18 months, Peters and Waterman gave over 200 speeches,
conducted more than 50 workshops and wrote their first book.

Suddenly the world was interested. Peters signed a contract
with Harper & Row to deliver a book based on the *Business Week*
article. It was not a multimillion dollar contract. In fact, it was
some $995,000 short of being a million dollar contract. Harper &
Row advanced Peters a meager $5000. Then, in November 1980,
Peters had a car accident and, again with time on his hands, began
writing the first draft of what was to become *In Search of Excellence*.

Throughout 1981 Peters gave speech after speech. The first
draft of the book was finished late in the summer of 1981. It
contained all the Siemens research – mainly because no additional
research had been done since the Siemens presentation a year
before. During the fall of 1981, Peters taught a rough draft of the
book on one of his periodic returns to Stanford. At this stage, *In
Search of Excellence* was a substantial 1300-page manuscript.

It was, Peters now admits, poorly written. He was no writer. His
previous writing experience was distinctly limited – he had
completed various academic assignments and had churned out a
succession of McKinsey reports. Even the *Business Week* article had
had to be rewritten by Lew Young.

Up until this point, the book was a solo effort. Indeed, the initial
idea was for Peters and Waterman to write separate books. It is
difficult to see how this could have worked given that they were
writing about the same thing, using the same research material.
"Though he had worked on the research for Siemens, Waterman
was not involved in the first draft. It was my book contract
following my article in *Business Week*," says Peters. "In the middle
of 1981 I asked Waterman if he wanted to be co-author though

nothing happened until I had the first draft. Waterman thought the first draft of *In Search of Excellence* sucked."

So, in November 1981, Waterman began revising the draft manuscript to a book which was way too long and which he had grave reservations about. More drafts followed. It began to take shape. "I was up in Maine on vacation when I got a draft of the book for the fourth time," says Bill Matassoni, retelling the story with his customary gusto. "I thought they don't pay me enough to read this again. But I did and faxed them back saying I thought it would be a bestseller – I was thinking 100,000 copies."

At this point, the book was called *The Secrets of Excellence*. Honed and polished, the manuscript was delivered to the New York offices of Harper & Row in March 1982. Harper & Row printed the dustjacket as the book was put through its final editing. Then, at a McKinsey meeting in the late summer of 1982, the subject of the book came up. McKinsey's founding father, Marvin Bower intervened and said the title had to be changed as it sounded as if Peters and Waterman were giving away the secrets of McKinsey's clients. It was a decision guaranteed not to please the publishers or the authors. But, in McKinsey, Bower's word was usually final. "It was a fiat from God," says Peters. "Bob and I were devastated. Once you have a title you become attached. I was in a funk for a couple of days." The only other title contender was "Management By Walking Around." This was rejected. "In the end we came up with *In Search of Excellence* but I've no idea where the idea came from." Excellence was born.

TWO

THE BESTSELLER

" *It all but had the frigging
flag on the cover of the
damn thing* "

Tom Peters[25]

From Humble Pie to Apple Pie

In Search of Excellence appeared to an apparently uninterested public in October 1982. Tickertape was not released over Broadway. Readers did not flock to their local book store in search of the latest research from management consultants. "We had no reason to believe it would be different from any other business book," Waterman later observed.[26] Business books did not sell, period. An initial print run of 15,000 was hardly an optimistic endorsement from the publishers. (Harper & Row had wavered over whether to order a print run of 10,000 or 20,000 copies – they decided on an obvious compromise.)

There were reviews. But these were far from glowing endorsements. "Much of the appeal of the authors' precepts comes precisely from the fact that in our heart of hearts we've known all along that that's the way to do things," noted Walter Kiechel in his favorable, though not overwhelming, review in *Fortune*.[27]

"*In Search of Excellence* was seriously trashed. The *Wall Street Journal* and *Fortune* loved it. The *New York Times*, the *Harvard Business Review*, and *LA Times* savaged it," recalls Peters overstating what was generally a tepid response.

The fact that there were reviews at all was something of a triumph. McKinsey's communications guru Bill Matassoni had helped oil the wheels. "I started talking to Walter Kiechel of *Fortune* and took him out to Cody to one of these organization practice meetings. I also got close to Adam Meyerson of the *Wall Street Journal*. Tom knew Jim Fallows at *Atlantic*. When the book came out we had reviews in *Fortune*, the *Wall Street Journal*, *Time*, and *Atlantic* in the first two weeks. That was big time launching." As acknowledgment of his role in promoting the book, Peters and Waterman gave Matassoni a framed certificate renaming him "Dr. Fame."

Whatever the reviews, *In Search of Excellence* was a book with a simple formula and even simpler intention. The subtitle is straightforward: "Lessons from America's best-run companies." Here is what works; here are successful companies, and this is why they are successful. "In a way, the whole notion behind our excellent company research is: If you really want to learn, watch the best. Watch what they're doing," said Waterman. "It's done all the time in sports, but to our minds it's done very little in business. In business – so far at least – it's been as if, in order to learn how to succeed, you went out and looked at everybody else's mistakes and told yourself, 'Don't do that'."[28]

In fact, Waterman's observation doesn't hold up to a great deal of examination. The most popular business books have always been about successful companies (from Henry Ford's *My Life and Work* to Alfred P. Sloan's *My Years with General Motors*, from Thomas Watson's *A Company and Its Beliefs* to Lee Iacocca's biography). Books on corporate failures have generally been failures for the simple reason that executives believe that reading books on what not to do increases the likelihood that that's exactly what they will do. For similar reasons, budding authors are not advised to write about crisis management.

Simple though it was, the entire premise of *In Search of Excellence* was also extremely bold – and its boldness would come back to haunt its authors. "The notion of deciding you were the arbiter is ludicrous. The idea of excellence seemed audacious," says Peters with a rare enthusiasm for understatement. "My title would have been a few good ideas which seem to work." Marvin Bower might also have gone along with this alternative.

Audacious or not, *In Search of Excellence* was enticing. "Let us never underestimate the market for hope. *In Search of Excellence* appeared when the industrial self-confidence of the West was at its lowest ebb ever. 'You, too, can be great' was the message. No surprise then, that it found a mass audience," says Gary Hamel, co-author of *Competing for the Future*. "The dividing line between simple truths and simplistic prescription is always a thin one. For the most part, Peters and Waterman avoided the facile and the tautological. Indeed, the focus on operations research, elaborate planning systems, and (supposedly) rigorous financial analysis had, in many companies, robbed management of its soul – and certainly had taken the focus off the customer. Peters and Waterman reminded managers that success often comes from doing common things uncommonly well."[29]

As Hamel observes, people like good news. *In Search of Excellence* glowed with good tidings. It radiated *bonhomie*. "The findings from the excellent companies amount to an upbeat message. There is good news from America. Good management practice today is not resident only in Japan," proclaimed Peters and Waterman. "But, more important, the good news comes from treating people decently and asking them to shine, and from producing things that work."[30]

And people like good news all the more when they are fed a constant diet of bad news.

In 1982 bad news stalked every corner. American industry was, by common consensus, held to be on its knees. The oil-crisis of the mid-seventies was the portent of a period of navel examination, self-analysis. President Carter talked of a "malaise," while business people contemplated their poor-performing companies and their underproductive workforces with bemusement. By the beginning of the 1980s, American industrialists and their counterparts in Europe were willing to hold their hands up and admit "We've screwed up." They would also have quickly moved onto blaming irresponsible unions and greedy sheiks for this sad situation before desperately professing that they had little clue as to what to do next. The death knell of post-war industrial optimism and unquestioning faith in the mighty corporation was sounding. Only the profoundly deaf carried on regardless – and there were many who chose to ignore the signals.

As the death knell rang out, there was no shortage of obituary notices. The most famous and accurate came from two Harvard Business School academics, Robert Hayes and Bill Abernathy. Their article "Managing our way to economic decline" came out in the July/August 1980 issue of the *Harvard Business Review*. It proved grim and highly influential reading.

Hayes and Abernathy had wrestled with the demons of decline and emerged dismayed. "Our experience suggests that, to an unprecedented degree, success in most industries today requires an organizational commitment to compete in the marketplace on technological grounds – that is, to compete over the long run by offering superior products," wrote Hayes and Abernathy. (It is astounding in retrospect that such commercial facts of life needed restating.) "Yet, guided by what they took to be the newest and best principles of management, American managers have increasingly directed their attention elsewhere. These new principles, despite their sophistication and widespread usefulness, encourage a preference for (1) analytic detachment rather than the insight that comes from 'hands on' experience and (2) short-term cost reduction rather than long-term development of technological competitiveness. It is this new managerial gospel, we feel, that has played a major role in undermining the vigor of American industry."[31] Hayes and Abernathy went on to champion customer orientation as a vital ingredient in reversing the apparently irreversible trend. Their message was that management was the problem. Forget about union militancy, forget about foreign competition, look upstairs to the boardroom.

The popularity of Hayes and Abernathy's article was a signal of what was to come with *In Search of Excellence*. An article buried in the *Harvard Business Review* does not usually excite or ignite debate. This one did. Hayes and Abernathy announced that corporate America was approaching its final hours; people were ready for its resurrection.

Managers were anxious to make sense of the spiral of decline they seemed to have inadvertently joined. They were desperate. And desperate people buy books in the hope – usually forlorn – that they will offer an escape route. "By 1982, people were prepared to listen. There was a whole new readiness to accept that Americans don't walk on water. The economy went deep south and people were ready to listen in a way they hadn't been earlier," says Peters. "The handbook/MBA logic was the logic of world management. That's not a grotesque exaggeration. Hayes and

Abernathy trashed American management and wrote it in the Harvard manual. They could say we piggy-backed on their work, but they put a shot across the bows of received wisdom and we continued with it." Received wisdom was being rewritten and, somewhat ironically, the purveyor of the rewriting was Harvard Business School which had done so much to create what its best minds were now set on undermining.

Hayes and Abernathy's findings were not exactly news to Peters. In fact, he had established links with one of Hayes and Abernathy's Harvard colleagues, Wickham Skinner, early in the excellence research. Skinner, like Hayes and Abernathy, had long been warning of the terminal decline he observed in US manufacturing industry. The eager Peters was a regular visitor to Skinner. "I got to know Tom when he used to call in on me when he was with McKinsey. Tom called every year or so for a while when he was working on the excellence research with Waterman. He was interested in my work in manufacturing and was one of the first to recognize that manufacturing in the Western world was being managed poorly and falling behind competitors in Japan," says Skinner. "He was very interested in manufacturing while most consultants and scholars were interested in marketing, finance, and information systems. He got beyond conventional views and insights. The recognition of the need for excellence in manufacturing was a very rare insight and he was one of the few to have it."

The bad news was not only America's manifest industrial and managerial limitations. To rub salt into the wounds, the Japanese were increasingly lauded as the managerial model for our times. A succession of books caught the spirit of the moment (and exasperated Peters and Waterman by appearing before their book). In 1981, William Ouchi's *Theory Z* venerated Japan's employment and managerial practices and, after their work with Peters and Waterman, Richard Pascale and Anthony Athos had published the bestselling *The Art of Japanese Management*. It played a crucial role in the discovery of Japanese management techniques as Pascale and Athos considered how a country the same size as Montana could be outstripping the American industrial juggernaut. "In 1980, Japan's GNP was third highest in the world and, if we extrapolate current trends, it would be number one by the year 2000," warned Pascale and Athos.[32] Harsh home truths lurked on every page of *The Art of Japanese Management*. "If anything, the extent of Japanese superiority over the United States in industrial competitiveness is underestimated," wrote Pascale and Athos, observing that "a major reason for the superiority of the Japanese is their managerial skill." In its comparisons of US and Japanese companies, *The Art of Japanese Management* provided rare insights into the truth behind the mythology of Japanese management and the inadequacy of much Western practice.

Among the key components of Japanese management identified by Pascale and Athos was vision, something they found to be notably lacking in the West. "Our problem today is that the tools are there but our 'vision' is limited. A great many American managers are influenced by beliefs, assumptions, and perceptions about management that unduly constrain them," wrote Pascale and Athos. The book, they said, was "not an assault on the existing tools of management, but upon the Western vision of management which circumscribes our effectiveness."[33] *The Art of Japanese Management* also featured the Seven S model.

Not surprisingly, since they'd shared a room for a week to pool their collective knowledge, Peters and Waterman sang from the same songbook as Pascale and Athos (though they largely ignored Japan – it rates only ten index references in *In Search of Excellence*). Peters and Waterman directed their fire closer to home. Western management was in gridlock headed down a dead-end. "The problem in America is that our fascination with the tools of management obscures our apparent ignorance of the art," they wrote. "Our tools are biased toward measurement and analysis. We can measure the costs. But with these tools alone we can't really elaborate on the value of a turned on ... workforce churning out quality products."[34]

What differentiated *In Search of Excellence* from *The Art of Japanese Management* was that Peters and Waterman sugared the bitter message. You could churn things out and they could still be good. Common people could do uncommon things – even if they weren't Japanese. There was room for optimism and in this positive message lies the secret of the book's long-lasting success. Andrew Campbell, formerly a McKinsey consultant, says: "*In Search of Excellence* gave hope to generations of managers who were dying under the weight of bureaucracy. It was common sense and anti-establishment; Peters talks endless common sense and cooks it up as a radical statement." Later, in *A Passion for Excellence*, Peters and his co-author, Nancy Austin, noted: "*In Search of Excellence* disgorged no magic: it simply said, 'Stay close to your customers; wander around.' The absence of magic – 'Practice common sense' – turned out to be its biggest selling point. And its biggest source of frustration: no sure-fire formulas for productive wandering around, no ten-step guides, how to begin, how to learn, and above all, how to teach yourself to sustain success for decades."[35] *In Search of Excellence* was home-made apple pie after a diet of humble pie. It was common sense at a time when common sense appeared a radical alternative.

Hayes and Abernathy's article identified the malaise in America's corporate world. But, the last thing a sick person wants to be told is that they are sick. They want to know how and when they will get better. This is exactly what *In Search of Excellence* provided.

Looking back, Peters argues that the good news element of *In Search of Excellence* was tempered by the underlying bad news. "Consultants live with problems. That's what they get paid for. So we were always working with broken things. *In Search of Excellence* was the first book written about things that work. It was purposeful," he says. "Admittedly, the logic of the book was that American management was fucked up. It was a brutal, upfront attack on American management and McKinsey thinking. Okay it was 75 percent about islands of hope but that was what they were: exceptional. I consider *In Search of Excellence* a bad news book." At the time, the public disagreed.

Back to Basics

The recipe for the home cooking was attractively straightforward. Peters and Waterman eschewed exhaustive analysis and labyrinthian charts. What's the point of a strategic five-year plan which covers the wall and never actually happens, if you can't get the best out of people? "The excellent companies require and demand extraordinary performance from the average man," wrote Peters and Waterman.[36] In other words, release the innate potential of people to set your business free. Allow the average person to fulfill their potential instead of treating them as untrustworthy and unknowing. Tune in and turn on.

In Search of Excellence was a back to basics book. It was the literary equivalent of returning to nature and discovering you're not a bad sort of person after all. Peters and Waterman sat in their log cabin in front of a comforting fire, poured themselves some coffee, and returned to first principles. And the basics, as mapped out by Peters and Waterman, began with customers. "Amid all this mainstream world management theory, no-one had talked about customers for 25 years," says Peters. "We weren't the first. MIT people were writing about internal entrepreneurship but we were making commonsense observations which had been pushed aside."

In Search of Excellence said forget the bullshit. Forget the charts. Forget being rational about every move you make. Business is about people. Here is a large dose of common sense. "Far too many managers have lost sight of the basics, in our opinion: quick action, service to customers, practical innovation, and the fact that you can't get any of these without virtually everyone's commitment," wrote Peters and Waterman.[37] They did, it must be noted, add a caveat: "We distrust simple answers and aren't trying to push one ourselves."[38] What you need to do is simple, but doing it right is not so simple.

In the 1990s talk of customer service and moving quickly has entered the realms of cliché. In 1982, amazingly and depressingly, it was fresh and forceful. Somewhere, somehow, management had left people behind. The almost total dominance of strategic management in the sixties, as well as the pursuit of corporate size and the mastery of mass-production, had dispensed with the humanity of management.

The corporate icons of the sixties and seventies were people like Alfred P. Sloan of General Motors and Harold Geneen at ITT. They were hard-headed, rational, and remorseless. Sloan's managerial classic, *My Years with General Motors,* achieves the almost impossible task of discussing over four decades with General Motors with hardly a personality in sight. To Sloan, human interest was of no interest. The then powerful unions are ignored. So, too, are key figures such as Charles Kettering (who invented the self-starter) and William Olds (of Oldsmobile). At first glance such omissions are not altogether surprising. Sloan's system was aimed at eliminating, as far as was possible, the deficiencies and eccentricities of managerial behavior. "It is perhaps the most impersonal book of memoirs ever written," observed Peter Drucker. "And this was clearly intentional. Sloan's book . . . knows only one dimension: that of managing a business so that it can produce effectively, provide jobs, create markets and sales, and generate profits."[39]

Management in one dimension, the world of Sloan and Geneen, was everything McKinsey extolled. Helping large corporations make sense of their empires was the job of McKinsey. Making complex strategic analyses and impressive charts was the job of McKinsey. The central thrust of *In Search of Excellence* was to encourage managers to cast off much of what McKinsey stood for. Peters and Waterman weren't exactly biting the hand which fed them, but they were giving every impression of wanting to.

There is an obvious irony here. At the time *In Search of Excellence* was written, Peters and Waterman were McKinsey consultants. Waterman may have fancied himself as an artist and Peters may have liked reading novels, but that shouldn't detract from what they were actually spending their time doing. "Wooden analyses" were their business. Big companies paid McKinsey, and McKinsey paid them – they weren't Sloan and Geneen but they were guilty by association.

"When Bob Waterman and I wrote *In Search of Excellence,* the cracks in the facade of American economic hegemony were starting to show. Practitioner and professor alike were looking for answers. There were dozens of books and articles on matrix organization structures. Strategists, in clear ascendance, ceaselessly debated the shape of 'experience curves.' Decision tree experts polished their tools for calculating expected values, and their students (MBAs) learned to plant, prune, and harvest 'decision trees'," wrote Peters later.[40] Of course, the world of experience curves, decision trees, and MBAs was precisely the world inhabited by Peters and Waterman. They had undoubtedly pruned their own decision trees and played their part in an awful lot of strategies which would never see the light of day. Now they shook the past off. It was like escaping from a bad hangover and realizing that your body still functions.

In retrospect, a lot of the targets were easy hits – MBAs, managers who never did any "real" work, companies who didn't listen to their employees or customers. But, such outright criticism and condemnation had not previously made any impact. Perhaps the nearest equivalent is Robert Townsend's *Up the Organization* which, in 1970, said many of the same things as *In Search of Excellence.* The trouble with Townsend's book was that it was also outrageously funny and this overshadowed the serious import of many of his observations. The tone of *Up the Organization* is set from the start, in a memorandum on how to use the book. Written over a decade before *In Search of Excellence,* the echoes of Tom Peters are strong. "In the average company the boys in the mailroom, the president, the vice-presidents, and the girls in the steno pool have three things in common: they are docile, they are bored, and they are dull," observes Townsend. "Trapped in the pigeonholes of organization charts, they've been made slaves to the rules of private and public hierarchies that run mindlessly on and on because nobody can change them."[41] (Townsend and Peters later worked together on an audio package called *Excellence in the Organization.*[42])

As well as nonmanaging managers and clueless MBAs, Peters and Waterman even got the ritual dig in at economists (though this is perfectly understandable) – "We have been exposed to a great deal of micro-economic theory, and it sometimes appears that there is only one thing that economists are absolutely sure about after several hundred years of labor: wheat farmers in perfectly competitive markets don't have high margins. We don't have any wheat farmers in our survey, but we got pretty close."[43]

They didn't have any wheat farmers (and, in fact, they didn't get close) but Peters and Waterman championed the regular guy doing a regular job who was generally ignored. "Many of today's managers – MBA-trained and the like – may be a little bit too smart for their own good," they wrote. "The smart ones are the ones who shift direction all the time, based upon the latest output from the expected value equation. The ones who juggle hundred-variable models with facility; the ones who design complicated incentive systems; the ones who wire up matrix structures. The ones who have 200-page strategic plans and 500-page market requirement documents that are but one step in product development exercises. Our dumber friends are different. They just don't understand why every customer can't get personalized service, even in the potato chip business."[44] The fact that Peters (an MBA) and Waterman had spent the last few years producing exhaustive reports was conveniently forgotten.

The professionalization of management had, said Peters and Waterman, produced managers who were highly "professional" in the narrowest sense. Peters' disdain for the professional manager continues – "The undeniable fact is that we continue to pay an awful price for the narrow view encompassed by so-called professional management," he wrote in 1994.[45]

The thing is, Peters and Waterman were right. In the late 1970s and early 1980s, American managers were out of touch – though that's not to say they are particularly in touch now. At the time, the smart people at the top were usually regarded as beyond reproach. Out of touch, they were also out of sight. In 1982, virtually every corporate vice-president had a parking space outside the office and ate in the executive restaurant. (Some anachronistic vice-presidents still do.) Those at the top had created a neat cocoon of well-carpeted offices, expense accounts and executive perks. Though such an untouchable aura was plainly difficult to justify (or was plainly wrong), apportioning blame fairly and squarely on the shoulders of managers was also a strictly limited diagnosis. If Peters and Waterman had asked their "dumber" friends, they would have found that they often didn't care about the company or the customers. All they wanted was a regular, larger, pay check.

It is easy for well-paid consultants to criticize less well-paid managers and extol the virtues of those lower in the corporate pecking order. Many do so – witness the flurry of books on empowerment – but it is usually as grounded in reality as dreams of an English Wimbledon champion. How many of their "dumber" friends did Peters and Waterman talk to? Not many it seems. A look through *In Search of Excellence* generally reveals the opinions of CEOs and chairmen rather than those lower down the corporate hierarchy.

Smart or dumb, Peters and Waterman's message was distilled down to eight points – a simple marketing trick in itself (select ten points and it looks as if you decided on ten and then made the contents fit; pick more than ten and they are instantly forgotten), and, at the time, novel. Peters later dismissively referred to the eight as "rather homely tactics . . . eight disconnected principles we teased from our research."[46] Excellent companies, said Peters and Waterman, had eight dominant characteristics:

1. **A bias for action**
    (In the 1980 *BusinessWeek* article this point was slightly more ambiguously titled "a bias towards action.") The excellent companies got on with doing the job. They didn't linger awaiting the next strategic plan. They acted. "'Do it, fix it, try it,' is our favorite axiom," wrote Peters and Waterman.[47] Again, it is unbelievably obvious – but not at the time when

think about it, write it down, add up the figures, collect some more figures and write it down again was the dominant approach.

The largely undeveloped corollary of this first point was that bureaucracy is an enemy of excellence. "We didn't fathom that 'close to the customer', for example, was so much blather unless you destroy 90 percent of the headquarters staff (and perhaps the headquarters itself), thoroughly entwine local units with their customers – and then hold those units fully accountable for results," Peters later noted.[48]

2. **Close to the customer**

This is, perhaps, the most famous of *In Search of Excellence*'s octet. Remember customers. Many large American corporations had forgotten them long ago. "The excellent companies really are close to their customers. That's it. Other companies talk about it; the excellent companies do it," said Peters and Waterman.[49] In an era of poor service, businesses had never been further away from their customers. Companies produced what they wanted to produce in the numbers they wanted. Whether customers wanted the products was largely ignored – until they didn't buy them. Later, in *A Passion for Excellence*, Peters and his co-author Nancy Austin noted: "When Peters and Waterman 'discovered' the 'close to the customer' principle in business, they couldn't have been more embarrassed. How obvious. How trite. We are no longer embarrassed."[50] There is, in fact, little sign of embarrassment in *In Search of Excellence* – the book begins with a story of a concierge in a hotel remembering Peters and Waterman's names when they arrived late one evening, rather than a catalog of their research methodology.

3. **Autonomy and entrepreneurship**

(Originally, the wordier "operational autonomy to encourage entrepreneurship.") At the beginning of the 1980s the world's rediscovery of the entrepreneur was hardly off the ground. Before long, the newspapers were profiling entrepreneurs by the thousand. Margaret Thatcher was proclaiming the new entrepreneurial age where deals were struck over mobile phones at every opportunity. Anyone who opened a corner store was an entrepreneur. Contrast this with previous decades – if Alfred P. Sloan had been called an entrepreneur he would have been speedily reduced to apoplectic anger. Peters and Waterman did not conceive of the entrepreneur as a greedy, deal-maker. Instead, they thought of entrepreneurs as regular people letting their irregular thoughts loose, investing their intelligence in their organizations rather than leaving it at home. (Peters has memorably defined entrepreneurship as "unreasonable conviction based on inadequate evidence.")

4. **Productivity through people**
   In the late seventies, the corporate thinking was simple. Productivity increases come from economies of scale. Period. The only alternative route to enhanced productivity was the technological dream of replacing the unenthusiastic dullards on the factory floor with Japanese workers or neat metallic robots which didn't answer back and didn't expect a pay check every month. Peters and Waterman advised: forget the robots. They argued that people made the difference because they did the work and knew the job. They quoted a GM worker laid off after 16 years making Pontiacs: "I guess I was laid off because I make poor quality cars. But in 16 years, not once was I ever asked for a suggestion as to how to do my job better. Not once."[51] (This was typical of the *In Search of Excellence* approach. A great quote which says a lot. But where does it lead? How could GM organize itself, change its thinking, transform its engrained attitudes?)

5. **Hands-on values driven**
   The companies and managers extolled by Peters and Waterman had a keen sense of values. (Initially, this point was "stress on one key business value.") They knew what mattered and their managers were willing to dirty their hands to get the job done. "The word manager in lip service

institutions often has come to mean not someone who rolls up his or her sleeves to get the job done right alongside the worker, but someone who hires assistants to do it," bemoaned Peters and Waterman.[52]

6. **Stick to the knitting**

The excellent companies were not distracted from what they knew they were good at. Pointless diversifications were not for them. This has become a constant refrain in management literature ever since – companies now seek to identify their core competencies which boils down to much the same. The caveat to this must be that what you are good at now is not necessarily what you need to be good at in the future. Stick to the knitting can be corporate suicide if you are sticking to the wrong kind of knitting or stick to it too long; too many companies cast on when they should be casting off.

7. **Simple form, lean staff**

"One of the key attributes of the excellent companies is that they have realized the importance of keeping things simple despite overwhelming genuine pressures to complicate things," wrote Peters and Waterman.[53] The excellent companies were not fascinated by size or complexity.

8. **Simultaneous loose–tight properties**

This was probably the least defined and most easily forgotten element in the eight attributes of excellence. The excellent companies managed to combine the free-wheeling flexibility of smaller companies with the carefully structured (and reassuring) rigidity of large organizations. They managed to get the best of every world.

The eight points are all-embracing truisms, attractive simplified solutions to perennial problems. In fact, the eight points raise more questions than answers. They are catchy and memorable – more Hare Krishna than the Gregorian chants of strategic management. People remembered them. Whether or not this helped them stick to the knitting or keep things simple was another matter.

Death to Rationalists

In Search of Excellence was more than eight generic points. Central to its argument was its dismissal of the rational model of management, the roots of which lie in Frederick Taylor's Scientific Management, formulated during the first years of the century.

Scientific Management emerged from Taylor's work at the Midvale Steel Works, where he was chief engineer. Taylor's "science" came from the minute examination of individual tasks. Having identified every single movement and action involved in doing something, Taylor could determine the optimum time required to complete a task. Armed with this information, the manager could determine whether a person was doing the job well. "In its essence, scientific management involves a complete mental revolution on the part of the working man engaged in any particular establishment or industry – a complete mental revolution on the part of these men as to their duties toward their work, toward their fellow men, and toward their employees," Taylor wrote.[54]

While Scientific Management didn't ignite a revolution, it undoubtedly shaped the working patterns of the twentieth century. Henry Ford's development of mass production was the natural progression from Scientific Management. To Ford, people were a complication. In his book, *My Life and Work*, Ford gives a chilling insight into his own unforgiving logic. He calculated that the production of a Model T required 7882 different operations. Of these 949 required "strong, able-bodied, and practically physically perfect men" and 3338 required "ordinary physical strength." The remainder, said Ford, could be undertaken by "women or older children" and "we found that 670 could be filled by legless men, 2637 by one-legged men, two by armless men, 715 by one-armed men and 10 by blind men."[55]

In 1982, the basic Taylorist principles remained in place (and still do in some organizations). Peters and Waterman wanted to reverse Taylor's revolution. They believed it was built on lack of trust and a fundamental lack of humanity. Reading Henry Ford on human resource management you can see their point. Instead of being cogs in an enormous machine, Peters and Waterman saw people as the heart of all business activities. (There was a certain irony in Peters and Waterman's anti-Taylorist agenda – after all, Taylor was the man who really started off the twentieth-century management consultancy industry, though, at $35 a day, Taylor came cheaper than a pair of McKinsey consultants.)

In terms of management theorizing, Taylor's sociological twin was the German, Max Weber, who remains something of a *bête noir* of the corporate world. Weber "pooh-poohed charismatic leadership and doted on bureaucracy; its rule-driven, impersonal form, he said, was the only way to assure long-term survival" observed Peters and Waterman in *In Search of Excellence*.[56] Weber's *The Theory of Social and Economic Organization* argued that the most efficient form of organization resembles a machine. It is characterized by strict rules, controls and hierarchies, and driven by bureaucracy. This, Weber termed, the "rational–legal model." At the opposite extreme were the "charismatic" model and the "traditional" model in which things are done as they always have been done, such as in family firms in which power is passed down from one generation to the next.

"Experience tends universally to show that the purely bureaucratic type of administrative organization – that is, the monocratic variety of bureaucracy – is, from a purely technical point of view, capable of attaining the highest degree of efficiency and is in this sense formally the most rational known means of carrying our imperative control over human beings," Weber wrote. "It is superior to any other form in precision, in stability, in the stringency of its discipline, and in its reliability. It thus makes possible a particularly high degree of calculability of results for the heads of the organization and for those acting in relation to it. It is finally superior both in intensive efficiency and in the scope of its operations and is formally capable of application to all kinds of administrative tasks."[57]

In Peters and Waterman's eyes, Taylor and Weber had a lot to answer for. They may have been engineers, but viewing people as corporate machinery was beyond their comprehension. "Bureaucracy is basically just machinery for mistake avoidance," observed Waterman. "The whole emphasis is negative. And of course you can always figure out why something shouldn't be done. But before the fact, it's very hard to figure out why something *should* be done."[58]

Weber-style bureaucracy had created needless layers of management. Scientific Management had led to organizations populated by managers who distrusted their employees – and vice versa. For Peters and Waterman, the legacy of Taylor and Weber was the target of their disdain. Managers had become little more than bean counters and overseers, woefully out of touch. "Many readers of that book claimed it vindicated American management practice (at a time when Japanese approaches were the rage). I think that's wrong. *Search* was an out-and-out attack on the excesses of the 'rational model' and the 'business strategy paradigm' that had come to dominate Western management thinking," wrote Peters in *Liberation Management*. "What it counseled instead was a return to first principles: attention to customers ('close to the customer'), an abiding concern for people ('productivity through people'), and the celebration of trial and error ('a bias for action')."[59]

The excellent companies offered an antidote to rationalism. They succeeded – in Peters and Waterman's eyes – precisely because they didn't measure everything or treat people like cattle. They defied rational wisdom. "If there is one striking feature of the excellent companies, it is this ability to manage ambiguity and paradox. What our rational economist friends tell us ought not to be possible the excellent companies do routinely," wrote Peters and Waterman.[60]

Even so, it is an exaggeration to say that *In Search of Excellence* was an out and out attack on anything. As befitted consultants, Peters and Waterman watered down their dismissal of the rational model. At times, *In Search of Excellence* read not so much as a dynamic quest, but a rather timid afternoon stroll. Rationality was not all bad, conceded Peters and Waterman. "We don't argue for drastically tilting the balance toward either pathfinding or implementation. Rationality is important. A quality analysis will help to point a business in the right direction for pathfinding and will weed out the dumb options. But if America is to regain its competitive position in the world, or even hold what it has, we have to stop overdoing things on the rational side."[61] Hardly revolutionary.

As a counterpoint to over-reliance on rationality, Peters and Waterman championed the soft side of the Seven S model – style, skills, shared values, staff. "As we worked on research of our excellent companies, we were struck by the dominant use of story, slogan, and legend as people tried to explain the characteristics of their own institutions," they wrote. "All the companies we interviewed, from Boeing to McDonald's, were quite simply rich tapestries of anecdote, myth, and fairy tale. And we do mean fairy tale. The vast majority of people who tell stories today about T.J. Watson of IBM have never met the man or had direct experience of the original more mundane reality."[62] Excellent companies were as soft as you like, but hard around the edges.

While detailed reading quickly reveals caveats and get-out clauses, the *tone* of the book was undoubtedly revolutionary. The softer sides of management had not been so openly celebrated for decades.

"His contribution to the soft versus hard debate should not be underestimated," explains Andrew Campbell, author of *A Sense of Mission*, a book which deals with corporate values. "Peters and Mintzberg have been the two great peddlers of realism, humanism, and soft-side thinking. Without them, the rationalist bias of academics and consultants would have drowned out the lesser voices. The Peters phenomenon forced others to be more balanced in their thinking."

Big Is Beautiful

The central irony of *In Search of Excellence* was that, though it proposed a shake-up of organizations and the way they managed their people, its selection of "excellent" companies largely featured the corporate giants which had dominated US industry over the previous three decades. Companies such as IBM, Procter & Gamble, Johnson & Johnson, Western Electric, and Exxon were no young upstarts, but long-established, conservative corporate names; fixtures in any corporate hall of fame. They were the kind of companies McKinsey wanted to have as clients. (Though, in fact, none were McKinsey clients at the time.)

Excellent perhaps; original, they were not. "When I worked on *In Search of Excellence,* from 1978 to 1982, my eyes still mostly turned eastward (Detroit etc.), toward yesterday's big manufacturers. Now my gaze has shifted," Peters later commented.[63] In 1982, Peters and Waterman couldn't escape the temptation to assume that big was beautiful. Detroit still dominated views of the industrial world. Ten years later, Peters noted that "The book's chief failure, in retrospect, was that Waterman and I – both from conventional roots – mainly examined conventional firms."[64] The final "sample of 62 companies was never intended to be perfectly representative of US industry as a whole" wrote Peters and Waterman.[65] What, then, was it representative of?

In Search of Excellence attempted to get the best of both worlds. It condemned contemporary management as lacking in passion, being out of touch with reality, more concerned with balancing the books than with motivating people or delivering quality products and services. It proclaimed "Small is beautiful," celebrating 3M's "small, independent venture teams," Johnson & Johnson's "small divisions," IBM's teams, GE's "bootlegging teams," and "small, ever shifting segments at Digital."

Simultaneously, *In Search of Excellence* continued the veneration of big manufacturing businesses. It celebrated IBM, perhaps the most obvious choice in the book (at the time) and acknowledged General Motors. It echoed the eulogies to corporate might delivered by John Kenneth Galbraith and Alfred Chandler in his 1963 book, *Strategy and Structure*. A decade later, Peters wrote: "Make no mistake, Bob Waterman and I, who came of age in the '50s and '60s, were Galbraith's and Chandler's offspring!"[66]

The 62 "excellent" companies were chosen using a model which is strikingly traditional. Peters and Waterman selected six industry categories – high technology, consumer goods, general industrial, service, project management, and resource-based. They then identified six key financial measures – compound asset growth, compound equity growth, average ratio of market to book value, average return on total capital, average return on equity, and average return on sales. The most successful companies in each industry sector were then identified. From the 62 companies only 36 passed "all hurdles" to consider themselves excellent. Seven more privately-owned companies joined the excellent group as Peters and Waterman estimated they passed the criteria. A final group of 43 excellent companies emerged.

Aside from these financial measures, the selection – like any other – was subject to objective judgments. Take the example of one company. Daniel T. Carroll (who was to review *In Search of Excellence* far from favorably in the *Harvard Business Review*) met Peters on a plane from Brussels to New York a while before *In Search of Excellence* was published. "He was an impressive, superbly trained person," Carroll remembers. "After that he would send me materials from time to time on the excellence research. I was intrigued and my expectations were heightened. He then called and asked if he could pay me a visit. At the time I was CEO of Gould in the Chicago suburbs. He came over to see me in Rolling Meadows, Illinois, and spent a couple of hours in my office. A few months later I received an inscribed copy of *In Search of Excellence* thanking me for my contribution. I had mixed feelings because I didn't feel we had interacted to that extent. I felt it was an overstatement. I put the book aside. When I came to read it I was really disappointed because he had included Gould in the near misses. But he didn't know a damn thing about the company."

Carroll was studiously unimpressed, labeling *In Search of Excellence* as "careless, anecdotal stuff." "I was saddened because this fine individual with all his academic training was producing something so pedestrian." Carroll went on to air his annoyance in the *Harvard Business Review* where he reviewed the book. This came about soon after he received his signed copy from Peters. Carroll gave a talk in Florida attended by the editor of the *Harvard Business Review*, Ken Andrews. "He said if I put the stuff down in writing he would publish it," says Carroll. "He did and I thought I should write something about Peters and Waterman because people were running around as if *In Search of Excellence* was some kind of religious tract. I thought it was dangerous because it was so far from the truth." Carroll wrote his damning review, eventually titled "A disappointing search for excellence," and posted it to Ken Andrews asking his advice on who to send it to. He needed to look no further. Andrews called Carroll and said he agreed with what he had written. "He said it was an egregious piece – and that description has stuck in my mind. He stopped the production schedule to make sure it went in," says Carroll. The review appeared in the November/December 1983 issue of the *Review*.[67]

Carroll's criticisms of *In Search of Excellence* were wide-ranging. He questioned the basis of selection – hardly surprisingly since he was skeptical of how much Peters and Waterman knew about his own company. "The authors presume a definition of excellence that is almost certainly too narrow," wrote Carroll. He was also dismissive of Peters and Waterman's claims to be propounding a new management theory – "eight attributes do not a theory make," he suggested, before going on to examine the justifications given for the eight attributes of excellence. "As eager as one can be for quick and sure solutions to business dilemmas, the solutions' worth inescapably depends on the quality of the supporting evidence, which in the case of all eight is based neither on the excellent companies nor for that matter on any described research." Carroll was scathing of some of the "research" quoted in the book – conversations with someone who worked for McDonald's as a 17-year-old high school student or a conversation overheard in a Palo Alto bar did not strike him as grounds for any conclusions. He cited research "based heavily on secondary sources, non-excellent companies and unfortunate anecdotes" as bad enough, but what made *In Search of Excellence* worse in Carroll's eyes were "the unsupported generalizations that litter the chapters dealing with the eight attributes of excellent companies."

Much of what Dan Carroll said in his review of *In Search of Excellence* was accurate. Despite the years of preliminary research, conclusions are often drawn from flimsy – or unexplained – evidence. From the 43 excellent companies, Peters and Waterman noted that 14 stood out, linked by the fact that "each is a hands-on operator, not a holding company or a conglomerate." As a result of such vaguely inclusive criteria, the research base of the book rests uneasily with its contents. Indeed, the link between the research identifying the excellent companies and the contents of the book is often forgotten. Of the 62 "excellent" companies listed in *In Search of Excellence*, 15 aren't mentioned at all in the remainder of the book and the majority, 42, are mentioned less than five times. One of the select group of 14, Bechtel, is only mentioned six times. As a result, merely a handful of organizations are actually examined in any depth. If excellence is actually gauged by coverage in the book, there were only seven truly excellent companies: Dana, Hewlett-Packard, Texas Instruments, General Electric, Procter & Gamble, 3M and McDonald's.

Another obvious limitation of *In Search of Excellence* and its selection of companies, one mentioned in passing by Carroll, was the fact that it was purely American. Originally there were 75 companies in the sample gathered by Peters and Waterman. Of these 13 were European. The latter were weeded out as they did not "represent a fair cross-section of European companies."[68] Somewhat peculiarly, the French company, Schlumberger escaped the ax and remained in the final selection.

Despite the curiosity of having a research base with little relevance to the rest of the book's contents, Dan Carroll and other reviewers were reviewing a new type of business book. Despite the years of research, *In Search of Excellence* wasn't research-based in the same way as virtually every other book of its kind (though one academic reviewer hailed it as a classic of "exploratory research" preceding conventional analysis).. It did include stories from bars and passing conversations from which general conclusions were extracted. It was more indiscreet than its predecessors, more willing to venture an opinion and wait for corroboration, more willing to encompass vagueness.

And yet, despite this, the book's appeal proved truly international. "It still amazes me to this day that *In Search of Excellence* became a bestseller overseas," says Peters. "The Siemens research had a European component which I hadn't more interviews for. Looking at the research data it wasn't coherent enough. It wasn't a good look at Europe so Herb Henzler and I decided to drop the European stuff." Unburdened, the book took off.

The Excellence Companies

Excellent but did not meet all the criteria

1. American Airlines
2. Arco
3. Exxon
4. General Electric
5. General Foods
6. General Motors
7. Gould
8. Ingersoll-Rand
9. Lockheed
10. McDermott
11. NCR
12. Polaroid
13. Rockwell
14. TRW
15. United Technologies
16. Western Electric
17. Westinghouse
18. Xerox

Excellent and met the criteria

1. Allen-Bradley
2. Amdahl
3. Atari (Warner Communications)
4. Avon
5. Blue Bell
6. Bristol-Myers
7. Chesebrough-Pond's
8. Data General
9. Disney Productions
10. Dow Chemical
11. DuPont
12. Eastman Kodak
13. Frito-Lay (PepsiCo)
14. Hughes Aircraft
15. Intel

16. K Mart
17. Levi Strauss
18. Marriott
19. Mars
20. Maytag
21. Merck
22. National Semiconductor
23. Raychem
24. Revlon
25. Schlumberger
26. Standard Oil (Indiana)/Amoco
27. Texas Instruments
28. Tupperware (Dart & Kraft)
29. Wal-Mart
30. Wang Labs

Exemplars of excellence
1. Bechtel
2. Boeing
3. Caterpillar Tractor
4. Dana Corp
5. Delta Airlines
6. Digital Equipment
7. Emerson Electric
8. Fluor
9. Hewlett-Packard
10. IBM
11. Johnson & Johnson
12. McDonald's
13. Minnesota Mining & Manufacturing (3M)
14. Procter & Gamble

Breaking the Mold

In Search of Excellence was narrow in perspective; often strikingly banal in its insights; contradictory in its selection process; nationalistic; and written by two unknown management consultants.

Yet, *In Search of Excellence* broke the mold. After slipping quietly onto the nation's bookshelves, *In Search of Excellence* took on a life of its own. "You couldn't troop an airplane aisle without seeing several business people reading it," recalls Peters.[69] "We would get sales reports from book stores. The Basking Ridge book store near AT&T headquarters was selling 2000 copies a week." *In Search of Excellence* was published in October 1982 and reached the *New York Times* bestseller list in April 1983 where it stayed for two years. It was the first management book to ever rank number one on the bestseller list – and Peters' sequel, *A Passion for Excellence,* was the second.

In Search of Excellence has now sold nearly six million copies. Its success has been truly international. It sold 100,000 copies in three years in the notoriously skeptical French market and proved a bestseller virtually everywhere else in Europe and beyond. When, in 1988, Peters made his first trip to China, he met at least five different publishers who had bestselling Chinese editions of *In Search of Excellence.*

When hardback sales reached the unprecedented figure of one million, after a mere 11 months, Peters and Waterman arranged a party (which, Peters is quick to point out, they paid for). Harper & Row's top management team were among those flown over to San Francisco to celebrate the book's success. Peters' mother,

Evelyn, was also among the celebrants in a Palo Alto restaurant who watched a plane fly past with a congratulatory banner trailing after it. "I can't really remember much of that time," says Peters. "Bob and I were in a state of suspended animation. This state of shock lasted for two or three years."

Even now, the book's impact remains strongly imprinted on people's minds. The man who hired the plane was a Swedish consultant, Sven Atterhed, who contacted Peters when he read the initial *Business Week* article. "*In Search of Excellence* picked up what some people felt intuitively, but no-one had spoken about those things in a way that made sense," says Atterhed. "We were stumbling around experimenting but Peters and Waterman had done the research."

"It was very exciting," says former McKinsey consultant, George Binney. "It was from the best traditions of American research – rigorous, practical, and helpful. It was clear that it was a different type of business book, a new generation." Jim Balloun, formerly in the San Francisco office, moved to Tokyo and found that best practice in Japan struck a chord with Peters and Waterman's work on excellence. "When I got to the Tokyo office I found that many of the things written about in *In Search of Excellence* were being put into practice in Japan. *In Search of Excellence* was a wonderful benchmark."

McKinsey's Bill Matassoni observes: "*In Search of Excellence* took off and had an enormous impact – though I am not sure about its impact on McKinsey. It was a different animal to any other business book. Tom brought people into the business bookstore for the first time." The effect was more specific than that, says Harriet Rubin, executive director of Doubleday's Currency Books: "It created a whole new audience of readers – men. It was the first such book to bring men into the bookstores in big numbers."[70]

The world was taken by surprise by this macho-success. There was no inkling that *In Search of Excellence* would succeed. Harper & Row began by ordering reprints of 15,000 but then had to raise it to 50,000 to meet demand. Matassoni had sat through the Cody gatherings, plowed through earlier drafts and had helped garner early publicity, but he was astonished. McKinsey colleagues of

Peters and Waterman were equally taken aback. There was not a McKinsey consultant who believed the book would sell. "No-one anticipated its success. Until then a really big business book would sell perhaps 10,000. This sold millions," says Jim Balloun, a veteran of 31 years with McKinsey. The publishers must have pinched themselves before ordering yet another reprint.

What was also unusual was the passionate nature of the response. The people who bought *In Search of Excellence* and liked it, became true believers, undaunted by jibes from their more cynical colleagues. The believers then sought out converts. The British industrialist, Sir Peter Parker, was given 17 copies of the book in two years by converts anxious that he join the bandwagon. Sir Christopher Hogg, then chairman of textile company Courtaulds, was an enthusiast. He bought copies for a few of his executives. Among them was John Harris, now CEO of Amtico, who became a convert. His story is typical. "I remember reading the book *en route* to the US and was so impressed I read most of it again on the return flight. It put a frame around what we were instinctively trying to do and provided a valuable tool to explain the West's best were doing the same. We then bought 50 books, distributed them throughout the company and held staff meetings to discuss how we might implement some of the ideas that were new to us and strengthen our resolve on those already being practised." Harris' enthusiasm remains undimmed – his company bought Peters' tapes, sends people to Peters' seminars, and works with the UK arm of his company. "Whilst there are cynics among the MBAs I employ, the rest of us believe the philosophy expounded is the way forward."[71]

The success of *In Search of Excellence* was, of course, not universally celebrated. "I hear that six people at Harvard Business School went into psychotherapy because they were so upset and somehow I didn't deserve this," Peters has light-heartedly observed.[72] There were doubters and skeptics as well as adherents. Dan Carroll was not the only one to bridle at the book's message. "Tom Peters, in his much acclaimed book, *In Search of Excellence*, accidentally discovered mediocrity," observed one unimpressed commentator.

Among the skeptics was the stately voice of Peter Drucker who gave *In Search of Excellence* a half-life of six months. "Half of the two or three million books they sold were graduation presents for high school graduates," caustically observed the doyen of management writers, adding, "The great virtue of the Peters and Waterman book is its extreme simplicity, maybe oversimplification. But when Aunt Mary has to give that nephew of hers a high school graduation present and she gives him *In Search of Excellence*, you know that management has become part of the general culture."[73] There was more. "The strength of the Peters book is that it forces you to look at the fundamentals. The book's great weakness – which is a strength from the point of view of its success – is that it makes managing sound so incredibly easy. All you have to do is put that book under your pillow, and it'll get done," concluded Drucker.[74] Over a decade later, Peters shrugs his shoulders at Drucker's barbs. "One of the great services we did was that Peter Drucker started giving interviews," he says.

The book's success owed something to a fairly indiscriminate, and uncontrived, marketing campaign mounted by Peters and Waterman. Prior to publication they actually copied 15,000 of the fabled "Orange Book" and sent them to interested parties. Unbeknown to them, they were starting a groundswell. The publishers were, not surprisingly, unimpressed by such largesse – it seemed as if these two first-time authors were intent on giving all their possible sales away before the book was even published. "We could not have more effectively marketed the book if we had planned the process meticulously," Peters later concluded.[75]

In Search of Excellence also benefitted from the kudos associated with McKinsey. "Managers beset with seemingly intractable problems and years of frustration with strategy and structure shifts were finally ready for a new view by 1980. Moreover, putting the stamp of McKinsey, long known for its hard nosed approach to management problem solving, behind the new model added immense power," Peters and Waterman admitted in the book.[76]

Until *In Search of Excellence* McKinsey had not been an active breeding ground for aspiring authors. "From a publishing standpoint McKinsey had always been rather nefarious. Marvin Bower sponsored a *sub rosa* connection to the *Harvard Business Review* but the product was mild mannered stuff. We wanted to go more visible," says Peters. This was not exactly a bold ambition –

McKinsey's prime vehicle of disseminating its latest thinking, the *McKinsey Quarterly*, makes the *Harvard Business Review* look like *Playboy*.

That *In Search of Excellence* was more visible cannot be doubted. The previous year's publications from the McKinsey stable included such predictable non-sellers as *Mathematical Planning Procedures* and *Sales Force Planning and Control in Insurance Companies*. Indeed, book writing was more likely to be regarded as a distraction from the real business of billing clients. The fact that McKinsey was willing, somewhat unenthusiastically and skeptically, to support a book represented something of a change in direction. Its riposte, under Ron Daniel, to the emergence of Boston Consulting Group as a genuine competitor was to broaden its ambit. From a position where it blithely asserted that it had the smartest people on the block, McKinsey began to cultivate its smartness, making it clear to the outside world that it invested in people who knew the optimum solutions to business problems. *In Search of Excellence* was part of this process.

From 1982 onwards, McKinsey has produced a steady supply of mainstream management books. Nineteen eighty two also saw the publication of Terence Deal and Allan Kennedy's *Corporate Cultures* and Kenichi Ohmae's *The Mind of the Strategist*. (Kennedy was part of McKinsey's organizational practice and credited Peters as "the intellectual and spiritual godfather" of his and Deal's book.) Since then there have been Richard Cavanagh and Donald Clifford's *The Winning Performance* (1985); Joel Bleeke and David Ernst's *Collaborating to Compete* (1992); *Real Change Leaders* (1995) by seven consultants; Max Landsberg's *The Tao of Coaching* (1996); and over a book a year from the prolific Kenichi Ohmae who has now left the company.

Not that McKinsey's principles were compromised along the way. For all its bestseller status, *In Search of Excellence* was an archetypal McKinsey book. Even now, its cover is free of endorsements or embellishments, unsullied by the usual crass marketing. Instead, it is gold (the premium color) and black: serious, high quality.

Within McKinsey, the success of *In Search of Excellence* made waves – not surprising when the Sargasso Sea becomes the Pacific

Ocean. "Everyone was shocked and genuinely pleased at the book's success. The idea of writing a business book was a non-event. Most people thought of business books as textbooks," says then McKinsey consultant, Michael Lanning. "There was some mild cynicism, but people didn't really care that much. It wasn't considered key to McKinsey's success. With a smaller firm it would have been a much bigger deal. We didn't follow up on *In Search of Excellence* in any way, though it may have opened a few doors. Some people in the firm thought it was great and tried to use the eight principles but that was short-lived. The principles weren't analytical or strategic enough. McKinsey's work doesn't lend itself to the eight principles."

Another former McKinsey consultant, George Binney, provides a more positive angle: "*In Search of Excellence* put McKinsey in a different bracket. Its enormous coverage brought McKinsey a different profile – it was not just a firm which did organization studies but one concerned with really helping people to run businesses."

The ideas championed in *In Search of Excellence* weren't the ones normally associated with McKinsey and it was not prepared to roll over and wholeheartedly embrace them. Indeed, McKinsey managing director, Ron Daniel, wrote a foreword to Pascale and Athos' *The Art of Japanese Management* rather than to *In Search of Excellence*. McKinsey now insists that it retains control over books written by its consultants.

But, most of all, *In Search of Excellence* succeeded because the timing was right, exactly right. "*In Search of Excellence* was genuinely new and the timing was right," says Lennart Arvedson. The unvarnished truth is that with *In Search of Excellence* Peters and Waterman got lucky, very lucky. You couldn't say that *In Search of Excellence* is a better book than *The Art of Japanese Management* or William Ouchi's *Theory Z*. It is researched and efficiently written, but it is not earth shatteringly comprehensive, authoritative or poetical. It is good, but not that good.

"*In Search of Excellence* is a garden-variety 'excellent' product – a pretty good product blessed with impeccable timing. 'Timing' is a word that business persons by and large prefer to 'luck,' because it makes it sound as if you might have played at least a little role in the outcome," says Peters. "What was the magic of *In Search of Excellence*? It was launched during the month in 1982 when US unemployment hit 10 percent for the first time since the Great Depression. People were in the midst of a big 'downer.' And the book purported to be about 'great American companies.' Moreover, the best-selling management books of all time up to that point – *Theory Z, The Art of Japanese Management* – had said, in effect: 'Everything that's good and new in management is going on in Japan.' The authors of those books, all close colleagues, had gotten to the market a year before Bob Waterman and I did. Our delay, which irritated us at the time, was a god-send – yet another synonym for luck. People were fed up with 'their' message, and welcomed ours. *In Search of Excellence* was about wacky ideas – 'the rational model has led us astray.' If they'd been presented by a professor, well forget it. But our book came out in a conservative black-and-gold cover and was supported by a conservative consultancy, McKinsey and Company. I say all this, I reiterate, with the benefit of hindsight. We had not a clue about the importance of these or a thousand other things at the time."[77] As Peters and Waterman no doubt reflected, such is life.

In Search of Excellence redefined the marketplace for business books. Books such as Ruff's *How to Prosper During the Coming Bad Years* (1979) with sales of 450,000, Casey's *Crisis in Investing* (1980) which sold 439,000 copies, and Cohen's *You Can Negotiate Anything* (1981) with 205,000 sales had suggested that there could be a mass market. *In Search of Excellence* revealed that the market really did exist and was bigger than any published dared dream about.

The Legacy

Given its sales and the surrounding hubbub, it is difficult to be objective about *In Search of Excellence*. It is akin to discussing *Citizen Kane* simply as a movie, or *The Beatles* as a pop group. Looking again at *In Search of Excellence*, it is striking that, in many areas, its ideas appear hackneyed and obvious. In the late 1990s, they *are* – but, at the time it was published, they were not.

With unusual candor, especially for management authors and consultants, Peters and Waterman argued in the book that what they were saying wasn't new or original. "Most of the theory has stood the scientific test of time and defied refutation. It merely has been ignored, by and large, by managers and management writers," they wrote.[78] This is a clever way of introducing a management book – our theories already exist so deride them at your peril!

Some of the book clearly stands up to reexamination. "The first 70 or 80 pages were, at the time, and might still be, the best précis of social psychology and motivation you can find," says Lennart Arvedson. But, in its identification of excellence with big companies, *In Search of Excellence* is now plainly out of step with our times – and Peters' own thinking.

At the same time, closer analysis of *In Search of Excellence* shows that Peters and Waterman concentrated their attentions on the roguish offshoots of big corporations. Of the excellent companies, they noted: "Perhaps the most important element of their enviable track record is an ability to be big and yet to act small at the same time."[79] "Things of quality are produced by craftsmen, generally requiring small-scale enterprise, we are told. Activities that achieve cost efficiencies, on the other hand, are reputedly best done in large facilities, to achieve economies of scale. Except that that is not the way it works in the excellent companies. In the excellent companies, small in almost every case is beautiful. The small facility turns out to be the most efficient; its turned-on, motivated, highly productive worker, in communication (and competition) with his peers, outproduces the worker in the big facilities time and again."[80]

Peters and Waterman were attracted to lack of structure – a 3M executive is quoted in the book saying "The 3M structure, if you just look at it on paper, doesn't seem to have anything that is terribly unique." And, in even stronger language, a 3M executive observed: "Structural form is irrelevant to us."[81]

Structural flexibility was, therefore, identified as a vital ingredient in excellence. In the years since, such flexibility has become the core of many managerial theorists and a profusion of books – including those by Peters himself. Another aspect of this, which *In Search of Excellence* anticipated, was the need for speed – "Innovative companies are especially adroit at continually responding to change of any sort in their environment," observed Peters and Waterman.[82] Again the need for speed of delivery, or of anything else, has become a corporate cliché.

Underpinning many of Peters and Waterman's arguments was the question of corporate values. They considered that companies without values were, literally, valueless. (Interestingly, among their McKinsey colleagues in San Francisco was Robert Haas who went on to champion values and ethics as chairman of Levi Strauss.) Again, recent years have seen a great deal more interest in corporate values. *In Search of Excellence* pointed in that direction without being truly categoric. "What one is simplistic about is vitally important. It's a focus on the external, on service, on quality, on people, on informality . . . And those may very well be things – the only things – worth being simplistic about," wrote Peters and Waterman.[83] "It appears that the real role of the chief executive is to manage the values of the organization."[84] (The use of "appears" is typical – a potentially sweeping statement is tempered by a word of caution. *Hold on, now – let's not go too far.* Such uncharacteristic caution is attributed by Peters to his academic training. The average PhD thesis is littered with such qualifications.)

Elsewhere, Peters and Waterman dipped their toes tentatively into what were to become big ideas. They signposted the route to the future rather than taking us there – the title of the book was highly accurate. "Excellence was a brilliant objective – an uplifting ideal," says Andrew Campbell. "You have to remember that the term 'competitive advantage' had only recently come into common business language. Managers had only started thinking deeply about competitiveness in the late 1970s. Excellence, with its people orientation and with Peters' passion, was totally seductive in a way that competitive advantage has never been. It signposted so much that came after – total quality, just in time, six sigma objectives – in other words the search for a score of 10 out of 10. Before Peters no one was aiming that high."

Another signpost was one for empowerment – "The message that comes through so poignantly in the studies we reviewed is that we like to think of ourselves as winners. The lesson that the excellent companies have to teach is that there is no reason why we can't design systems that continually reinforce this notion; most of their people are made to feel that they are winners;"[85] the learning organization – "The excellent companies are learning organizations;"[86] and more fluid corporate structures.

But, *In Search of Excellence*'s greatest impact was in its championing of customer service and quality. "We repeatedly found examples of those who pursue quality with quixotic zeal," wrote Peters and Waterman.[87] They ignited the interest in those issues. Soon after, they exploded into a wave of quality initiatives, and led to the belated discovery of the quality gurus, Deming and Juran. Peters and Waterman cannot take credit for the Western discovery of quality, but they firmly pushed Western businesses in that direction.

Finally, *In Search of Excellence* changed the language of management. Peters and Waterman talked about people rather than employees. They eulogized over customers and coined neat phrases to make management less mysterious and more accessible. (They also, lest it be forgotten, introduced the word "stuff" into the management vocabulary.) "We need new language. We need to consider adding terms to our management vocabulary: a few might be temporary structures, ad hoc groups, fluid organizations, small is beautiful, incrementalism, experimentation, action orientation, imitations, lots of tries, unjustified variations, internal competition, playfulness, the technology of foolishness, product champions, bootlegging, skunk works, cabals, and shadow organizations. Each of these turns the tables on conventional wisdom. Each implies both the absence of clear directions and the simultaneous need for action," they wrote.[88]

This accessibility – criticized by Peter Drucker – was at the heart of *In Search of Excellence*'s success and of its message. It struck a chord. The mystery of management was stripped away. "Tom made management popular. While a lot of the academic stuff which went before was not enjoyable, he managed to make it more fun, a part of life," says Max Worcester of *Frankfurter Allgemeine Zeitung*.

Among the converts was Herb Kelleher of Southwest Airlines: "My first impression of Tom and of his work was that he was bringing a new, refreshing and welcome perspective, insight and emphasis to how to do business successfully and humanistically at the same time. When I read his earlier works, I said to myself: 'That's what I have been trying to do and now I *know* what I'm doing – and why'." Many thousands of managers echoed Kelleher's sentiments.

THREE

CORPORATE MAN

" *I'm an engineer by training – and disposition* "

Tom Peters[89]

December 2nd, 1974, San Francisco

The 32-year-old Tom Peters arrived at the San Francisco offices of McKinsey & Company promptly – 9.00 a.m. on the dot. It was his first day and he knew of McKinsey's reputation for punctuality. Anyway, he was nervous as hell and hadn't slept. Five years in the Navy and four as a Stanford student are preparation for many things. But were they preparation enough for the world's top consultancy firm?

Peters checked in at the McKinsey & Co. office on the forty-eighth floor of the Bank of America world headquarters. Company credit cards were handed over. He got the keys to the office – he would be working late. And that was that. Half an hour into his McKinsey career he was ready for work.

He looked around. The office was all but deserted – something he would quickly become used to. There was no sign of Jon Katzenbach who had hired him. He had been assigned to a team, so looked around to find the members. A few minutes later he had located his colleagues, or at least he thought he had located them. People seemed unsure, but the safest bet seemed to be that one was in Oklahoma, another in Iowa, and the other in New York City. Some welcome, thought Peters.

The office chief passed by to brief him on his first assignment. He seemed mildly surprised that Peters was still there and not at San Francisco airport. "You're working on a project for Skelly Oil," said the chief. "It's a new ammonia plant . . . $150 million-worth of investment they want to get right." Peters heard the message loud and clear – he had received enough orders in his life: get it right, don't screw it up, we're talking big bucks.

"I think you should get yourself to New York and take it from there," said the chief as he started to leave. *"There's a flight this afternoon."*

Peters examined a pile of papers which was neatly stacked on his desk. His name was carefully written on the front. This was it. His first assignment as a consultant. He leafed through the file and found his instructions. He was to arrange to meet up with a microeconomics expert to talk fertilizer. There was, he thought, a lot of fertilizer to come. Next he was to head for the Skelly plant in Clinton, Iowa.

He sorted out his flight and read through the background. It made sense. You get an expensive consultant in and what does he do? He hires another consultant who knows about fertilizer. When Peters arrived in Clinton he was freshly briefed on fertilizer. He headed to the downtown hotel where his elusive team-mate had been staying. He had already left, destined for Skelly HQ in Tulsa.

Peters went out for a coffee. He pondered the 25-year cash-flow projections the client wanted and stared at the granules as he worked out a means of discovering the likely cost of feedstock for the next quarter of a century. Two days into his McKinsey career he had yet to meet his team or his team leader. There were nearly 1000 McKinsey consultants and over 170 partners spread throughout the world. He knew more about fertilizer than he ever thought there was to know, and here he was, in Clinton, Iowa, at the customer site for the first time. He thought about the sizable daily fee McKinsey was charging Skelly for his presence. He was on his own, situation normal.

After introducing himself to Skelly, Peters received further instructions. His next port of call was to be Calgary, to assess Canadian supply and demand for agrichemicals over the next 20 years. After a day trawling through reports and statistics, Peters determined he needed help – the consultant desperately needed a consultant. He went out and hired a two-person firm, which he determined knew the ins and outs of the Canadian agrichemical industry, to undertake a week long study. Still there was no word from the team leader.

The Development of
a Corporate Man

The Tom Peters who hesitantly walked through the doors of the
Bank of America building on a Monday morning in 1974 was
dramatically different from the man who now stalks stages in a
flurry of sweat, energy, and opinion. He was the archetypal
corporate man.

"If they had known what they were getting, it's doubtful that
McKinsey, with its clipped, sharp, staid young overachievers
would ever have hired him," concludes Art Kleiner in *The Age of
Heretics*.[90] There is no doubting that Peters has never been
clipped. But he was – and is – sharp; he could look as staid,
though not perhaps as neat, as the next man in a dull suit, and he
was an achiever. In fact, in 1974, Peters was McKinsey material
par excellence.

McKinsey always fills its vacant positions with the same kind
of person. Its principle is: if they work don't change them. Former
McKinsey managing director, Ron Daniel, has outlined the
company's recruitment philosophy: "The real competition out
there isn't for clients, it's for people. And we look to hire people
who are: first, very smart; second, insecure and thus driven by their
insecurity; and third, competitive. Put together 3000 of these
egocentric, task-oriented people, and it produces an atmosphere
of something less than humility. Yes, it's elitist. But don't you think
there has to be room somewhere in this politically correct world
for something like this?"[91]

Tom Peters fitted – and fits – the McKinsey bill as mapped out by Daniel. He is smart – no-one bluffs their way into McKinsey. He appears insecure – "I know nothing" is his constant refrain. And he is highly competitive. In addition, Peters came from a post-war generation weaned on the overbearing power of monolithic corporations – "I was born in 1942 and reached semi-adult awareness during the Tasty Kake Eisenhower years," he says. "Young men about to enter the world were admonished 'keep your nose clean, don't make waves' – and collect your gold watch after 40 years of labor for reliable old XYZ Widgets."[92] His entire upbringing and the spirit of the times was that large organizations were the most efficient means of making capitalism happen. Big meant economies of scale and, from the perspective of employees, a benevolent paternalism (in theory, at least). Noses were assiduously kept clean – when they were freed from the corporate grindstone.

The corporate ethos was all-embracing and there is no evidence to suggest that the young Peters was the kind to buck the system. Peters was in his early thirties when he arrived at McKinsey, and by then he had worked in some of the highest profile and tightly disciplined environments in the world. Now he was ready for his own XYZ Widgets.

Shaping The Man

Peters' father, Frank Peters, had found his XYZ Widgets in the shape of Baltimore Gas & Electric Co. where he worked for 41 years. Frank's career was typical for the times. "He was pretty sure, from one year to the next (from one decade to the next), what door on Lexington Street he'd enter at 8.30 a.m. any given Monday through Friday," says his son.[93] Peters' grandfather had arrived from Germany around 1870 and Frank Peters carried on the German work ethic. "He was a formal fellow; there was a bit of Prussian left," says Peters of his father.[94] Even so, Frank Peters is remembered by his son as "an exceptional fella – bright, engaging." "I now respect my father intellectually though we argued like cat and dog. I was often pissed off at his points of view but then found myself parroting them." Frank Peters died in June 1980, four days before his son's first nationally published article – a column on the op-ed page of the *Wall Street Journal*.

Thomas Jacob Peters was born in Baltimore and raised near Annapolis, Maryland, south of Baltimore. His affiliation to the city is now restricted to long-standing support for the Baltimore Orioles and a fading talent for lacrosse. Frank and Evelyn Peters were not poor, but far from rich, and Tom was an only child. When they bought their first car in 1951, a Chevrolet, it was a major event. Such was the family's excitement that, Peters later reflected, his father wouldn't have taken the car back even if it had been delivered without an axle.[95]

Peters grew up in the age of segregation – he remembers the "colored" and "white" toilets at the local service station. But he had an unexceptional, happy, childhood. "I had lots of friends and it was a neat little community," he says. Among his childhood distractions were occasional weekend visits to the JF Johnson Lumber Co. in Annapolis, ten miles away, to buy lumber for one of his father's projects. "I still remember the pungent odor of fresh sawdust, which covered my clothes upon our return home, and watching the powerful blades rip through a sheet of plywood in seconds. The tough old fellows at the saws often had a finger missing, a stern warning to any youngster dreaming about a career in home carpentry," he later recalled.[96]

Peters' mother, Evelyn Peters, was a teacher. His parents took him out of the state school and he went to a small private junior high school, called Severn, in 1955. After that Evelyn Peters taught the fifth grade in a nearby suburban elementary school. Her influence on her only child was far-reaching – and continues even now she is in her eighties. She is acknowledged at the start of *In Search of Excellence* – "Tom owes special thanks to his mother, Evelyn Peters, who inculcated the restless curiosity that led to this research."[97] She encouraged his voracious reading, directing him towards history books – "My mother force-fed me history from the age of four and a half," says Peters. Evelyn Peters had high aspirations for her son though she did not imagine him becoming a captain of industry.

Peters' 1994 book, *The Tom Peters Seminar*, is dedicated to "Evelyn Peters, a talker who raised a talker." Peters recalls her "making four friends in an elevator between the ground and fifteenth floor." "That is not an apocryphal story. I've seen it happen."[98]

At school, Peters was academically successful, especially at math ("math was off the charts") but failed to excel in sports ("I was lousy, really lousy. I'm just not co-ordinated"). The young Peters also won an award for his involvement in extra-curricular activities. "I had this fabulous teacher who got me into debating, and I edited the yearbook and a zillion things like that. But I was not interested in things that chief executive officers always do. I was not a leader in student government."[99] Conventional, unexceptional and middle-class, the young Peters was not an automatic candidate for stardom. He was no rebel – "I was not rebellious in the sense of our current commander in chief who went to Oxford and, according to the right-wingers, rebelled against his country"[100] – just a smarter-than-average kid growing up in an average American environment of the 1950s and early 1960s.

Slowly, Peters' ambitions turned towards going to university. "I grew up in a small town and went to a prep school which had been a prep for the US Naval Academy. It wasn't one of those schools which fed kids into the Ivy League system automatically," he says. But, Frank and Evelyn Peters were keen for their son to carry on his education – "My parents would have starved themselves for me to go to university," says Peters. "I was pushed, but not excessively so, by people at high school. Going to university was a step which just seemed to evolve."

Building Bridges

After graduating from high school, Tom Peters went to Cornell to study architecture. "I wanted to be a chemist, then an architect, and now I haven't a clue," he admits. Architecture proved the wrong choice. "My only fascination was with architecture though I dropped out of the course at Cornell after one semester because I had as much artistic talent as a sea slug," recalls Peters. "These were the just post-Sputnik days when engineering was everything so I switched to engineering. Building things is still around on the back-burner. I am fascinated by design."

Indeed, the engineer in Peters remains strong. He wants to take things apart to see how they work. "I'm an engineer by training – and disposition," he later admitted in *Thriving on Chaos*."[101] His masters degree in engineering featured a then state-of-the-art treatise on combining probabilistic time distributions in multitask PERT (Program Evaluation and Review Technique) design. Peters claims later to have created the world's most complex PERT chart. This is a dubious distinction.

It is perhaps difficult to imagine now, but Peters the engineer still thinks of himself as a "traditional manager" reared on a diet of rationalism, numbers, and measurements. "I was trained as a civil engineer. I cotton to build bridges, dams, and other very lumpy objects. I went on to business training – where the hard, cold numbers, Joe Friday's 'just the facts, ma'am' attitude, prevailed."[102]

At Cornell, Peters graduated number two in a class of 60 and emerged as a Bachelor in Civil Engineering. Ithaca's College Town may be an intellectual hot-bed, but Peters regrets the limitations imposed by his course of study. "My training in engineering was anti-literate. I am still mad at Cornell because I went for five years without reading anything apart from the crap you have to read in engineering text books."[103] But read them he did.

Curiously, Peters' time at Cornell coincided with that of two others who would eventually write business bestsellers: John Naisbitt (of *Megatrends* fame) and Kenneth Blanchard (author of *The One Minute Manager* and a host of variations). Blanchard and Peters were in the same fraternity and lived for a while in the same house. During 1983, these three Cornell alumni filled the top three slots in the *New York Times* bestseller lists.

Peters received a scholarship from the US Navy for his Cornell studies. To him, it seemed a natural enough thing to do. "I grew up in the shadow of a the US Naval Academy in Annapolis and lived by the river so boats and things that floated were natural to me. I also had an uncle who was in the Marine Corps who I greatly admired," he says. "In the context of the time, joining the Navy wasn't unusual. Everyone was in some kind of training corps. You knew that you had to do military service anyway so you might as well do it with some stripes on your arm. If you signed on for four years instead of two they paid for your tuition." Having taken the Navy's shilling, he had to carry out his side of the bargain. (The payback had already started – before graduating from Cornell, Peters served a stint as a US Navy midshipman on a British warship, *HMS Tiger*.)

Peters' Cornell training was put to immediate use. "The Navy paid my way through Cornell and I paid them back with four years of service," he says. In the Navy, Peters' first port of call was supposed to be Antarctica until President Johnson intervened. In 1966, Peters left for Vietnam as a 24-year-old US Navy ensign in an 800-person Seabee (construction) battalion. "I put on a boiler suit and avoided the bridge, and ended up in the Seabees," says Peters. It was his first real job. In the next four years he went through two tours in Vietnam, a spell in the Pentagon, and earned a Navy Commendation Medal, a Meritorious Service Medal, and various other decorations.

The Seabees, the Navy Civil Engineering Corp, were invented

in World War II to support the Marine Corps by being their construction arm. "Their logo was 'Can Do,' which was fairly merited. Breaking rules was par for the course. It was a cantankerous outfit," says Peters.

He found himself in Da Nang, Vietnam, building bridges, airstrips, and gun emplacements. (Over 16 months, his unit was responsible for $20 million-worth of construction.) War or not, Peters loved it. "I had a ball in Vietnam. The military in time of war is a rule-less society. It is about improvisation. You wore the clothes but other than that it was improvisational theater. The fog of war is all-improving. You come out of regimented university and regimented society and there are no rules. You're told to build a gun emplacement when you hadn't done one before."

Headstrong, talkative, and smart, Tom Peters was not a submissive recruit for Uncle Sam. He tended to forget when to salute ("You really ought to salute, Tom, I *am* your commanding officer," said his military boss) and, in Vietnam, would sometimes disappear for several days to contemplate a particular project. (It was a habit he kept up in his later career, sometimes extending his absences into weeks – and, on one occasion, months: he was fired.) A Naval citation noted Peters' "unusual initiative, thoroughness, and diligence."

His commanding officer, Captain Dick Anderson, didn't receive the salutes his rank merited but provided lasting inspiration. Peters recalls it as "almost instant growth and flowering. Dick was a demanding taskmaster (all the best coaches are), but he was demanding because he cared."[104] "Dick (as I learned to call him *many* years later) chuckled at my utter disregard of his eminence – and my preoccupation with the task at hand. He'd gently chide me about it from time to time . . . but he was clearly a supporter. Which I never forgot: As a sometime boss, I've spent the last quarter-century trying to emulate him."[105]

In 1968 Lieutenant Peters was assigned to the Pentagon and worked for Lt. Commander Joe Key. Again, Key provided an example the young Peters carefully noted. "Joe was fearless. He'd charge into an admiral's office and ask a question. The stunned admiral (who hadn't hung around with lieutenant commanders for years) gave him the answer," says Peters.[106]

Authority, the young Peters learned, was there to be challenged and those who held it were human – and sometimes humane – after all.

Back to School

Lured by a scholarship, Tom Peters originally signed up for four years with the Navy. He left in April 1970 and so escaped the fury of his mother who did not relish the prospect of her son remaining a naval builder of bridges. But what next? While in Washington, Peters had done some part-time work as a financial planning consultant and a real-estate salesman. The naval builder of bridges could have carried on building bridges. Peters decided otherwise. "I didn't know what to do after the Navy. I didn't have any better ideas than doing an MBA," he says. It was a move not exactly fired by a burning interest in the subject he would be studying. "I went to business school because that's what people were doing. My half dozen best friends had decided the MBA was hot. The MBA became a popular phenomenon at the time and two thirds of my buddies went to Harvard," says Peters.

Already looking to the future, he applied to the Harvard and Stanford MBA programs in January 1970. His selection was not the result of a great deal of research. "There was a magazine, *MBA Magazine* or something, and it rated Stanford as the number two school behind Harvard. It appeared to be the coming place so I applied to Stanford and Harvard. Looking back I can't believe I was so arrogant. I applied in person within moments of the last date for admission. I went to Boston on a typical January day. It was gray and miserable. Then I went to the San Francisco Bay Area and it was just after a storm – it was 50 degrees, the air was clear, and the palms were doing what you expect palms to do. Hedonism was the central factor in my decision to go to Stanford. I looked around at the Bay Area and thought it was time for good weather."

In the interim, Peters needed to find a job in the civilian marketplace. He had no driving ambition to work in any particular area. Thoughts of being an architect had disappeared and building bridges seemed a road to nowhere in particular. "When I left I didn't know what to do. But I needed a job so I worked for Peat, Marwick in Washington, DC for a few months. It was not a formative experience, tantamount to nothing though I learned a few things," he remembers. His brief spell with Peat, Marwick (now KPMG) was Tom Peters' first taste of the world of management consultancy (and earned him a base salary of $16,800).

After Peat, Marwick the newly awakened hedonist headed West to Stanford Business School, a place not known for its willingness to countenance hedonistic distractions. While Harvard is the premier business school, period; Stanford is the premier West Coast business school. Founded in 1885, Stanford University is 35 miles south of San Francisco and a few miles north of the high-technology center of Silicon Valley. Today, Stanford has nearly 25,000 students, faculty and staff from 50 states and 100 countries. Its pedigree is long and impressive, if you are impressed by pedigrees. The current US Secretary of State and four of the nine Supreme Court justices are all Stanford graduates. Herbert Hoover was founder of the Business School. Stanford Business School's 21,000 living alumnae include six members of the American Academy of Arts and Sciences, two members of the National Academy of Sciences, one member of the National Academy of Engineering, two John Bates Clark medallists in economics, and one Nobel laureate in economic sciences, as well as two former US cabinet secretaries – Secretary of Health, Education and Welfare, John Gardner, and Secretary of State George Shultz. Stanford is not for lightweights.

The Stanford MBA is tough. Like many other such programs, it demands a degree of masochism. You have to be highly motivated, committed, and very ambitious. It is also helpful to be a speed-reading insomniac with an obsessive streak. (Put like this you begin to wonder why MBAs are so highly prized and why corporations give the mental misfits a job at the end.) In his book, *Snapshots from Hell,* Peter Robinson describes the trials, tribulations and caffeine soaked late-night sessions involved in tackling a Stanford MBA. Peters enthusiastically endorsed the book ("Fabulous . . . it's fun, it's wild, it's weird. I loved the book"). Robinson's account is, in reality, far from wild or weird; it's simply a tale of hard work and nightmarish lectures with heavyweight intellectuals and a classroom of people who want to be merchant bankers or McKinsey consultants. Robinson remembers particularly the trauma of cold calls in lectures when the lecturer randomly selected a member of the class and put them on the spot – "roughly the classroom equivalent of the right to launch tactical nuclear weapons on unprotected populations," concluded Robinson. After four years of the chaos of real warfare, Stanford posed a different kind of challenge for Peters.

He took the first year of the MBA program and then transferred to a PhD on organizational behavior along with two other students, Bob Le Duc and Phil Fisher. Unlike the MBA program, the PhD was unstructured, with the students following their own research interests. Peters carried on attending the MBA classes as well as studying for his PhD. Le Duc and Peters were to form a long-lasting friendship which later developed into a business. "I remember Tom's high energy. He developed a reputation as someone who read a book every day – and he probably did," says Bob Le Duc.[107]

At Stanford, Peters met some of his intellectual mentors. The most influential was Gene Webb who died in 1995.

Webb was "a marvelously thoughtful and creative teacher" says Stanford colleague James March.[108] Also under Webb's wing at Stanford was a Swedish doctoral student called Lennart Arvedson. "I started in 1969 and Tom began his MBA in 1970. Tom was an intense, intelligent, and productive guy," says Arvedson. "At Stanford, Gene Webb was our mutual mentor and we met in his office. We both had close relationships with Gene. He was incredibly intellectually stimulating and personally extremely caring; not only a mentor but a friend. Gene and I were only five years apart in age – I was an old student and he was a young professor – he had got his PhD in his early twenties. Gene was a *bon vivant*. He enjoyed the good things in life and shared them with people. He was extremely supportive to me personally though

I'm not sure anyone was as close to Gene as Tom who saw him a few weeks before his death."

Peters recalls Gene Webb as a professor with boundless intellectual curiosity. "A discussion of any management topic was typically enlarged by analogs from fourteenth-century politics, arcane mathematical theorems, the traits of 50-year-old Sauternes – and all those who came and still come under his sway were rewarded time and again by original notions that were influenced by such catholic tastes."[109] Mimi Webb, his widow, recalls that "Tom always had an unconventional, dominating presence. I imagine that quality of his personality was well-developed long before his arrival at Stanford."[110]

Also influential was Harold Leavitt. "I liked and admired Tom from our earliest meeting. His energy was endless and so was his daring. He was far too wordy, so we faculty were forever trying to get him to cut his writings in half. We did not succeed," Leavitt remembers.[111] Leavitt and his colleagues are not alone. A series of editors at some of the world's leading publishing houses have also failed to rein in Peters' capacity to expand sentences into paragraphs and chapters into book-size dissertations on anything and everything.

Leavitt also recalls an early instance of Peters' ability to work with an audience. "He and I together once did a gig for a company in Pittsburgh. I thought I was pretty good and Tom just a youngster I'd brought along. Of course they invited him back, and didn't invite me."[112]

"I think some of my writings and conversations probably had a little influence on the early Tom Peters, but none in recent years," says Leavitt. "I think my movement in the direction of more open and less pompous organizations perhaps gave him a bit of academic support in his early days. Gene Webb and I worked closely together and saw the world in the same way. Gene's influence was far greater than mine, but in the same direction."[113]

Stanford is traditionally a liberal environment – though it lacks the rebellious streak of Berkeley or Santa Cruz. The prospect of Ronald Reagan's presidential library being located at Stanford, for example, drew a wave of protest – the idea was dropped. "I am a lifetime, reasonably active Democrat. When I was at the Stanford

Business School getting an MBA in 1972, my picture was on the wall of the school newspaper's office; the caption: 'Mr. Big Government' – I was enamored with the social policy experiments being mounted at the time," says Peters.[114]

Peters, recently returned from Vietnam, was now in the midst of protests against the war. The Stanford MBA class of 1972 was unusual. It had a large number of Vietnam vets. The average age was 30 and many students were married and had children. "Stanford was not a radical place and Tom was not active in student politics. But the relatively conservative student body was against the government over Vietnam. In spring 1971 there was even a student strike," recalls Lennart Arvedson.

According to Peters: "There was no real anti-Vietnam feeling at Stanford's business school. It wasn't a hotbed of protest, and by 1970 US involvement was going to be wound down anyway. There wasn't much contact between the business school and the university across the road. Out of the MBA class, probably 306 out of 310 were male and 70 or 80 percent were veterans. There was a Stanford Workshop on Social and Political Issues which I was involved in. Stanford wasn't an extreme sort of place – though I remember one activist, Julien Phillips, who later went on to join McKinsey."

His Stanford days were a formative period for Peters, but he has since been a vehement critic of the MBA system. "Though MBA students may take a few specialized courses in their second year, the fact is that these so-called citadels of professional learning turn out dilettantes (would the degree better be called PBA, for Pastiche of Business Administration?) who walk away with an acceptable technical vocabulary but little in-depth knowledge and, worse, because of the abiding focus on finding jobs, little taste for perpetual learning and true mastery," he wrote in *Liberation Management*.[115] To Peters, MBA programs are too concerned with technique and not enough about people.

Peters obtained his MBA in 1972 and, in February 1973, took his final written exam for his PhD. Armed with an MBA from one of the world's leading business schools, he was anxious to earn some money. Perpetual learning and true mastery would have to wait. The usual poverty of student life, preceded by four years in

the Navy, had further heightened his desire for a life of comparative indulgence – "I was sick of eating lentils," is how he phrases
it.

Opportunity took him back to Washington, DC, where he
worked in the US Government Office of Management and Budget
(OMB) from April 1st, 1973, first as director of the Cabinet
Committee on International Narcotics Control and then as
assistant to the director of OMB for Federal Drug Abuse Policy.

His time in Washington pushed Peters into making a crucial
change in direction. He became "completely and hopelessly
fascinated by complex organizations. I watched people being
vilified by bureaucracies; people slithering through bureaucracies.
I watched a huge organization from a small corner." After studying
organizational behavior in theory, Peters found himself with a
grandstand seat viewing the tortuous reality. Cocooned in the
Office of Management and Budget, Peters enjoyed the experience
of watching people struggling with the all-embracing "system"
though he didn't really understand why. "We had heads the size
of melons – I look back with disgust at myself. I became a
garden-variety mathematically adept executor of strategic projects," he says.

During his time with the OMB, Peters took the opportunity to
travel the world – monitoring the narcotics trade had one advantage: drugs had been a global business long before the legitimate
business world discovered globalization. Instead of sitting at his
desk, Peters confounded conventional wisdom by leaving town
before crucial meetings to pay a visit to the people on the spot. He
found that the fact that he had actually been to Thailand or
wherever to see the problems at first hand added power to his
arguments. It sounded good when he said "Well, when I was
talking with the ambassador in Bangkok this time last week,"
though it must also have proved highly irritating for his colleagues
and superiors.[116]

While Peters was becoming adept at using the complex systems
of Washington life, other dramas were unfolding next door in the
Nixon White House. Peters and his colleagues, however, were
buried too deeply in the system to notice what was happening.
"Days before the impeachment vote in the House of Repre-

sentatives, we really couldn't imagine that Nixon was on his last legs – we who, in theory, were closest to the scene were about the last 500 people in the US to figure out what was up!' he says.[117]

By the summer of 1974, Peters was growing tired of the unreality of Washington. "I'd got caught up in the world of DC and decided to leave. I wanted to go back to the Bay Area but didn't want to return to academic life. So, I applied to McKinsey."

His interest in working for McKinsey had actually begun before he was at Stanford. Quite why Peters was keen to join McKinsey is difficult to determine (apart from the money, of course). The most obvious answer is that his brief time with Peat, Marwick had given him a taste for management consulting. There may also have been some peer pressure – Stanford is one of McKinsey's traditional hunting grounds and many of his student colleagues aspired to work for the consulting colossus.

Whatever his motivations, Peters wasn't initially welcomed. "I applied to McKinsey before my MBA and was rejected out of hand. Then I applied at the end of my first year at Stanford for a summer job with McKinsey. Again they turned me down. I was told to get a life because I was interested in economics. They said that wasn't plausible and that I needed to know marketing or something like that," says Peters.

Two of Peters' Washington colleagues encouraged his interest in McKinsey. At the time, Roy Ash was running the Office of Management and Budget, and his two deputies were seconded from McKinsey and Peters knew them. Whose idea it was for Peters to re-apply is unclear, but in May or June of 1974 he applied to McKinsey's Los Angeles and San Francisco offices supported by an introduction from one of the McKinsey secondees, Dolph Bridgewater.

The blind confidence of youth made the entire thing appear ridiculously straightforward. "The interview process for McKinsey was not particularly onerous," Peters recalls. "It wasn't at all like the crap business school graduates now have to go through. I was so shockingly arrogant that I couldn't think that they wouldn't welcome me with open arms, My assumption was that it was a coronation. It was easy."

The coronation went without a hitch. Peters was interviewed

in Los Angeles and San Francisco and received a job offer from both offices. He left Washington in August 1974 and bummed around before starting work for McKinsey at its San Francisco office on Monday December 2nd, 1974.

The Firm

Insiders in the consultancy McKinsey & Company always call it "the Firm." There is an assumption that when it comes to management consultancy, McKinsey operates on a different plane – where the bills are larger, the hours longer, standards higher, the results better, and the people brighter.

The Firm is more than a mere consultancy. It is an ethos. Staid suits and professional standards. Clean-cut and conservative. It is obsessively professional and hugely successful; a slick, well-oiled financial machine. (McKinsey's revenues in 1995 were $1.8 billion – well over double what they were in 1987 – generated by 3650 consultants.)

Eulogies to McKinsey are easy to find. Most examinations of the world of management consultants lead back to the company's portals. "The most well-known, most secretive, most high-priced, most prestigious, most consistently successful, most envied, most trusted, most disliked management consulting firm on earth," is how *Fortune* described McKinsey.[118] Tom Peters prefers to observe that "McKinsey has a stratospheric belief in itself." There is no hyperbole in Peters' observation. It is simple, matter of fact.

In management consultancy, belief is everything. Consultants have to have the faith; they have to believe wholeheartedly that they and their company have the answers to corporate nightmares. Like politicians, consultants have all the solutions to our problems. And, like politicians, they tend to leave the unpleasant part – who foots the bill or actually gets the job done – to last. Instead of "Read my lips: no new taxes," the consultancy chorus is "Read my report: now pay the price." And, at McKinsey the prices are as high as the belief. McKinsey is driven by belief; faith in the McKinsey doctrine. Self-effacing modesty is not on the agenda.

McKinsey's occasional bouts of self-analysis are more notable for their farcical air of seriousness than their genuine urge to probe the organization's deepest mysteries. "McKinsey likes to compare itself with the Catholic Church and US Marines. 'Is its lofty attitude out of tune with the times?' was a headline in an article published internally."[119] You can easily imagine the *Catholic Times* or *Vatican Chronicle* running a story along similar lines – generally any organization which needs to ask itself if it is out of tune is as out of tune as a bar-room piano.

While McKinsey's continuing success suggests it is certainly not out of tune, it would be fair to say that any organization which contemplates comparisons with both the Catholic Church and the Marines is unusual. Given its self-assurance and success, it is little wonder that McKinsey has its doubters. "I think the Firm takes itself a little too seriously. For what it does, it's probably the best in the world. But in the grand scheme of things, maybe what McKinsey does just isn't as important as it thinks," Robert Waterman has reflected. "McKinsey thinks it sells grand strategies and big ideas when really its role is to keep management from doing a lot of dumb things. They do great analysis, but it won't get your company to the top."[120] Such views are best expressed at a distance from McKinsey headquarters in New York.

What is so special about McKinsey? It is not the oldest consultancy company – Arthur D. Little can trace its lineage back to the 1880s. Nor is McKinsey the biggest consultancy company in the world – Andersen Consulting dwarfs it in terms of revenues and numbers of consultants (but not, significantly, in revenue per consultant). McKinsey is special because its unshakeable conviction that it is the best has created the widely held belief that it *is* unquestionably the best.

Many of the world's leading corporations and their executives are believers. They are willing to pay millions of dollars for the privilege of receiving McKinsey's wisdom. Indeed, such is McKinsey's standing that simply by announcing that you have brought the Firm in to rectify some apparently terminal corporate problem can bolster your share price. Belief fosters belief; belief creates believers.

Of course, it doesn't always work. McKinsey does make mistakes, like any organization, but it retains its enormous self-belief. This is where Peters the corporate man now was. "There was a time, before he broke loose, when McKinsey was the natural place for him to go. He's smart and had MBA stamped on his forehead," says consultant Don Laurie.

Though it may have been a logical career move, Tom Peters did not find life at McKinsey easy. In fact, he found life at McKinsey is designed never to be easy. The theory is that smart minds, like Olympian bodies, thrive on perpetual challenge. MBA graduates sign on for much of the same – the salaries and opportunities win golds – but they still require an awful lot of caffeine to survive. "The freedom I experienced . . . was exhilarating," says Tom Peters. "But for seven years I suffered from almost constant headaches because of the expectations. In McKinsey's 'ambiguous,' project-centered, never-work-with-the-same-people-twice world, the standards of integrity and attentiveness to clients and peers were skyscraping. I paid through the nose for my freedom, in other words. (And, mostly, it was a good bargain – though it took me years to see it that way.)"[121]

McKinsey's version of "freedom" was – and still is – a permanent state of heightened insecurity. "Seniority in McKinsey correlates directly with achievement," states McKinsey's web site with impressive simplicity. Would any other organization – outside of the Catholic Church – state things with such grand matter of factness?

In his seven years with the company, Peters "grew up professionally" but, along with his colleagues, he never knew what his next assignment would be. Or where. Or even who he'd be working with. In seven years, he never worked with the exact same team twice. "I did know that if I hustled and kept picking up new skills, some project manager somewhere would recruit me before my current assignment was over, that maybe a couple of high-profile project managers would actually fight to sign me up," he says.[122]

The project team approach and McKinsey's faith in its own brilliance is part of a unique corporate culture. Its creation can largely be attributed to Marvin Bower, who joined the business in the 1930s. Bower's heritage and the McKinsey corporate culture are safeguarded by the company's rules which mean that in the spring every three years McKinsey's senior partners – over 150, known as directors – vote in an open ballot to determine the managing director. Admirably democratic, the election of a McKinsey managing director has, somewhat appropriately, more in common with the selection of a new Pope than the usual machinations of choosing a CEO.

Indeed, McKinsey constantly asserts its difference. "My vision was to provide advice on managing to top executives and to do it with the professional standards of a leading law firm," said Bower.[123] Consequently, McKinsey is always the Firm rather than a corporation tainted by its obvious commercial *raison d'être*. Its consultants are "associates." McKinsey has "engagements" rather than mere jobs, and is a "practice" rather than a business. It is laden with pretension, but generates money in a thoroughly unpretentious manner. "The entire ethos of McKinsey was to be like a Wall Street bank," says former McKinsey consultant George Binney. "We wanted to be very respectable, the kind of people CEOs naturally relate to. That's the enduring legacy of Marvin Bower."

Bower's gospel was that the interests of the client should precede increasing the company's revenues. If you looked after the client, the profits would look after themselves. (High charges are not a means to greater profits, according to McKinsey, but a simple and effective means of ensuring that clients take McKinsey seriously.) Bower's other rules were that consultants should keep quiet about the affairs of clients (that's why he blanched at the original title of *In Search of Excellence*); should tell the truth and be prepared to challenge the client's opinion; and should only agree to do work which is both necessary and which they could do well. To this he added a few idiosyncratic twists, such as insisting that all McKinsey consultants wore hats – except, for some reason, in the San Francisco office – and long socks. The sight of a consultant's flesh was deemed too much for clients to bear.

Tom Peters has fond recollections of Bower. "Marvin Bower

and I got on well. I'm not sure we weren't dealing with things he hadn't already dealt with. Marvin is genteel, polite. A couple of times I got letters from Marvin out of the blue," he says.

The fact that he was working in the hatless San Francisco office may have helped Peters. "The San Francisco office was McKinsey's weird office. It attracted McKinsey intellectuals who weren't good at making money but were full of intriguing ideas. I fell into the McKinsey phenomenon and the cast of characters at McKinsey."

The Myth of the Renegade Consultant

At McKinsey, whether you are in San Francisco or London, the pressure to deliver is immense. Working at McKinsey is no cozy sinecure. Expectations are enormous, as Tom Peters discovered. Only the best will do. McKinsey's traditional hunting grounds are the leading business schools – Harvard, Stanford, Chicago, MIT's Sloan, Kellogg at Northwestern, Wharton at the University of Pennsylvania, and France's INSEAD. McKinsey's current managing director, Rajat Gupta, was originally turned down when McKinsey did its annual trawl through Harvard but he wrote to the company asking it to reconsider. It did and he was elected managing director of the Firm in March 1994.

McKinsey's bright, energetic MBA graduate recruits are thrown into the fray immediately. A McKinsey consultant is reckoned to peak at around 45 (Lou Gerstner, now of IBM, holds the record at thirty-one of being the youngest person ever to become a senior partner) and, by the time they reach their fifties, they are slowing down, cutting out the exhaustive committee work and retiring at 60. They work hard and are paid very well.

Inevitably, many fail to stand the heat and leave or are speedily dispatched to lesser lights in the consultancy world (or to the real world of running companies). The consultants know where they stand. McKinsey's recruitment brochure says: "If a consultant ceases to progress with the Firm, or is ultimately unable to demonstrate the skills and qualities required of a principal, he or she is asked to leave McKinsey. This 'up or out' policy is applied throughout The firm. It is a way of ensuring that we continue to maintain the high-performance people we must retain, and maintain our ability to provide superior client service."[124] Its reputation and the rewards are such that McKinsey has around 50,000 applications every year from which it recruits around 550 new consultants.

Up or out, is not the vocabulary of a benign humanistic organization. But, as Tom Peters soon appreciated, McKinsey is not XYZ Widgets. "To my dad, my life at McKinsey looked chaotic. To the entry-level employee of the fifties, who went to work in the GM plant (or the purchasing department), it looked positively nutty. He knew exactly what he'd be doing and where he'd be doing it for the next 30 years or so – barring war, a bad back, or a liver that revolted against ritual after-work pub stops," he later observed. "To me, my glamorous life as a consultant . . . felt humdrum. Another damned 12-hour plane trip from San Francisco to London. Another client company in another industry to put under a microscope. Another three colleagues (from England, Germany, and Japan) to learn to work seamlessly with. And, in six short weeks, a progress report was due to the client chairman. Blow it and you were in trouble."[125]

And then there was the matter of report writing. Given his ability to write 100 pages when ten are required, it is little wonder that Peters struggled to fit his prose into something as limiting as a house style. The final neatly bound McKinsey report to its clients was based on an uncreative "pyramid style." This moved the client through a brilliantly logical framework offering the McKinsey slant on issues and trends. The top of the pyramid was an august conclusion in which McKinsey mapped out the best future moves. The aim was watertight logic so that the client would gasp in amazement at the sheer beauty of the report. Given these parameters Peters struggled. "Though I had a successful sojourn at McKinsey, I never mastered the corporate style. My attempts at pyramid building usually ended up producing piles of scattered rocks and pebbles. I was continually accused of circular reasoning, but even my circles had gaps."[126]

Despite such hiccups, Peters' gadfly, hyper-energetic approach fitted in with the company to some extent. "McKinsey is not

conceptual," says Don Laurie. While other companies sell packaged theories and neat one-dimensional products, McKinsey does
not. Its package is its all-round brilliance. It is not tied to a
particular gospel. It is not hidebound by theory. (If there was a
theory in the 1960s, it was Bower's general statements of aims and
values which were more to do with good housekeeping than good
management.)

Since they left, both Peters and, to a lesser extent, Waterman
have given the impression that they were renegades caught in
McKinsey's authoritarian system. "I met abnormal McKinsey
people," says Peters. But "abnormal" McKinsey people do not
wear kaftans and read Kerouac; they wear ties with more than one
stripe and admit to reading novels occasionally. Any attempts to
portray Peters as a wayward hero in an all-consuming system are
probably best described as retrospective mythology. No rene-
gade lasts seven years with McKinsey unless they are delivering
exactly what McKinsey demands. The San Francisco office may
have been off-beat but it was still moving to the same rhythm in
which intriguing ideas were peripheral to actually doing the job.
One way or another, Peters delivered, even if he didn't have to
wear a hat.

There is no room for loners in McKinsey. Project teams have
long been its *modus operandi*. "People forget that Tom was part of
a practice here. They weren't renegades, though sometimes Tom
portrays it that way. There were a lot of people who wanted to
shake up the company and he was one of them. Look at Ken
Ohmae. He was just as much a rebel as Tom, but he stayed quite
a while," says McKinsey's Bill Matassoni.

Peters has indeed created the impression of being a wild spirit,
at odds with the dictates of the Firm. In *Liberation Management*,
he says: "McKinsey had a very tough time tolerating us [Peters
and Waterman], and eventually both of us left on the basis of a
very mutual desire to part ways. In short, the squeaky wheel at
McKinsey usually gets discarded, not oiled."[127] Elsewhere he
suggests that while McKinsey talked to chairmen, he and Waterman talked to divisional directors.

The desire to portray himself as something of a rabble rousing
rebel can be seen in other of his recollections. In the Navy, for

example, Peters mentions his failure to salute and his unconventional habit of disappearing to contemplate. While he was undoubtedly more opinionated and willing to voice his opinions, Peters was still more corporate man than corporate skunk.

Even so, the research prior to *In Search of Excellence* saw McKinsey and Peters growing steadily further apart. It was not an instant separation. Peters now reflects that the signs of mounting disaffection had been there for some time. "McKinsey and I were becoming alienated. I didn't bother to tell them I was off for a year. I grew my hair! By McKinsey standards it was outrageous behavior. The roar of the crowd was influencing me. I was having fun but having to bear McKinsey partners criticizing me. I was pushing McKinsey farther than it liked to be pushed. Subconsciously, leaving must have been in my mind." If you have any doubts in your mind, McKinsey is not the place to be. It is built on belief. Doubters are quickly cast out into the wilderness.

Part of the problem was that Peters and Waterman saw their consulting work as of limited long-term value. Great ideas and neat solutions led to great reports but not necessarily implementation. It was like discovering a new chemical combination and then not being allowed to buy the chemicals to see if it worked. On the genesis of *In Search of Excellence* Waterman says: "We had gotten bored working for big, OK companies that would pay big money, accept our recommendations, and then do a half-assed job of implementing them."[128]

Peters echoes his former co-author's complaint: "Waterman and I often observed a Grand Canyon between the icy clarity of the strategies we concocted and the halting execution of those strategies by our worldly clients. The client may have nodded at our inexorable river of logic until he was in need of chiropractic help, but when he left the boardroom he'd be distracted by another earthy personnel problem that had arisen in the two hours he was away from his desk."[129]

McKinsey's Bill Matassoni sees Peters' departure as a fairly inevitable and natural parting of the ways. "I won't speculate on his reasons for leaving McKinsey. He appreciated the place but just decided he wanted to do something else. He was happy here, he liked the team working, and we gave him as much room as you can. Despite all the analogies about the Marines and the Catholic Church, we're fairly loose. Tom ran pretty wild and all the time he was shaking up our own thinking. He was a kind of a superstar with McKinsey – outspoken, passionate, his style was a little different. Eventually Tom wanted to become a business guru and that's not McKinsey's style. We're a little more buttoned-up than that." By 1981 Peters was intent on loosening the buttons.

Leaving The Firm

Tom Peters left McKinsey & Co. in December 1981, after almost exactly seven years. Bob Waterman was instrumental in securing an attractive deal – especially in retrospect. "I left and McKinsey paid me a retainer to finish the book – that was Waterman's doing. The retainer was for $10,000 a month for five months. The agreement said I would pay back $50,000 from royalties and they would get half of the royalties. Waterman didn't get a penny until a few years later. I spent the next four or five months finishing *In Search of Excellence*," says Peters.

In *The Age of Heretics*, Art Kleiner suggests that Peters' departure was actually Waterman's idea: "At McKinsey, he felt more and more isolated, and acted more and more obstreperous, until several months before the book's final deadline, Waterman asked him to quit McKinsey, if only for his own good. To help make the exit smooth, Waterman negotiated a deal in which Peters would get to keep his royalties. Nobody thought they would amount to much."[130] Given that expectations of future sales were so low, McKinsey's agreement was generous. It couldn't have held out a great deal of hope of receiving back any of its retainer to Peters.

As Peters left ten months before the publication of *In Search of Excellence* he can't be accused of cashing in on the book's success – though this criticism has been aired. "Peters and Waterman left McKinsey – in a dispute partly over whether profits from their book should have gone to them individually or into the McKinsey pot," said a 1993 *Fortune* article.[131] As the book contract was with Peters there would appear little doubt about where the money should legally have gone. However, McKinsey's understandable pique was down to the fact that the book was based on research it – and Siemens – had supported over a number of years. "My memory says royalties for *In Search of Excellence* were very straightforward," insists Peters. "No one was expecting the book to sell so I thought it was a fair deal. I knew nothing about publishing." Peters wasn't the only one – McKinsey had barely published a book and certainly not one which had sold in such large numbers. (In fact, McKinsey published only two books between 1960 and 1980, but has produced over 50 since.)

Whatever the machinations – and it is difficult to see how Peters can be accused of anything other than accepting a generous leaving present which he subsequently had to repay anyway – his departure to almost instant wealth and success was hardly guaranteed an enthusiastic reception among his former colleagues. "To this day he is viewed with mixed feelings at McKinsey but, at the same time, he has brought a lot of attention and value to the Firm," says Paul Cohen, formerly of the Tom Peters Group.

'There was some resentment of the riches which befell the two authors," says ex-McKinsey consultant, Michael Lanning. "People always said the firm struck a deal with Peters and Waterman on the basic understanding that the book wouldn't sell. People laughed when they heard that if it sold more than 50,000 copies, Peters and Waterman could have the money. No-one thought it could possibly reach that ceiling." But the book did reach that ceiling and Peters and Waterman were a lot richer as a result.

While Peters left, Waterman carried on working at McKinsey though his reservations were much the same as Peters'. "Leaving McKinsey, I was giving up a salary I hadn't dreamed I would make. Waterman had a bigger salary to give up," observes Peters. Waterman had been with the company far longer than his co-author and was not drawn to the media-hype of becoming a management guru. Waterman eventually left in 1984, apparently tired of fighting internal battles. "When Waterman left, he said the whole outside world is loving the stuff I do and yet I have to spend my time defending myself against McKinsey partners," says Peters.

Tom Peters now believes that the parting of the ways brought benefits to both sides. "Despite the acrimony, McKinsey benefitted from *In Search of Excellence*. The other project at the time didn't produce anything so that gave me some pleasure. McKinsey has become more participative and deals with the soft stuff," he says. The practices launched at the beginning of the excellence research established a model in McKinsey – "We now have 50 practices. The tradition is alive. More important than the book was getting people involved," says Bill Matassoni. For all its success, *In Search of Excellence* was simply an uncharacteristically high-profile blip in McKinsey's low-profile march forwards.

Mentors for Life

Looking over Tom Peters' career before *In Search of Excellence*, there seems little in the way of grand designs. Career planning wasn't exactly voguish in the 1970s and 1980s. Tom Peters, like many young people, now and then, fell into things, moved with the flow, and took what experiences were up for grabs. He was opportunistic and bright enough to seize the opportunities. He didn't really care that architecture and civil engineering had fallen by the wayside. His interest in the world of organizations and management had evolved without developing into an obsession. If it hadn't been for *In Search of Excellence* he may have stayed with McKinsey for the rest of his career. But, equally, he may have drifted back into academia or into another field entirely.

While there was no master plan, Tom Peters was fortunate. His career up to 1981 was marked by encounters with a series of inspirational long-term mentors. First, there was Dick Anderson and Joe Key in the Navy. Anderson tended to leave his young officers very much to their own devices and then demanded results. Not surprisingly, getting the job done was the important thing. He gave the young, recently graduated, Peters room to sort out problems for himself. Later, in Washington, Key showed Peters that those above simply needed to be well managed to deliver what *you* wanted.

Then Peters encountered Harold Leavitt and Gene Webb at Stanford. Webb exercised the most profound influence over Peters – and continued to act as his mentor until his death in 1995. In *In Search of Excellence* Peters acknowledged his debt by dedicating the book to Webb.

Peters' student friend, Bob Le Duc also fell under Webb's wing. His observations are interesting because they resonate very clearly with the person Tom Peters eventually became: "Gene Webb was a fun guy. He was very curious and inventive. He would just try things. He pushed your curiosity by trying off the wall stuff. It was fun. But he was also an intellectual and that attracted us to him. We had a great deal of respect for the academic life and a romantic notion of it which Gene lived up to."

Curiosity has remained an abiding motivation for Tom Peters. Only the curious learn. But Webb also inculcated into Peters the need to take risks, to be bold, and accept that neat ideas often bit the dust, while others would fly. "I'm lucky to have had several mentors whose sense of exploration rubbed off on me," says Peters.

After working largely unsupervised in Washington, Peters moved on to the intellectual powerhouse of McKinsey where he came under the influence of Waterman and a host of others. His influences at McKinsey reinforced his experience with Gene Webb. He found that the most interesting people had a broad base of knowledge and were fascinated by many things. Specialists they were not.

His brief spell with Peat, Marwick led to him encountering a bee-keeping boss who regularly contributed to the leading journal in the field. Many of his innovative ideas about organic management processes, which he applied to client R&D problems, were by-products of his passion for the ways and wiles of bees. Peters' first boss at McKinsey held degrees in physics and law (and not in business); and he remembers his first partner project manager as "one of McKinsey's weirdos." The British politician Dennis Healey says that the only politicians worth knowing are those with a "hinterland" of interests outside politics. Those who are totally political are shallow personalities. Peters' early experiences confirmed him in the same view. (This is something Peters continues – he is proud of the fact that the managing director of his company is a trained merchant seaman as well as an accountant.)

The people who inspired Peters defied convention and, in all these thoroughly traditional organizations, Peters was given more license than is normally the case. He pulled on the organizational leash and, instead of being reined in, was let go still further. This was due to a combination of his own forceful personality and of the often far-sighted people who were charged with "managing" him – "I've worked for some traditional outfits (for example, the Navy), but have rarely been burdened with bosses who were bent on oppression," says Peters.[132]

While the young Peters was undoubtedly keen to learn, he was also keen to find someone to learn from and look up to. He was, like most young people, a man in search of role models. To some extent this continues. Peters maintains a surprising reverence for many he now encounters as a globe-trotting luminary. "Most CEOs I've met are very bright. But Welch, Walsh, and Barnevik are almost in a league of their own. I, for one, am intimidated by each member of the trio!" he wrote.[133]

Peters may be wealthy and his name known throughout the world but he is still in awe. He is still a little boy from Annapolis, Maryland – waiting for the autographs of ballplayers, in a dingy alleyway behind Griffiths Stadium in Washington DC – when he encounters the powerful and famous.

Tom Peters was, after all, brought up on a diet of authority and convention. He was corporate man. The British guru Charles Handy was also a corporate man. He worked for Shell and recalls that "It wasn't an organization. It was a way of life. I'd never bought my own train ticket before I left Shell, or paid my own income tax – it was all done for you."[134] The Tom Peters of 1981 had been through a similar experience. Nearing his fortieth birthday, he hadn't yet touched down in the real world. From Vietnam to Washington, Stanford to McKinsey, he had circum-navigated the fringes of reality, spending his time ensconced in the unreality of warfare, academia, and the hyper-unreality of consulting. Reality loomed.

FOUR

PETERS THE CORPORATION

" I became a rock star after McKinsey "

Tom Peters

Back to Unreality

At the end of 1981 Tom Peters was freed from McKinsey. A year later he had a runaway bestseller on his hands. Suddenly, and unexpectedly, everyone wanted a piece of the bestselling author and, for the first time, Peters was outside of the institutions which had organized and driven his career.

It all came easily. "I anticipated phones ringing like they had done after the article in *BusinessWeek*. And the phone rang. Obviously in retrospect what was happening could be explained: I gave more speeches and became good at platform delivery," says Peters. He was in demand and available while Waterman remained with McKinsey for another three years. "Waterman is very self-effacing and was sheltered at McKinsey. I was a loud mouth so I got more of the phone calls," admits Peters.

He was on his own, almost. "At the end of 1981 I had a beer and a burger with Bob Le Duc," recalls Peters. "We decided to go into business and aimed to earn $60,000 a year – which was less than I earned at McKinsey."

Since leaving Stanford in 1974, Le Duc and Peters had kept in touch. Le Duc had gone on to teach at Harvard Business School and from there to Hewlett-Packard's training division where he provided some help to Peters and Waterman during the excellence research. The meeting with Peters came at the right time for Le Duc who was thinking of leaving Hewlett-Packard. "Tom was committed to leaving McKinsey and I was thinking of doing something else so we thought we would start a two-man consultancy company. The aim was to do some interesting things and have some fun," says Le Duc.

Le Duc left Hewlett-Packard in October 1982 and on November 1st was primed for the start of the duo's new adventure based at Peters' home in Palo Alto. Their first seminar booking was with the Young President's Organization. It was canceled through lack of interest. It was an inauspicious start but, unworried, Le Duc headed off on vacation for the remainder of 1982. He returned in the New Year to find that things were changing as *In Search of Excellence* slowly began its upward curve.

"Remember we didn't know *In Search of Excellence* was going to be such a great success. Though Tom was hopeful he certainly wasn't taking anything for granted," says Le Duc. The two did some work for GE's executive development center at Crotonville and for Northrop. With seminars on top of this work they hoped to have enough money to pay the bills rather than to take over the world.

Untutored in the perils and complications of self-employment, Peters and Le Duc found fortune favoring them. "I was charging $1000 a speech at that time though after the book my speaking fees edged up to $2000 or $3000 and I had a couple of people working for me," Peters recalls. After seven years of expense accounts and executive travel Peters was back to reality. An air of unreality quickly resurfaced. "I slept in one half of the apartment and worked in the other. One day I came back from a trip and my assistant said I was speaking to Arthur Andersen and I was charging $10,000. They had asked what my fee was and she thought she would try $10,000. They agreed and so my fee was now $10,000." There is some irony in McKinsey's rival, Arthur Andersen, inadvertently feathering the nest of one of McKinsey's progeny.

Some got in early and managed to book Peters before Arthur Andersen upped the price. Dr. Albert Vicere of Penn State was one of the lucky ones. "We had a faculty member who was director of a two-week program on leadership. He had met Peters at Berkeley and was designing a new program at the time *In Search of Excellence* was published. It was in 1982 so the book was out but not yet a success. Peters was unknown," says Vicere. "We hired Tom for $800 to come to Penn State to do a one-day seminar. It involved him coming from the West Coast. When he arrived he was covered in red blotches because he had caught himself in some poison ivy. Even so, he did a great job and the people loved him. He said he would love to come back in 1983. By then his name was known and his fee was $4000. It worked wonderfully. Then in 1984 he spoke for half a day on a different program – this time for $5000. After that we simply couldn't afford him."

Vicere remembers Peters as "very personable and outgoing. There was almost an air of the absent-minded professor to him. Arriving at the hotel he was unkempt and his shoelaces were untied. His delivery style reflected his personality. If you talked to him he shared his ideas and had opinions, and was opinionated. But he listened to what you had to say and was interested."

Vicere was fortunate. From the beginning of 1983 until the spring of 1984, Peters and Le Duc traveled hectically. Their itinerary made Peters' globetrotting at McKinsey appear positively sedentary. Time zones were crossed almost daily. If Tuesday was Denver, Wednesday was sure to be New York. After a Northrop management retreat at Palm Desert, California, Peters and Le Duc reviewed their progress. "It was successful," says Le Duc. "We'd been running around for 15 months but thought we could either carry on as we were or get serious and make it into a business. We decided on the second option even if it wasn't likely to be as much fun."

In 1983, Peters, the corporate man, was transformed into Peters, the corporation. Bob Le Duc, Peters, and business adviser Ian Thomson created the Tom Peters Group (TPG) based in Palo Alto (described accurately in *In Search of Excellence* as "a prototypical upper-class community") close by Stanford.[135]

"TPG started off innocently enough," says Peters. "It had two forms of innocence. Since the phone was ringing a lot I needed an admin assistant. The first incarnation was just a couple of people. As I gave more and more seminars, especially the longer ones, I would be asked to follow up with a company. I started, half-inadvertently, discussions with Bob Le Duc and he started a training company called the Palo Alto Consulting Center." With the Palo Alto Consulting Center, Le Duc and Peters focused on serving a small number of bellwether companies – including Apple Computer, People Express, and Mervyn's (a Dayton-Hudson subsidiary).

Low-key consulting for a select bunch of clients is hardly Peters' style. You get to know the people and the businesses, but it doesn't make a splash, it doesn't really change things or bring ideas to a wider audience. And, in the mid-1980s, demand for Peters was enormous. Riding on the tide of the book's success Peters traveled the world giving seminar after seminar. "I became a rock star after McKinsey," he reflects. The crowds flocked and Peters traveled and traveled. Between 1982 and 1985, he estimates that 100,000 to 200,000 people witnessed his seminars. (One seminar, in November 1983 at Boca Raton featured the triumphant Cornell alumni, Peters, John Naisbitt, and Ken Blanchard.) Looking back Peters is staggered by his own stamina. "I recently found a single month's calendar from 1985. I came close to vomiting. I was doing over 150 seminars a year at the time, sometimes doing two speeches in different cities on the same day. I was either very strong or conned myself."

From being an unknown management consultant, Peters was catapulted to prominence and fame. He talked and preached. "I met Peters after a conference. I was astonished at his enthusiasm. He had been on the platform all day and yet still wanted to talk until very late about his subject," says Philip Sadler, formerly of Ashridge Management College, who saw Peters in one of his forays into Europe where *In Search of Excellence* was equally successful.

Lennart Arvedson who had known Peters since their days at Stanford was taken aback by the size of what was happening. "I was awed by the scale of his success. I also knew him when it was happening and he was in awe himself. He would rise very early and on Sunday mornings he would quickly find out where the book was on the *New York Times* bestseller list. He worked hard and was lucky. Tom was running around at a frantic rate. I would never have dreamed of trying to keep up." Peters himself could barely keep pace.

Trying to find time to speak to Peters was a major logistical exercise. Swedish consultant Sven Atterhed first came across Peters with the *BusinessWeek* article in 1980. "I contacted him because it was close to what we were doing and thinking. It resonated. Then the book came out and his answering machine was melting with the number of calls. He had just one part-time secretary at the time," says Atterhed. "He had so many engagements, eventually we met on a private chartered plane he was flying on from San Carlos airport in the Bay Area to San Diego on March 23rd, 1983. The plane departed at 4.00 a.m. so we met in the dark and then had two and a half hours on the plane. We talked our heads off."

Even Peters' business partner had difficulty getting hold of him. Peters and Le Duc found themselves meeting in Ramada Inns in the middle of nowhere to save time in their chaotic schedules. For those working closely with Peters, the explosion of interest was astonishing. "It was strange. A friend asked what's it like working so close to the sun," recalls Bob Le Duc. "My relationship with Tom was open and honest, and our styles were different. If I'd have been a Tom Peters-type it would have led to jealousy, but I am not. Instead, I became convinced that he really did know what was happening and what was going to happen to business and the competitive environment. I was in awe of that to some extent, but it gave me a fair degree of confidence in where we were going. If Tom was the visionary, I was the nuts and bolts type."

In the fledgling business, one thing led to another. "Tom liked the idea of having a company. It gave him a chance to dabble in other things with varying degrees of personal commitment," says Paul Cohen, formerly of TPG. As Peters roamed the world preaching excellence, his small corporate empire grew. "Tom didn't want to have separate divisions, but separate companies which people had genuine responsibility for," says Bob Le Duc. "We didn't want to just license things. We wanted to be full partners."

Peters and Le Duc brought in Ron Myers to work on the Center for Managerial Excellence, the precursor of what was to become TPG's training business. Myers had been director of the President's Association of the American Management Association (which had keenly supported *In Search of Excellence*.) The Center conducted 40-person, four-day workshops a half dozen or so times a year – "intense personnel and organizational evaluation of the wellsprings of strategic competence is the object," explained

Peters somewhat mysteriously in *A Passion for Excellence*. Nancy Austin came in as the communications person and started TPG Communications. Austin had been co-author of *The Assertive Woman* and had worked with Le Duc when she ran Hewlett-Packard's management development.

Growing in numbers and looking more and more like a "real corporation," TPG then discovered the decidedly uncorporate world of the skunk.

The Skunk Goes Camping

Small, free-wheeling groups of innovative people were what Tom Peters was trying to achieve with TPG. The whole endeavor was an antidote to the dullness Peters regards as endemic in organizations – "Most organizations bore me stiff. I can't imagine working in one of them. I'd be sad if my children chose to. Most organizations, large and even small, are bland as bean curd."[136]

To sum up the kind of organization Peters hoped to create, the phrase Skunk Works was taken up. In *A Passion for Excellence* Peters defines Skunk Works as "a highly innovative, fast-moving, and slightly eccentric activity operating at the edges of the corporate work."[137] It was the antithesis of everything he had previously experienced in his working life – and a million miles away from the conservative regime of McKinsey. "If I were a perfect reader of tea leaves, parts of the corporate skunk were already visible when I was in the Navy and later when I worked at the White House," says Peters. "But if you forget about the Navy and Washington, and think about McKinsey, the first couple of years there were straight."

The phrase Skunk Works has its origins in the work of Clarence "Kelly" Johnson at Lockheed's Design and Development Center in Burbank, California sometime after World War II. Someone asked what Johnson was doing. The reply was, "I guess old Kelly's stirring up a little kickapoo joy juice." Kickapoo joy juice was a violent moonshine drink brewed by the mountain hillbilly family featured in the Al Capp cartoon *Li'l Abner*. Now and then, the hillbillies were seen in the comic strip tossing a skunk into the pot to give the brew an added kick. The Lockheed team became known as the Skunk Works.

To develop the Skunk Works idea, Le Duc and Peters began to organize five-day Skunk Camps – a kind of summer camp for executives. The first Skunk Camp was held in September 1984 at Pajaro Dunes outside of Monterey. "It was originally conceived as an opportunity to say thank you to the people who we'd learned the most from during the previous two years," says Bob Le Duc. "We were scared to death when most of the people accepted the invitation." Its 47 attendees included academics, such as Peter Vaill of George Washington University and Jerry Porras of Stanford, and business people, including Tait Elder of Allied, Don Burr of People Express, Stew Leonard of Stew Leonard's, Ken Stahl of Xerox, and Bill and Vieve Gore from WL Gore & Associates. The Camp was a success though Le Duc and Peters were preaching to the already converted. "Seldom, if ever, have we learned so much or felt so much," noted Peters and Nancy Austin in *A Passion for Excellence*.[138]

The second Skunk Camp was a profit-making venture. It was held in January 1984. Among those attending was Robert Buckman of Buckman Laboratories in Memphis. "I had read *In Search of Excellence* and then got a flier. I thought it was appropriate. I think we've sent more people than anyone else to Skunk Camps," says Buckman. "Even then, Tom was energetic, a little crazy, with lots of ideas." The issues facing Buckman's company were typical of those encountered by Skunk Camp participants. "My father had run the company from the top. All decisions went through him and came from him. He died in 1978 and I was left with 28 vice-presidents and general managers looking to me to make decisions. I knew it wouldn't work. We had to get people to assume responsibility and to make things happen," says Buckman. The Skunk Camp was part of this process.

The Skunk Camps quickly became highly popular. Bob Le Duc brought in yet another Stanford alumni, Reuben Harris, to take charge of the burgeoning Skunk Camp business. Harris had also been on the Stanford PhD program, though a year before Le Duc and Peters. "The premise was that the Skunk Camp was a feeder for the consulting business but we never got the consulting right," admits Le Duc. While companies were happy to send their executives along for five days of motivational debate, few went on to use TPG's consulting services – Buckman Laboratories was one of the few which did. "The people who went to the Skunk Camps were an extraordinary audience. They'd come and work hard and have fun and then go back and start doing this stuff. We'd contact them and offer our help. But by and large they thought they could do it themselves," says Le Duc. The dividing line between the Skunk Camps and consulting work proved difficult for TPG to manage – internally at least.

The Skunk Camp enabled Peters to continually amass new stories and material. Away from the office, executives aired their real concerns, what was really close to their hearts. "The Skunk Camps were Tom's laboratory. There would be one every three or four weeks. You rarely found big company people there – it was middle managers from Domino's Pizzas and the like," says consultant Don Laurie, going on to describe his experience at one of the camps. "The Skunk Camp was a week long and very informal. We stayed in condos at Pajaro Dunes. Tom explored his developing ideas. He would get up and chew over a subject and then send people away to do an exercise. It was very clever and then you'd see the ideas crop up someplace a few months later."

Generating material and ideas was one thing but Laurie believes the idea of using the Skunk Camps as a supply-line of consulting clients was fatally flawed from the outset. "The idea was to create a consulting business. The trouble is that the lifeblood of consulting is concepts," says Laurie. "If Tom gave a speech and it led to some interest, the consultants would go in with no concepts so it was hard for them to deliver anything. In consulting, big companies are where the money is. But middle managers from smaller companies went to TPG's events. The consultants would end up with three-day assignments." Somewhat ironically, the companies which sent managers to Skunk Camps were the conservative organizations increasingly lambasted by Peters.

Laurie believes that the failure of the Skunk Camps to provide a flow of consulting clients had a deeper more substantial cause. "Tom's weaknesses are, first, that he is not conceptual. None of the things he writes about have a concept behind them. In that sense he is more of a journalist. Second, he doesn't have any *how tos*. He'd give a speech and people would be cheering because he was saying managers were doing a lousy job. But they couldn't translate what he said into action. He never thought it was up to him to provide that."

Bo Burlingham of *Inc.* observed the Peters phenomenon at first hand. He, too, identifies the lack of a practical way forward as a stumbling block to perceptions of Peters. "In fact, Tom doesn't know a helluva a lot about management or business. His own company's a mess. What he is interested in is innovation and you can get burned out on that. All the time, you've got to find the next new thing. Innovation is the hidden message of his books," says Burlingham. "We would meet people who were tremendous admirers but hadn't the faintest idea of how to do stuff in their own companies. They wanted to emulate but had no tools to do it."

Bob Buckman remains a Peters enthusiast, arguing that the ideas can be converted into real business achievement. "I didn't let him off the hook. I said I had to change the way people think and had to bring about major cultural change. I can see why there is a lot of resistance to the things Tom says but he is right. Just because people don't like it doesn't mean it's not right," he says. "At our company, we have eliminated the gatekeepers of information, closed the gap with the customer and made ourselves more egalitarian. That's hard data not fluff."

With TPG's consulting business looking increasingly likely to be buried in fluff, the emphasis began to shift to communications and training. One of the new avenues for these ideas was a TPG newsletter which Jayne Pearl was recruited to produce. Her introduction to the new corporate world of Tom Peters was not unusual. Things were moving fast and Peters eschewed corporate conventions. "I was working in a radio station and we lost our funding. A friend of mine had written an article about Tom Peters and heard he was starting a newsletter," says Pearl. "I called the office and sent my resume. They called me in New York and said could I come tomorrow. I flew out and was interviewed by the people there. Then Tom came up the elevator with a messy T-shirt." The interview was, by most standards, informal. "He asked why should they hire me. I told him they'd be crazy to hire me because I'd never read any of his books and didn't know anything about newsletters. He said, you're hired. I asked about money and logistics and he said they'd pay enough. I started two weeks later in October 1985."

Pearl had previously worked on *Forbes* and found herself ill-prepared for the free-flowing business she had crossed the country to work for. "On my first day, I sat with Tom and some others. I asked if there was a prototype, an outline, a mission or a marketing study for the newsletter they'd hired me to produce. They said no, nothing. But they thought they *should* be producing a newsletter. Tom felt that articles were too limiting space-wise. He wanted a vehicle to explore things."

So, TPG Communications fell into the newsletter business – the first issue of *On Achieving Excellence* appeared in December 1986 (with a skunk appropriately on the masthead). "The mission was to find things that were working," says Jayne Pearl. "At *Forbes* you talked to the CEO and a few analysts. If you were doing a marketing story you talked to the VP for marketing. You didn't talk to people. With the newsletter, you talked to everyone." After seven years of being steered through corporate doors straight to the board room, Peters wanted to connect with the real world.

The newsletter was just one of the signs of what Peters was fast becoming. It overflowed with good news. Excellence is here! Just look around. Each issue featured a signed homily from Peters, now reincarnated as plain Tom. Thomas J. Peters of *In Search of Excellence* fame was, a handful of years later, being reinvented. The newsletter continues. Its circulation is small – 5000 to 6000 – but with a hefty annual subscription it is a nice little business of its own.

Meanwhile TPG was also producing videos and expanding its training activities. Nancy Austin's company, Not Just Another Publishing Company, along with its Massachusetts cousin, Excel/Media, was responsible for audio, video, and print products. Later, Jim Kouzes arrived from Santa Clara University to the

Center for Managerial Excellence – "Jim came with a reasonably well-developed reputation which has since become a great reputation. He is a fabulous pedagogue," says Peters. After joining TPG, Kouzes co-authored the best-selling *The Leadership Challenge* and became something of a leadership guru in his own right. (Kouzes now charges a daily rate of between $10,000 and $20,000. His TPG colleague Oren Harari, also an ex-academic and now a senior consultant with the company, charges $5000 to $10,000 for a day of his time.) Kouzes is now chairman and chief executive of TPG/Learning Systems, part of TPG. "Jim Kouzes has his own ideas and has linked himself with Tom. It's not in conflict with Tom's philosophy but it is not really building on it," observes Lennart Arvedson.

TPG's horizons rapidly broadened. TPG started selling overseas via a joint venture the year it was set up and, in 1986, TPG Europe came to life in Stockholm, Sweden, under the direction of Peters' old friend Arvedson. "During my various return visits to Stanford, Gene Webb and I had talked about a US–Swedish exchange. In the fall of 1985 the exchange took place and TPG helped to fund it," says Arvedson. "A group of Stanford professors came to visit Sweden and I organized their visit. Ian Thomson from TPG came along for the ride and we talked. I'd been with the Business and Social Research Institute in Stockholm for seven or eight years and had decided to leave. I was looking around, then Tom called and asked if I would be interested in joining up. I joined for the adventure."

Arvedson saw the potential for a European version of *In Search of Excellence*. "Originally the concept of TPG was to be research rather than consulting-oriented. What I wanted to do was a European study following the *In Search of Excellence* approach. I liked the notion of learning from success stories rather than dissecting failures. One of the first things we did was organize a research seminar on organizational excellence in the US and Europe. There were about 30 participants – academics and managers from around Europe." (The European version of *In Search of Excellence* was eventually produced – but not by TPG.)

TPG Europe was another ill-defined "good" idea. "My brief was pretty open. I wrote some memos on what I thought we ought to do," says Arvedson. "TPG was a combination of ideas and consultancy, benefitting from name recognition and some of Tom's ideas."

Another Swede, Michael Pieschewski, joined Arvedson soon after. Formerly with SAS, Pieschewski was never formally part of TPG though he collaborated on a number of projects. "TPG Europe began by organizing presentations and seminars run by Tom, but that was very limited as Tom wasn't in Europe a lot. Then it was a question of how to capitalize on Tom's ideas without Tom," says Pieschewski. "The idea was to develop some kind of package around Tom's ideas so we could market it and sell it. We worked with Bob Le Duc and others from TPG and developed the package." (The package was called "Creating value for the customer" but it proved unsuccessful – at one presentation an executive concluded by saying: "So you want me to buy a program which will undermine my own power and give it to other people? You must be joking.")

The challenge was to use the Peters brand name without using the person. The trouble was that the brand, still only a couple of years old, struggled to exist without Peters' physical presence. "The phone calls to TPG Europe would be of various kinds," says Lennart Arvedson. "First you would get the stuffy staffer from XYZ Corporation saying they were running a weekend retreat in Capri and they would like Mr. Peters to deliver an address after coffee. Then there were calls from intelligent staffers saying they were organizing a management conference and the CEO had said he would like Tom to talk to the conference as many of his ideas were reflected in what the company was trying to achieve. We would talk to them and sometimes Tom would go if his taking part played a genuine role in the organization attempting to achieve something. The final kind of call we received would be from executives who had read the books, watched the videos, and now wanted to find out if Tom could help them implement his ideas. In several companies this led to fairly major consultation assignments, sometimes with and sometimes without Tom's involvement. But we did not have the wherewithal to build a thriving business on this basis."

Still trying to come to terms with its nebulous brief, TPG

Europe then relocated to London where it temporarily shared an office with another consultancy, run by the American consultant Don Laurie. There was talk of a joint venture between the two, but it never materialized. Indeed, there were many grand plans. In the first few months of 1990, Lennart Arvedson initiated a project called the Palo Alto Center for Management Studies. The idea was for a global non-profit research center built around Peters. Arvedson put together a group of people including Charles Handy; Christopher Lorenz of the *Financial Times*; Gay Haskins who was then with the European Foundation for Management Development; Jan Lapidoth of SAS; Max Worcester of *Frankfurter Allgemeine Zeitung*; and a Korean business professor, Boo Ho Rho. The upshot was a plan for a Festival of New Organizational Practice to be held at Canary Wharf in London. Handy proposed that it should be a kind of organizational fashion show, and a date was even decided on. The meetings were sometimes stormy as the future of organizations was debated. On one occasion Peters and a Canadian academic had a violent disagreement in a hotel lobby in Dresden. Meanwhile, back in Palo Alto, TPG's Ian Thomson was keen to see a financial return from the debate. "It was a wonderful dream while it lasted, then the idea died after a year of discussions," says Arvedson. The group's ambitions were a little higher than its capabilities (and, as a suitable postscript, Canary Wharf crashed). This was really the beginning of the end for TPG's European designs.

Arvedson left TPG at the end of 1991 and Michael Pieschewski remained alone in London running his own business. "It was kind of turbulent at that time because Tom had an accountant, Ian Thomson, who was a tough guy, hard to deal with. There were the nice guys – Tom and Bob Le Duc – but Ian was tough," says Pieschewski. "The way I saw it was that Ian Thomson protected him, like an old Italian godfather. When you dealt with Tom you didn't actually deal with the real issues like money or investments. Ian dealt with that. TPG had all those people he knew from school or university. They were there to protect him. It was a safe environment. A lot of charismatic and famous people work with people they knew or worked with earlier in their lives."

TPG included Le Duc, Arvedson, and Reuben Harris from

Stanford. Ian Thomson had been a good friend of Gene Webb's. The bean-counter Thomson was in many ways the fulcrum. "We wanted someone we could trust. Neither Tom or I could actually sign a company check – we didn't want to – so all the finance went through Ian, and more and more administration did as well. Tom counts on him. He is a wonderful guy," says Le Duc. Thomson remained distant from the euphoria – he prided himself on never having read a word of Peters' books nor attending any of his presentations. Free-wheeling TPG may have seemed, but its day-to-day management was decidedly retro. Peters may have been the arch-antirationalist but, in practice, his company was decidedly rational. Its job, as much as anything, was to rein in its owner, to offer some sort of control to the whirlwind. "I have never spent five minutes alone with Tom. He always has other people and there is someone arranging his meetings," says Michael Pieschewski.

Peters created a corporate cocoon. Occasionally he bucked against it and cleared his calendar, but it quickly filled up. He injected the chaos; the company was there to create order from it. "Tom is a disorganized guy even though he comes out of the Navy and McKinsey," says Don Laurie. While Peters was intent on making it up as he went along, Ian Thomson and the rest of TPG were there to ensure he kept to the script. With someone like Peters this is a hopeless task. "He is very undisciplined and generous. He will say he hasn't got the time, then spend two days with you," says Max Worcester of *Frankfurter Allgemeine Zeitung*. While Peters' corporate protectors allocate 30- or 45-minute meetings, he largely carries on oblivious, scribbling new appointments on the back of pieces of paper, staying to talk if he is interested and feels it is worth his while.

TPG kept Peters grounded in some sort of reality. It was – and still is – an expensive defense mechanism. "You can very easily upset Tom. He's very emotional, highly sensitive, and very vulnerable. I didn't know him before he was rich and famous, but he has a horror of being ripped-off," says Max Worcester. "At TPG, Ian Thomson is the lynch-pin. He ensures that Tom doesn't throw his money away, that he makes the right investments and hires the right people. Ian is his daddy. TPG has never got beyond Tom. It exists to market him."

By 1989 TPG's revenues were $7 million, dipping to $4 million in 1991 with five full-time employees.[139] Its numbers rise and fall according to Peters' prominence. "The emphasis shifted sharply to money-making rather than research," says Lennart Arvedson. "No-one has succeeded in building a Tom Peters Group. There is an entity in London but it has little connection with the scale of Tom's renown or the management revolution." The most recent incarnation of TPG Europe is the London-based TPG Partners. "Our focus is very much on the 'passion' side of the 'systems plus passion' combination so often a characteristic of excellent companies," it states somewhat nebulously.

"TPG has grown to 30 to 35 employees and is relatively profitable. It has never been an obsession. I never wanted to run a big company. I wanted TPG to be interesting," says Peters. Today, Peters is the chairman and the group is made up of Peters' personal service company; TPG Communications, which concentrates on the newsletter; and TPG Learning Systems, under Kouzes, which employs 90 percent of the people.

No Jack Welch

There is no escaping the fact that Tom Peters is TPG: he is the company. Without him it is nothing. Articles are not written about the interesting work being undertaken by the company or its clients. In fact, most of the work which comes its way, comes through Peters. Journalists and readers have eyes only for Peters. "I think Tom is disappointed in his business not developing, though he is the father of the disappointment. There is only one Tom Peters and they don't do anything without him," observes Jan Lapidoth.

TPG is a company with no real direction or *raison d'être* other than supporting the work of its eponymous star name. It is a vehicle. "Someone in TPG once said that you should never work for a company which has the founder's name," says Michael Pieschewski. (Perhaps Peters should have learned a lesson from McKinsey's founding father, Marvin Bower – with typical shrewdness, Bower did not want his name to be automatically associated with the company as this would mean that every client would require his involvement so when the company founder, James O. McKinsey, died, and the company split, the McKinsey name remained.)

The Tom Peters Group must be an unusual company to work for. "Like any organization, when you're new, it takes a few months to figure out. It was an informal and eccentric group," remembers Paul Cohen, editor of the newsletter, *On Achieving Excellence*, from 1989 to 1995. "I was always aware that with TPG your star is hitched to the fortunes of Tom. It was an ascending arc. The company was clearly there to support and advance the work of

Tom Peters. It was like being on the inside of a presidential campaign with a coterie of people supporting a powerful individual. It was great because there seemed no limit to the amount of work he could generate. The downside was that if he chose to stop, the company had no real reason to exist. It was a rollercoaster, but when a company is synonymous with an individual that is inevitable."

As Cohen was aware, the notion of Peters as a company has obvious drawbacks. "Tom Peters is the brand and with his company he wanted to leverage it," says Don Laurie. "He bought a building in Palo Alto and gave various people some space. TPG was an *ad hoc* group of people who worked under the same roof." The company does not seem to have gone beyond this. "There is a lot of good stuff in his books but there are no concepts. The books are full of good stories, but there are contradictions. If you put a lot of good stories together you don't have a business," says Michael Pieschewski. "Tom made a lot of money and provided the guys with the finance to support the company. It was dependent on Tom. He was the guy paying the salaries. In setting up TPG, Tom wanted to set up a business which wasn't just books and presentations. I'm not sure that any of the businesses were very successful."

Peters retorts that the entire *raison d'être* of the Tom Peters Group was never to become a consultancy. He had had enough of that world at McKinsey. "It was never intended to follow things up. My one intent in life was not to create a consulting company. Senior people in consulting companies sell young bodies at high prices rather than doing things which are different. Actually doing things interests me far more."

TPG was an attempt, it seems, at creating the archetypal Californian organization. Small and dynamic, its role models were the upstart computer companies of Silicon Valley rather than traditional organizations. Peters had swapped the Atlantic coast of Annapolis, Maryland, for the Pacific surf. The small, affluent, and intense world of Stanford and Palo Alto became the bedrock of Peters' thinking and perception of the world. And in this cosseted high-tech corner of the world, everything is possible.

Initially, TPG may have been an indulgence – albeit a serious one – but it has allowed Peters the luxury of avoiding the routine criticism of management gurus that they have never managed anything. This is largely true. "I would be a very poor manager, Hopeless. And a company job would bore me to death," says the doyen of gurus, Peter Drucker.

And, of course, Peters the management guru always encounters the problem of how far his own organization measures up to his ideas. When it comes to customer service, the Tom Peters Group is a hostage to the opinions of its founder. It is, from time to time, hauled over the media coals by journalists who don't get their calls returned by the champions of customer service. This is a fair criticism. If Peters' own, small company can't actually deliver what he propounds, what chance have other organizations?

My own experience suggests that TPG largely fails to practice what Peters preaches. Calls do go unreturned. There is the impression that the company is simply a means of screening Peters' calls. Peters' own busyness is their instant defense. (My requests for interviews with Ian Thomson and some of his colleagues, drew no response whatsoever.)

It is perhaps just as well that Tom Peters has no pretensions to being a manager. Peters is no CEO even though he half-jokingly refers to himself as the chief of the Tom Peters Group. "I never got turned on by the idea of meeting Jack Welch. The thought of running GE does nothing. Hanging out with CEOs has never been my bag. I am not interested in being a star fucker," he says. "The lifers at McKinsey think they can do it after seven years with CEOs, but I never went through that. I enjoyed running a 35-person platoon but I enjoy what I'm doing now. Drucker said he would be bored running a company. Working with a start-up and from my associations with start-ups it is hard psychologically demanding work. It was nothing I aspired to."

Indeed, though ex-McKinsey consultants often go on to hold some of the world's top management jobs, McKinsey does not actually give much in the way of managerial experience. Archie Norman, CEO of the UK retail chain Asda, spent 15 years with McKinsey. "There are very good people at McKinsey and it's a fabulously successful company, but – even though I say it myself – it would be wrong to see strategic consulting as management training. It's a very good business training, as it gives you an understanding of how companies work, but the only real management training is to have to manage something and to learn. Unfortunately, at McKinsey there's nothing to manage other than small teams of highly educated people. There's a sort of legend, a mythology that this is a great management training."[140]

While many who leave McKinsey finish up as senior executives, unless you finish up running IBM (as did ex-McKinsey consultant Lou Gerstner) virtually any managerial position is viewed by McKinsey as a step backwards. McKinsey likes to stand aloof. "I never went through the contempt McKinsey people have for CEOs. For every Lou Gerstner there are lots of failures," says Peters.

Peters' employees generally settle for the observation that Peters is many things but he is definitely, categorically, not CEO material. "Tom is not a manager. He doesn't try to be a manager," says Jayne Pearl. "Tom gives little direct feedback. He doesn't like to deal with or confront people if there is a problem. He's not direct in that way. Someone in Tom's position always has other people who can do the dirty work. He doesn't have to deal with a lot of that stuff. In terms of employee management he does not claim to have much interest," says Paul Cohen. "Tom didn't think I was being rigorous enough on editing his column. Two or three months into my stay, Ian Thomson, the managing director of the company, stopped by my desk and said casually that Tom thought it would be good if I was a little harder. It was a 30-second conversation but I discovered it was a stern alert. I changed my approach. You had to read between the lines."

Cohen's predecessor, Jayne Pearl, recalls an early introduction to working with Peters. "To get my feet wet and immerse myself I was editing his weekly syndicated columns and his various articles. On one of my first assignments he called me up and said could I come over to his farm. He said he wanted me to pack a bag and come over – as if it was a few miles down the road. He said bring a portable computer. I asked how long I should expect to stay. He said he had no idea. When I arrived the problem was that he had written over 100 pages for a ten-page article. He was so frustrated. So I spent the next four or five days editing the article. He wouldn't let me part with a single anecdote."

To Peters, anecdotes have always been precious. To him, a good story is preferable to a bar chart of sales figures any day of the week. Part Peters from his fund of illuminating and supportive stories and you would see him naked. Part him from his company and he would appear no different.

On the Road With a Passion

While corporate man was developing his own corporation and discovering the world of the skunk, there was the question of the sequel. This was always going to be difficult. Ask anyone who has had a bestseller with their first book (Harper Lee perhaps) or a hit with their first album. Three years of research had preceded *In Search of Excellence*, and, at that time, Peters had the benefit of McKinsey's resources, financial and intellectual. Also, the success of *In Search of Excellence* meant that its successor would be judged by entirely new and more demanding criteria.

Bob Waterman was unlikely to be the co-author. Having eventually left McKinsey, he was pursuing a radically different, low-key path to Peters'. Peters and Waterman had also, since the success of *In Search of Excellence*, dismissed Harper & Row as their publisher – "Bob and I got pissed off with Harper & Row. It was real petulance because we thought they hadn't moved as quickly as we would have liked them to," explains Peters. Ambitious talk of a partnership between TPG and Random House later led Peters to a new publisher.

By 1983, with *In Search of Excellence* top of the bestseller lists, Peters was gathering material. The emphasis was on collecting "implementation vignettes" of excellence in practice. The initial plan was for the book to be co-authored by Peters, Nancy Austin and Bob Le Duc. "Le Duc got distracted and never made his deadlines," says Peters. Le Duc was running a hectic schedule but admits that he was "a bit surprised" when it was decided that the co-author was to be Nancy Austin. (Though Austin was co-author, she was the sole author of the last 100 pages concerned with coaching.) *A Passion for Excellence* was completed at the end of 1984 and published early in 1985. Like its predecessor it reached the top of the bestseller lists, knocking Lee Iacocca's book off the top spot. Sven Atterhed hired another plane to fly past trailing a celebratory banner.

Despite its success in terms of sales, Peters couldn't win with *A Passion for Excellence*. It was either going to be slated because it was too similar to *In Search of Excellence* or too different. In practice, Peters was under pressure from all sides. The demand for a sequel was enormous – from publishers and readers – and the demands on his time were equally huge. Between the publication of *In Search of Excellence* in October 1982 and the completion of *A Passion for Excellence*, a little over two years later, Peters had started a confusing network of companies, circumnavigated the world a dozen times or so, given seminar after seminar, and along the way had to assemble a sequel to his bestseller. "*In Search of Excellence* came out of the Siemens research. It was nice and orderly. Then, following that, I spent a lot of time on the road giving seminars. Along the way I began to be exposed to new companies," says Peters. "I met people who I never met at McKinsey. I discovered different kinds of company and expanded my horizons. I was doing lots of seminars with middle managers." A new world opened up, but old world pressures remained as strong as ever.

Reviewers, perhaps in awe of *In Search of Excellence's* success, went easy on *A Passion for Excellence*. This was unfortunate, because *A Passion for Excellence* smacks of confusion and indulgence. Some things are very sad: middle-aged men who buy Harley Davidsons in the belief that a few thousand dollars' worth of machinery will enable them to recapture their lost youth; songs about peace and poverty by hugely rich rock stars; and consultants who seek to prove how in touch with reality they are. *A Passion for Excellence* is something of a mid-life crisis, a lengthy attempt at recapturing lost youth. Having spent the latter part of the sixties in Vietnam, it seemed as if Peters and Austin were seeking to recreate the summer of love. At times they were as whimsical as two lovers sharing a joint – "We interrupted (rudely to others involved, we're afraid) a busy schedule to spend 25 minutes watching a bricklayer at work – because he was an artist, with an artist's passion, and because the quality of his product reflected that."[141]

There was more. Peters and Austin were in touch with their senses – "We've developed a term, after careful thought: smell. Does your company smell of customers? Do you listen to them directly (via MBWA), act on what you hear, listen naively (i.e. consider their perceptions more important than your superior technical knowledge of service or product)? Do you love your salespersons (i.e. listen to them), despite their efforts to strain your resources – and patience – in response to what you see as customers' whims? Do you look for the dozens (hundreds, really) of tiny bases for differentiation – i.e. a small but measurable difference that is the winning edge for superb cookie makers and aircraft engineers alike?"[142]

To damn *A Passion for Excellence* with faint praise is to give it its due. "*A Passion for Excellence* is probably my sixth favorite of my six books," Peters admits. Even now, it is unaccountably riddled with typographical errors. "*A Passion for Excellence* was a collection of stories collected on the road. It is hopelessly disorganized, a haphazard collection of anecdotes awkwardly shoved into a framework. It came from me talking to zillions of people and doing seminars, so it wasn't the best-written book, and the published version is a nightmare, but people still come up to me about the vignettes. People read it for the soundbites."

The vignettes developed the approach, developed only slightly in *In Search of Excellence,* of taking snippets of conversation and turning them into much more. *A Passion for Excellence* took the "soft" side of the Seven Ss and expanded and glorified it. It reveled in the softness of the world of business: suddenly everything was intuitive, celebratory, exciting. Business was a ball. Peters and Austin quoted Jan Carlzon, CEO of Scandinavian Airline Systems: "All business is show business."[143]

A Passion for Excellence brought Carlzon's innovative work to a wider audience. Peters and Carlzon appeared at this point to have created a mutual admiration society. While Carlzon's brand of managerial magic was celebrated in *A Passion for Excellence*, Peters and Carlzon were never close friends. "Tom dug out a lot of success stories and almost made them his own successes. Take Jan Carlzon. Carlzon has probably not read a Tom Peters book," says Michael Pieschewski.

Indeed, Peters' advice occasionally ran totally contrary to what Carlzon was actually doing at SAS. Jan Lapidoth was a senior vice-president with SAS at the time. "I worked for three years with the senior management group of SAS in Houston, Texas. Someone thought it would be good to get Tom over and so I asked him. He dropped in for a couple of hours to a hotel where we all were," he recalls. "We'd embarked on an ambitious program to create synergies between hotels and airlines, and so on. Tom walked in, just off a flight. I had briefed him a little, but he was grumpy. Jan Carlzon was not there, which was just as well because before we'd got started Tom started bashing the entire idea of synergy. He said it just doesn't work. When Carlzon returned our enthusiasm for synergy had disappeared – eventually Carlzon went under in pursuit of that idea." To some extent, Lapidoth says, it was a clash of strong personalities. "Tom and Jan Carlzon had a few polite encounters but didn't really know each other very well. You have to remember that both are gurus in their own right and stars tend not to like each other a great deal."

In *A Passion for Excellence*, Peters and Austin fell in love with their vignettes. Instead of case studies they became breathless celebrations. "Many accused *In Search of Excellence* of oversimplifying. After hundreds of post-*In Search of Excellence* seminars we have reached the opposite conclusion: *In Search of Excellence* didn't simplify enough!"[144] they observed. "Leadership means vision, cheerleading, enthusiasm, love, trust, verve, passion, obsession, consistency, the use of symbols, paying attention as illustrated by the content of one's calendar, out-and-out drama (and the management thereof), creating heroes at all levels, coaching, effectively wandering around, and numerous other things. Leadership must be present at all levels of the organization."[145]

A Passion for Excellence was built around a triangle of care for customers, innovation, and people, with leadership at its center. Peters and Austin celebrated leadership, but put it into a more vibrant context. There was no talk of transformational and transactional leadership, no real theory. Instead, Peters and Austin gave a bravura eulogy. Leadership, as extolled in *A Passion for Excellence*, was the soft Ss run riot, so soft they became linguistic marshlands with words sinking into the mire. "Leadership (management) is symbolic behavior," they wrote.[146] "The concept of leadership is crucial to the revolution now under way – so crucial that we believe the words 'managing' and 'management' should be discarded. 'Management,' with its attendant images – cop, referee, devil's advocate, dispassionate analyst, naysayer, pronouncer – connotes controlling and arranging and demeaning and reducing. 'Leadership' connotes unleashing energy, building, freeing, and growing."[147]

Despite its deficiencies, *A Passion for Excellence* was notable in that it argued the case for what was to become yet another in the long line of managerial fashions: empowerment. "What drives the skunks to success when larger groups founder? We think that it is, above all, a sense of ownership and commitment," wrote Peters and Austin.[148] The book was also important in that it sought to bridge the gap between big and small organizations. It clarified – somewhat at least – what Peters and Waterman tentatively mapped out in *In Search of Excellence*. "A passion for excellence means thinking big and starting small: excellence happens when high purpose and intense pragmatism meet. This is almost, but not quite, the whole truth. We believe a passion for excellence also carried a price, and we state it simply: the adventure of excellence is not for the faint of heart."[149]

Bob Le Duc, almost one of the book's co-authors, defends *A Passion for Excellence* and believes it was an accurate reflection of the times: "It captured the positive, uplifting optimism we all felt." Even so, Le Duc became slowly disenchanted with the company, its work, and his role. "As time went on, customers seemed less interested in working through the difficult issues. I withdrew from doing the Skunk Camps in 1986. The initial plan was for the two of us to do consulting and teaching. But by then I was responsible for all those people. They were having fun but I was stuck in the office not having much fun at all. I was getting burned out and starting thinking of pulling out." In October 1987 Le Duc left to work as an independent consultant based at his home. He later returned to work in an office on the first floor of the TPG building in Hamilton Avenue, Palo Alto. After the first onslaught of fame, it appeared a chapter was closing. But not before fame bit back.

FIVE

THE
BACKLASH

*" In Search of Excellence's
eight principles have
survived intact – just the
companies haven't "*

Tom Peters

November 1984,
Palo Alto

The day's mail was piled high on a desk in reception. Tom Peters, running late yet again, bounded in and swept on – "Hi, how y'doing," he appeared to say. Another day in the vortex of Peters' energy beckoned for the staff of the fledgling Tom Peters Group. The phone rang. A call from Lew Young, champion of In Search of Excellence *who had just left the editor's chair at* Business Week. *Today, was the publication day of one of the first issues under the new editor Steve Shepherd.*

Peters came out a minute later. "Let's see it," he said and began to rifle the stack of unopened mail. Near the bottom of the pile he found the new Business Week. *The cellophane cover was ripped apart. "Shit," he said as he tore it off. A colleague looked over his shoulder as Peters contemplated the front cover and its simple headline: "Oops!"*

Fifteen Minutes of Fame

Book-buying executives weren't the only people who fell for Tom Peters' brand of exhortation and celebration. The media lapped it up. Peters was a journalist's dream – ready to talk, opinionated, quotable, and increasingly well-known. His face and his pithy, usually damning, quotes began to appear all over the place. Suddenly no management article was complete without the obligatory Tom Peters angle – and angles there were aplenty.

The first cover story featuring Peters(written coincidentally by an ex-McKinsey secretary) appeared in *Inc.* soon after *In Search of Excellence.* More quickly followed. After decades of frosty academics who couldn't condense their research into a readable book let alone a sound-bite, and cagy consultants anxious not to give anything away, the media found a flexible friend. "I met Tom soon after *In Search of Excellence*," says *Inc.*'s Bo Burlingham. "He was a breath of fresh air – someone who cared passionately, and who loved and cared about business. He made it exciting and I liked him tremendously."

Peters' principal media tactic was to talk to anyone about virtually anything. (An approach which has distinguished his career and his life.) "I answered the phone and shot from the hip. A lot of people don't talk to the media but no comment is the guarantee that your view won't see the light of day. I realized I would be misquoted from time to time, but I've looked at the media as allies. Seen that way, you have the entire business media working for you. Short of the *National Inquirer*, the average person working for *Forbes* or *Business Week* is a meticulous researcher so I've used that," he says. Indeed, Peters' books are littered with acknowledgments to columnists and journalists – the kind of people who scarcely rate a mention in other business books for the simple reason that most academics don't actually think of journalists as meticulous researchers at all. (Peters is also notably ethical in his acknowledgments – no line goes unacknowledged. This scrupulous fairness is something which clearly fosters friends in the media.)

Even so, it wasn't always plain sailing. "For 15 years now, I've been dealing almost daily with the press. I've been extolled, pilloried, quoted, and misquoted. The press has made me – and made me mad as hell." But, overall, it was a good deal. Peters admits that he was good for the media and the media was good for him. They fed off each other. "I had good media instincts and a lot of my subsequent popular success stems from that, in retrospect," he says.[150]

Every quote fueled Peters' fame and usually, one way or another, added to his fortune – and good fortune. "I was too dumb to be fearful of the balloon bursting," he recalls, going on to draw parallels with the sudden fame which came to runner Jim Fixx – "He wrote that book on running and then wrote a book about what it was like to write a very unexpected bestseller. He said he was just a half-assed jock and next thing he knew he was introducing presidential candidate Walter Mondale."

Peters wasn't (and isn't) a half-assed jock – or even quarter-assed – just a management consultant, caught up in the absurd maelstrom of fame. "I didn't catch my breath. It was so ridiculous that you didn't think. I've got a low self-concept so my shrinks tell me, low self-esteem. The reaction was so over the top, I hid. I couldn't handle it. A lot of people in those situations move to Manhattan. I could have moved there and joined the cocktail circuit. Instead I bought a farm in Vermont in the summer of 1984. I was supposed to spend the winter in China but ended up on the farm and loved it. It was a lark. I moved to Vermont planning to spend a month there every year, now I spend 80 to 90 percent of my time there. Psychologically it moved me away." Peters' bolt-hole has since been turned into his permanent home – or at least, as permanent as his peripatetic lifestyle allows.

But, despite having a geographical retreat, much of the rest of the time Peters flailed around. His low self-esteem did not manifest itself in public reticence. He has always been publicly voluble – and the assumption, therefore, is to assume that his reticence does not exist. "In the beginning he was so angry he was casting about in any direction," says Harvard's Wickham Skinner. "Now, he's not in so much of a hurry." The media was hungry and he fed them. "In *In Search of Excellence* and the work which immediately followed he tended to attack anyone who seemed to rival him. He trashed academics and others who seemed to him to be asserting some authoritative position," says Dan Carroll. "Then he seemed to put it behind him and stopped feeling the need to put others down. In that respect, he grew up. Tom has changed for the better. He now has greater self-confidence."

Inadvertently, Carroll himself turned the tables on Peters but only by being misquoted. "On one occasion I talked to a journalist. He quoted me as saying that Tom's conclusions in *In Search of Excellence* were fraudulent. In fact I said they were wrong. Tom called me quite upset, but next time I met him at an airport we had an amiable chat."

Others were drawn into the firing line. Tom Horton, then head of the American Management Association, gave an interview to a reporter in Detroit after giving a talk to the Economic Club of Detroit. It was not big news, but Peters found it and didn't like it. He was "appalled" and called Horton's comments "utter non-sense." Horton was nonplussed. "I had said that 'managing by walking around' was perhaps a good idea, especially for the sedentary executive; but there are times that one must sit still, develop strategies, do one's homework, and so on. Somehow Tom Peters took this as a criticism and then took me to task," Horton recalls.[151]

Peters has a thin skin which, considering he survived both the Navy and the politically charged McKinsey, is a little surprising. "I'm devastated when I get bad reviews," he says. "Waterman had the ability to not allow the barbs to affect him. He has Teflon skin. I smile a lot of the shit off but every wound is fatal." Peters loses sleep over apparently trivial things. He worries and turns things over in his mind. "He is a very human human being with pains and insecurities. He is very sensitive to criticism," says Lennart Arvedson. "I criticized what I thought was a draft of one of his columns and sent him a fax saying I thought he shouldn't publish it. It was too late but he told me that he had lost several night's sleep thinking about it."

At the same time, Peters' fame and fortune mean that he attracts a fair number of sycophants who are as likely to voice criticism as Thomas Pynchon is likely to hold a press conference. "He could always take criticism. He thrived on it because people were fawning on him all the time," says Jayne Pearl. "I wrote in a review of *Liberation Management* saying that though he was as egalitarian a boss as I'd ever had, hardly any women were quoted in the book. He rang me up to say I'd made his week and the criticism was justified."

Whether he was giving or receiving criticism, Peters' penchant for punditry put him in the firing line. Today's media darling is inevitably tomorrow's fall guy. "We create heroes fast, then smack them down fast if they get complacent or snooty. We'll try anything," he wrote in one of his columns.[152] All it takes is a remark taken out of context, an opinion too far.

Ironically Peters' nemesis was *BusinessWeek*, the magazine which had done so much to promote *In Search of Excellence* in the first place. Its long-time editor, Lew Young left to be replaced by Stephen Shepherd. Understandably keen to make a splash, Shepherd targeted the companies chosen by Peters and Waterman as excellent. He found plenty to write about.

Excellence Fails

On November 5th, 1984 *Business Week* covered 12 pages with a lengthy story entitled "Who's excellent now?" *Business Week* found that, two years on, the companies featured in *In Search of Excellence* were anything but excellent. Its front-page headline was "Oops!" The article claimed that about a quarter of the "excellent" companies were struggling – among them were Hewlett-Packard, Disney, and Digital Equipment.

The single and undeniable fact that the excellent companies of 1982 were not all excellent in 1984 has continued to haunt Peters. Indeed, mention his name and this is often the first thing people mention – "Ah, isn't he the one who got it wrong?"

The *Business Week* article appeared to mark the beginning of the end for Peters and the *In Search of Excellence* phenomenon. Almost exactly two years after the book's publication, the bubble of fame was pricked. The *Business Week* article was the end of the honeymoon when everything Peters touched turned to gold. Not many survive a mauling from such a big media name.

Behind the headline, the undeniable fact is that Peters and Waterman did get it wrong – and have been admitting so ever since. "We missed or glossed over other things, such as the on-rush of globalism. But the point is neither to defend nor denigrate 1982's work. *Search* provided a challenging message. Many of its lessons are timeless, yet almost all beg reexamination in light of new conditions," wrote Peters ten years later.[153] Excellence in 1982 was not excellence in 1984, and certainly not ten years later. In their defense, Peters and Waterman could have pointed to escape clauses inserted into *In Search of Excellence* – "We are asked how we know that the companies we have defined as culturally innovative will stay that way. The answer is we don't," they wrote.[154] But it is unlikely this would have done much good. The word was out.

"We started to get beaten up. When *Business Week* ran its 'Oops!' story it was a shitty week," recalls Peters. "I was certain the phone would stop ringing though I didn't understand the media then. I wouldn't disagree that I had been on the road too much and in that respect the *Business Week* article was a great wake up call. There's nothing the soul likes more than a great beating. You've just got to believe that 'Oops!' was all part of being in the marketplace of ideas."

At the Tom Peters Group, the *Business Week* article was not viewed as entirely disastrous. While it certainly caused the thin-skinned Peters to lose sleep, his colleagues were more sanguine. "We thought if that's the worst we're in great shape. We had a terror of being a fad," says Bob Le Duc. "They were looking for a shocking story to put in their new format. It was a nuisance but we felt vindicated."

Since *Business Week* set the ball rolling, analyses of the performance of the "excellent" companies have been somewhat gleefully assembled by an array of academics and consultants.

In 1995, Fred Reichheld and Jeremy Silverman of consultants Bain & Co. calculated that in the ten years from 1985 to 1995 two thirds of the stocks of the publicly traded excellent companies underperformed the S&P 500. They concluded that only one fifth of the original excellent companies remained excellent. "While [*In Search of Excellence* is] undeniably entertaining, it cannot by itself help anyone achieve (or sustain) the model of excellence it portrays," wrote Reichheld and Silverman.[155]

Dwight Gertz and Joao Baptista of Mercer Management Consultants provided similar damning evidence in their book, *Grow to be Great*.[156] It compared the performance of companies featured in *In Search of Excellence*, *Built to Last* by Stanford's Jerry Porras and Collins, Treacy and Wiersema's *The Discipline of Market Leaders*, and their own chosen companies. *In Search of Excellence* companies performed the worst of all. This makes for a good chart (see illustration 1) but little else. The performance criteria used

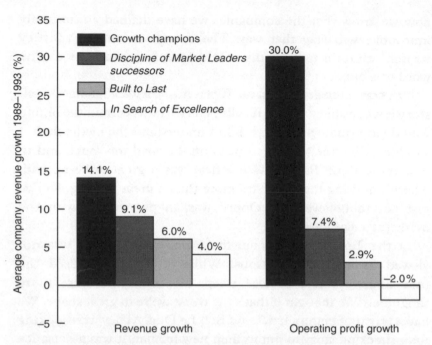

Illustration 1 Relative performance of the "excellent" companies 1989–1993. (*Source*: Mercer Management Consulting analysis)

by Gertz and Baptista covered 1989 and 1993 so the competition is a false one. No one, let alone Peters and Waterman, would have chosen the same companies in 1989 as in 1982.

Among those who have examined Peters and Waterman's failure is Richard Pascale who worked with them on the Seven S model. Pascale and Peters have taken different paths, and ones which are unlikely to converge. Pascale believes that Peters is offering simplistic solutions to complex problems and, as such, does a disservice to American business.

Pascale's 1990 book, *Managing on the Edge*, is undoubtedly one of the most cogent examinations of the modern managerial world. But, when it came to *In Search of Excellence*, Pascale was colorfully scathing. "We can, of course, learn from excellent companies, but *how* to learn from them is far more complicated than might first be supposed," wrote Pascale. "Simply identifying attributes of success is like identifying attributes of people in excellent health during the age of the bubonic plague. A study of the 'survivors' during the Middle Ages might have identified any number of spurious patterns: perhaps some drank only wine (or only water), were married (or celibate), were devout Catholics (or atheists). All of those patterns were foolishness, of course, yet hundreds of thousands of desperate citizens amassed like lemmings behind one credo or another in hopes of being spared. Sound familiar?"[157] The lemmings, presumably, are all those who bought *In Search of Excellence*.

Curiously, on the very next page, Pascale gives an abbreviated version of the state of the heath of the excellent companies. He identifies those which were still excellent five years on from *In Search of Excellence* – and, of course, by making such a judgment (the reasons for which are unexplained) Pascale repeats the same mistake as Peters and Waterman. In *Managing on the Edge*, Pascale identifies fourteen of the excellent companies as still excellent; ten as "solid but [experiencing] loss of leadership," eleven as in a "weakened position," and eight as "troubled." He does not elaborate on the grounds for these judgments. It is interesting that even Pascale's revisited list is flawed – among his companies regarded as still "excellent" was IBM which was by then on the verge of the biggest collapse in its history. Pascale's "weakened position" category includes Hewlett-Packard, which continues in rude good health, and his "troubled" group includes K-Mart, which subsequently revived and then stumbled again. Despite his criticisms, Pascale's "research base" for *Managing on the Edge* included 45 companies from the 62 included in the excellence research.

Critiques of Peters and Waterman's "excellent" companies continue to appear. The message, uniformly, is that their selection was fatally flawed. Indeed, it was. Any selection of excellent companies is doomed from its inception. As Peters said, it is ludicrous to set yourself up as an arbiter of corporate excellence. It is ludicrous for the simple reason that though such judgments offer a snapshot of reality they can never offer a long-term panorama. "When the excellence companies began to disappear down the toilet Peters was vilified. He was out on a limb," says Randall White of RPW Executive Development. "It's true that many of the organizations Peters has focused on have declined but that's true of any book which provides a benchmark. Benchmarks only bring you up to date."

As benchmarks go, there was little criticism of Peters and Waterman's selection at the time. The reason for this is simple, says Max Worcester of *Frankfurter Allgemeine Zeitung*: "Tom didn't get it wrong in *In Search of Excellence*. At the time, he was right. He pointed out the criteria for success at that time. But, for anyone who had been brought up in an European environment, there was little that was new in *In Search of Excellence*." While many of the issues raised in the book were well-known in Europe, understanding of how to implement them was generally limited to Scandinavia and Germany. The rest of industrial Europe was struggling in much the same way as American industry.

Interpretations of history tend to err on the negative side. Henry Ford is no longer regarded as an industrial genius, but as an inhuman corporate dictator. Perspectives change, best practice alters. In many respects the subsequent performance of the excellent companies has nothing to do with the book's worth. "So many people criticized Tom for saying the excellent companies were no longer excellent. But so what? Tom's contribution was to show that there are alternative routes; that it can be fun. You need zany models to do something," says Sven Atterhed.

The subsequent critical research tends to be selective. In their defense, Peters and Waterman could point to the fact that of the fourteen "exemplars of excellence" thirteen are still in the *Fortune* 200; or that Hewlett-Packard has moved from $1 billion in revenues in 1980 to $35 billion; or that, of seventeen American companies selected by Collins and Porras in *Built to Last*, eleven were from the *In Search of Excellence* selection. Some of the companies featured by *Business Week* – like Hewlett-Packard and Disney – have revived. Others have fallen – Wang registered for bankruptcy. Others – Fluor, Caterpillar, Digital Equipment – have yo-yoed from good times to bad. Others still carry on doing largely what they were doing in 1982 – Johnson & Johnson, Wal-Mart, Intel, Emerson Electric, Mars, 3M, Boeing, Merck – and some have lost their independence (including Data General and NCR). Reviewing their performance early in 1997, Peters estimated that 30 percent of the excellence companies deserved an "A" grade. "I still don't know what the answer is," Peters admits. "*In Search of Excellence*'s eight principles have survived intact – just the companies haven't."

Who's excellent now?

Revisiting the list of excellent companies is to witness corporate mortality at work. The numbers shown in italics next to the companies featured in *In Search of Excellence* are their rankings from the 1996 *Fortune* 500.

Excellent companies which did not meet criteria
1. American Airlines
2. Arco
3. Exxon   *3*
4. General Electric   *7*
5. General Foods
6. General Motors   *1*
7. Gould
8. Ingersoll-Rand
9. Lockheed
10. McDermott
11. NCR
12. Polaroid
13. Rockwell   *90*
14. TRW   *126*
15. United Technologies
16. Western Electric
17. Westinghouse   *135*
18. Xerox   *41*

Excellent and met the criteria
1. Allen-Bradley
2. Amdahl
3. Atari (Warner Communications)
4. Avon
5. Blue Bell
6. Bristol-Myers   *79*
7. Chesebrough-Pond's
8. Data General
9. Disney Productions   *102*
10. Dow Chemical   *36*

11. DuPont
12. Eastman Kodak   67
13. Frito-Lay (PepsiCo)
14. Hughes Aircraft
15. Intel   60
16. K Mart   16
17. Levi Strauss   198
18. Marriott   147
19. Mars
20. Maytag   410
21. Merck   55
22. National Semiconductor
23. Raychem
24. Revlon
25. Schlumberger
26. Standard Oil (Indiana)/Amoco   23
27. Texas Instruments   89
28. Tupperware (Dart & Kraft)
29. Wal-Mart   4
30. Wang Labs

Exemplars of excellence
 1. Bechtel
 2. Boeing   40
 3. Caterpillar Tractor   63
 4. Dana Corp   169
 5. Delta Airlines   98
 6. Digital Equipment   77
 7. Emerson Electric   128
 8. Fluor   140
 9. Hewlett-Packard   20
10. IBM   6
11. Johnson & Johnson   43
12. McDonald's   132
13. Minnesota Mining & Manufacturing (3M)   62
14. Procter & Gamble   17

The Myth of Permanence

Of all the companies featured in *In Search of Excellence*, IBM was the most obvious choice and, apparently, the safest. Big Blue embodied excellence. No one would have dreamed of questioning its right to be listed among the pantheon of business greats of 1982 or any other year. IBM, a company which once accounted for 70 percent of the global computer industry's profits, had the reassuring look of permanence.

In 1991 Peters wrote: "Consider IBM. No company has been praised more highly for adherence to soaring, widely shared values. Yet each of its three pillars of wisdom – service, people, perfection – has cracked if not crumbled." Service no longer gave IBM a competitive advantage, its paternalistic attitude to employees smothered individuality, and its quest for perfection led to unnecessary complexity. "We must comprehend how quickly values age, becoming hopelessly narrow, ludicrously elaborated – and at odds with a shifting marketplace! Ironically, the more virtuous the value (service, people) the greater the chance of long-term perversion. Why? Because the 'better' the value, the more the establishment makes sure you adhere to it *exactly*," noted Peters.[158]

Between 1991 and 1993 IBM accumulated losses of nearly $16 billion and in 1993 alone lost $8.1 billion. In his book, *Big Blues: The Unmaking of IBM*, Paul Carroll dismissed IBM's management as "like a music publishing company run by deaf people."

"This was a company that was very successful for several

decades, but the curse of success is that people try to codify it," IBM CEO, and ex-McKinsey consultant, Lou Gerstner has said. "My view is that you perpetuate success by continuing to run scared, not by looking back at what made you great, but looking forward at what is going to make you ungreat, so that you are constantly focusing on the challenges that keep you humble, hungry and nimble."[159]

Contrast IBM with another company featured in *In Search of Excellence*, Wal-Mart. Its selection was as much emotive as objective. "In *In Search of Excellence*, Bob and I took one big risk. We fell in love with a company and put it in the book. Everything we learned about it we liked. The risky company was Wal-Mart," says Peters. Wal-Mart managed to record 99 consecutive quarters of sales and earnings growth after it went public. It wasn't so risky after all.

The chief lesson of *In Search of Excellence* – for Tom Peters as well as anyone else – was that corporate excellence is a fleeting experience. Companies come and go, whether they are IBM or Joe's corner store. By the time *BusinessWeek* had got round to examining the performance of the excellent companies many were on the ropes. The most amazing thing about this was not that fortunes wax and wane, but that people were so aghast about what is a fact of business life. "I don't dismiss *In Search of Excellence* simply because some of the companies struggled afterwards. That happens to all companies," says Henry Mintzberg.

Richard Pascale's *Managing on the Edge* begins with the line "Nothing fails like success." "Great strengths are inevitably the root of weakness," writes Pascale. This fundamental truth is only slowly dawning on business awareness. Lew Platt, CEO of Hewlett-Packard (which also had its fair share of difficulties in the late eighties) says: "General Motors, Sears, IBM were the greatest companies in their industries, the best of the best in the world. These companies did not make gigantic mistakes. They were not led by stupid, inept people. The only real mistake they made was to keep doing whatever it was that had made them successful for a little too long."[160]

What made the companies excellent in 1982 did not necessarily make them excellent even a few months later. This truism has formed the cornerstone of Peters' work since *In Search of Excellence* and *A Passion for Excellence*. His work is now built on the mortality of corporations, rather than seeking to construct a route to immortality. Evidence of corporate mortality is rife and Peters uses it to reinforce his message of imminent danger.

In recent years this process of corporate attrition has accelerated. Churchill and Muzyka of INSEAD calculate that the "death rate" of *Fortune* 500 companies was four times as high in 1990 as it was in 1970.[161] In 1988, Arie de Geus, a former planning director at Shell, wrote an article showing that one third of the *Fortune* 500 industrial companies listed in 1970 had disappeared by 1983. Of the 1970 *Fortune* 500, 60 percent have now disappeared – either acquired or gone out of business. Between 1980 and 1990 alone, almost 40 percent ceased to exist. The average corporate survival rate for large companies in the early 1980s was only about half as long as the life span of a human being.

A look at *Fortune*'s, or virtually any other, listing swiftly provides evidence of the turbulence at work. The loss makers of 1995 included Time Warner, Tyson Foods, Comcast Corporation, Worldcom and Salomon. It is an international phenomenon: across the Atlantic, 43 companies ranked in the UK's top 500 listing left the list in 1995, probably never to reappear.

There were, however, a few organizations identified by de Geus which had survived for 75 years or more. De Geus suggested that the key to their longevity was their ability to conduct "experiments in the margin." They were always looking for new business opportunities which continually challenged the organization to grow and learn.[162] Interestingly, it was these marginal activities which Peters and Waterman picked up on in *In Search of Excellence*. The trouble is that their analysis did not go beyond identifying them as important.

Since *In Search of Excellence* Peters has learned that the companies which manage to retain their excellence rating have done so by sheer luck ("The survival of some organizations for great lengths of time is largely a matter of luck," notes Herbert Kaufman in *Time, Chance and Organization*) or by becoming radically different than their predecessors visited by Peters and Waterman. Look at General Electric, which failed to meet all the criteria laid down in *In Search of Excellence*. Its development over the past decade mirrors the development of Tom Peters' thinking.

Jack Welch took over at General Electric in 1981. Between then and the end of the decade, GE cut the average number of management layers between Welch and the very front line from nine to four. Its headquarters was slashed from 2100 people to fewer than 1000. The number of senior executives across the company was cut, first from 700 to 500, and then by another 100 between 1990 and 1994. The overall workforce was almost halved, from 404,000 to 220,000. Yet GE's revenues more than doubled through this period, from $27 billion to $60 billion. When Welch arrived, GE had an average of five or six people per manager. By the late 1980s its average had doubled, and is now at about 14, with some units reaching 25 or more.

"With that change has come a transformation in the way employees relate to 'their' managers, and in the nature of the management process itself," reported the late Christopher Lorenz of the *Financial Times*. "Since the only way for a single person to 'manage' two dozen people is to allow them more independence, management at GE really has changed from being a 'command and control' function to one of mainly 'coaching' people, and – providing their type of task allows it – unleashing their initiative as completely as possible."

The realization, reflected in changes at GE, is that excellence is transitory. Corporations need to constantly change, and to do so requires managers with radically different skills than their one-dimensional predecessors. Difference – both personal and corporate – has become the new necessity.

The trouble is that the rise of the professional general manager has encouraged corporate parents, and corporate managers, to be alike rather than different. "The manager is a hero in the Western world, but an impostor," says Andrew Campbell of the Ashridge Strategic Management Centre. "The concept of management has proved a huge distraction. The management side of running a company is trivial compared to the importance of being commercial or entrepreneurial, or having a particular specialist skill. Any organization needs to have people with the skills relevant to its business rather than concentrating on turning the marketing director into a rounded general manager."

Indeed, Campbell goes on to suggest that we have become preoccupied with creating immortal organizations rather than ones which work in the present. "Why do we want organizations to thrive for ever?" he asks. "On average organizations survive for less time than the working life of an individual. They become dysfunctional and, at that point, they should be killed off. What is encouraging is that, first through management buyouts and now through demergers, we are becoming more adept at bringing an end to corporate lives which have run their course and creating new organizations in their place."

Companies are human after all. Ten years after *In Search of Excellence* Peters wrote: "Hats off to 1982's 'excellent' chiefs who saw the need – and then had the gumption – to change. My condolences to the rest." He then mapped out the lessons he had learned from *In Search of Excellence*:

1. Changing large institutions, even in the face of clear market signals, is no lark.
2. Savaging bureaucracy is a must.
3. Adaptation is unlikely without radical surgery.
4. Listening to customers is no panacea.
5. Looking at the right "models" is imperative.[163]

For Peters the route to learning these lessons was the *Business-Week* article. Excellence – at least in its original form – was dead.

SIX

THE GURU
GRAVY TRAIN

66 *The only thing worse than
slavishly following
management theory is
ignoring it completely* 99

The Economist[164]

December 1988, London

Ten o'clock in the evening on a dull and wet winter's day in London. The city is still full of people, most drifting home after an evening's entertainment. From a hotel at the end of Piccadilly overlooking Green Park, Tom Peters walks on to the rain-soaked pavement and hails a passing black cab. He asks the driver to take him to the Four Seasons Hotel.

Along the way he is silent, gazing distantly out of the window as London slips by. At the Four Seasons he goes to reception: "Hi, I'm Tom Peters and I'm doing a seminar here tomorrow. Can you show me the room I'll be speaking in?" The receptionist looks sympathetically towards him. Obviously a newcomer to the speaking circuit, settling a few nerves before his moment in the spotlight. She shows him to the darkened room and switches the lights on. Peters thanks her, surveys the room for five minutes and turns the lights off before leaving.

In the morning, he is up at five. He calls one of his staff in California where it is nine the previous evening. He works on an article and an hour goes by. He rings room service and orders breakfast.

As he waits, he rifles through a pile of papers, finds the piece he wants and adds it to his seminar file. Over breakfast he reads through what he has prepared.

Three hours later he is on stage, in the spotlight. His audience is 300 managers from a major UK pub and restaurant chain. They are senior managers, divisional managers, and pub managers from throughout the country. Peters strides across the stage holding his notes in one hand. His other hand is by his mouth, as if deep in thought. The room is silent as the audience waits expectantly. Peters flourishes his notes.

"It amazes me how little I know. I know next to nothing. Nothing strange in that. The people who claim to know it all, usually know zero. Zip. We know that. We all know that.

"But what about corporations? What about the big names – the Fortune 500, the Fortune 100, the Fortune 50 – what do they know?

"I remember years ago, when I was a kid, you knew where you stood. You went to work and that was that. Day in, day out, you knew which office door you went through. My dad did that for over 40 years. Forty years with one company. Think what that would be like. Forty years.

"People like my dad stayed with companies for their entire working life because they thought the companies knew best. Companies knew it all.

"The trouble is we still believe it – or want to believe it – or have to believe it. But companies know nothing."

The audience sits transfixed. A few glance at their bosses to see if they can gauge their reactions. They, too, appear transfixed by the perspiring figure on stage who is now affecting a look of total disbelief.

"Look at General Motors. They don't get much bigger. GM knew it all. It knew so much that it ignored the oil crisis in the seventies. It knew so much that it never noticed the Japanese made cars as well. GM knew so much that it didn't even realize that women drove its cars.

"It worked on the premise for decades and decades that men bought the cars and therefore it was men who drove them. It knew so much that it forgot half of the fucking population. Think of the books telling us how smart GM was. It was smart at controlling its people. It was smart at changing its models. It was smart at getting its sums right. But it still knew nothing about its customers. And if you know nothing about your customers, you know nothing at all."

The audience is nodding. Some exchange whispered comments. They agree. He is right. The customer always comes first. Some parts of the audience are laughing – quietly – at GM's blindness.

"I can hear you laughing at GM's stupidity. Yeh, they were incredibly stupid, incredibly blinkered. They didn't see anything coming. But think again. Why the fuck are you laughing? Your company has only just realized that women go into its pubs."

There is a pause, a long pause. Peters takes his jacket off and puts it over a chair at the corner of the stage. Those in the audience are shrinking in their seats.

The Rise and Rise of the Guru Business

The "Oops!" article did not disrupt the triumphant progress of Tom Peters. It merely caused him to pause for a while. During the mid-1980s, he was at the peak of his fame. Along the way, as he passed through airports, forever *en route* to somewhere, Tom Peters was – unconsciously – doing something more than becoming rich and earning an awful lot of air miles.

In his masterly book, *The Practice of Management,* published in 1954, Peter Drucker confidently asserted that management had arrived as "a distinct and a leading group in industrial society. Rarely, if ever, has a new basic institution, a new leading group, emerged as fast as has management since the turn of the century. Rarely in human history has a new institution proved indispensable so quickly."[165] Over 40 years later, Drucker's bold pronouncement holds true.

Approaching the new millennium, the managerial stakes appear higher than ever before. The drama unfolding before executive eyes is no longer a small-scale domestic farce. Countries and governments have now joined the *dramatis personae*. Politicians embrace management. "Politicians are asking management theorists how to plan their day, organize their offices, and master their emotions. They are even asking them how to think about the world," notes *The Economist*.[166] Newt Gingrich's essential reading list distributed to fellow Republicans featured seven management texts; President Clinton spends his valuable time with management thinkers – even if it is sometimes on the golf course; and management gurus embrace the big issues of trade and government. (Peters has filled many column inches with his views on global trade.)

The agenda has broadened, as has the remit of those contributing to the agenda. Harvard Business School's Michael Porter is no longer simply a distinguished academic, but a consultant to entire countries, writing books about the competitive advantage of nations. Kenichi Ohmae is no longer a McKinsey consultant revealing the secrets of Japanese strategy, but an aspiring politician, drafting manifestos for the governments of the world. (It is reputed that when Ohmae left McKinsey to go into politics he said it was simply a question of changing clients, from corporations to all of Japan.) Charles Handy has become a best-selling social philosopher rather than a business school academic. And Tom Peters has expanded his repertoire to encompass everything from the rise of the Asian "Tiger" economies to the powers of Zen Buddhism.

Once again, Richard Pascale provides a note of caution. "I think it is a packaged goods business. There is an unquenchable thirst. If you take the premise, as I do, that corporations are the dominant social institutions of our age you have to reckon with the fact that corporations are very influential. Certain trappings go with the party – a whole group of jesters like me," says Pascale. "It is part of the fanfare surrounding these institutions. With that comes a constant churn of material for corporate chieftains to feed on. Because of their prominence in society this is always going to be with us, though, among the CEOs I speak to, there is a certain cynicism about the material."

Cynicism or not, expanding horizons have fueled ambitions. No longer does a new management idea aim to change one aspect of a particular job; most are intent on changing the world. The word "revolution" can increasingly be found on dustjackets (even though between the covers there is often little that is original let alone revolutionary). Though most managers are unlikely or unwilling revolutionaries, they either believe that their revolutionary potential lies smoldering beneath the surface or realize that there is a need for a managerial revolution in thought and deed. Change, in all its manifestations, is now a fact of corporate life; a continual process and coveted competence rather than a tool for the occasional quick-fix.

Espousing the revolution are the management gurus. They think big. Michael Hammer and James Champy claim that reengineering was concerned with "rejecting conventional wisdom and received assumptions of the past . . . it is about reversing the industrial revolution . . . tradition counts for nothing. Reengineering is a new beginning." The British academics Colin Williams and George Binney filed this neatly under hyperbole: "The last time someone used language like this was Chairman Mao in the Cultural Revolution. Under the motto 'Destroy to build', he too insisted on sweeping away the past."[167] Though the gurus may advocate it and wish for it, the past cannot be so conveniently swept away – something Mao discovered, and Champy and Hammer are also having to come to terms with as companies struggle with the full practical ramifications of their particular manifesto.

The managerial world is awash with such notions. There are brave new worlds – and words – aplenty. The sheer mass of new material suggests that quantity comes before quality. There is a steady supply of new insights into old ideas. Management theorizing has become expert at finding new angles on old topics. (*In Search of Excellence* was, after all, a 1982 reworking of the oldest managerial chestnut of them all: how can you be successful?) There is nothing wrong with this. Indeed, management is fundamentally concerned with seeking out modern approaches to age-old dilemmas. The final word on a subject such as leadership is unlikely ever to be uttered.

Even so, there is a great deal of skepticism about many of today's managerial ideas. Managerial thinking is tainted with ever greater hype and hyperbole – something Tom Peters has experienced and, his critics would say, championed. The emerging agenda can be seen as driven by the media as much as by the research interests of academics or the needs of business. Depending on your perspective, this can be attributed to the substantial financial rewards available for those with the next bright idea to sweep the globe, or as a sign of ever increasing desperation among managers to find ways in which they can make sense of the business world. Alternatively, and more positively, you can regard the merry-go-round of ideas as an indication of just how vital effective management is to the economies and people of the world.

Though they bellow their "revolutionary" credentials from the highest rooftops and loftiest platforms, management thinkers do not like the label, guru. They are appalled when you ask: "Do you think of yourself as a management guru?" Indeed, it is worth asking because it irritates them so much. After a hard day earning $50,000, or more, the last thing they want to confront is a cynical smart-ass. The trouble is that when it comes to dealing with the media, these people are good. They are well used to the question. They gather themselves from outraged indignation and field it with a well-rehearsed answer.

Ask Rosabeth Moss Kanter, ex-editor of the *Harvard Business Review* and author of, among other books, *The Change Masters* (the thinking man's *In Search of Excellence* according to one reviewer) – "I reject the term guru because it is associated with pandering to the masses, providing inspiration without substance. There is a little bit of the shaman in a guru," says Kanter.

Ask Henry Mintzberg – "There is a lot of obnoxious hype about being a guru, to the extent that the medium can destroy the message," says the author of *The Rise and Fall of Strategic Planning*.

Ask Peter Drucker, the doyen of management thinkers. Drucker argues that the "g" word has only become popular because "charlatans" is too lengthy for magazine and newspaper headlines.

And ask Tom Peters. "According to the press, I make my dough as a 'guru.' Revolting! That's not my take. I just talk about stuff I've seen; try to confuse people I talk to. Yet most who attend my seminars are looking for answers. Thanks for coming, but how tragic. There are no answers. Just, at best, a few guesses that might be worth a try."[168]

Peters and the other star names may well be right. The term "guru" cheapens their trade, but for better or worse it is the best available shorthand for what they are.

Inventing the Guru

Saying that there were no real management gurus before Tom Peters is like saying there were no rock stars before Elvis. In the 1950s we find Douglas McGregor, Frederick Herzberg, and Abraham Maslow. In the 1960s it was a role filled by Alfred Chandler, Ted Levitt, and Igor Ansoff, followed in the 1970s by Henry Mintzberg. At the time, they were recognized as significant thinkers in the relatively minor field of management. They wrote books which didn't sell in huge numbers but were respected and influential. They wrote articles in academic journals, gave the occasional seminar, and worked as consultants for a few large corporations. As virtually all of them worked for a major business school with generous salaries, they did just fine. It was a good business to be in, but nothing special. In the 1960s and 1970s you *did* get paid more if you ran an organization.

Peters reinvented this cozy academic business. Yes, there were gurus, but Peters created the guru industry. He was the first, and he was original. "Tom created a new market for management thinking. They weren't new concepts, but a new way of looking at them. He has taken it to the masses in a way never done before," says Ralph Ardill, marketing director of the Peters case study company, Imagination.

Instead of being eccentric, academic, peripheral, or occasional figures, gurus have gone mainstream. "In the past decade, management gurus have done well enough to qualify for a place in their own case histories. Having once been unexceptional, leading gurus are now exceedingly rich. Tom Peters makes $65,000–90,000 for a day-long seminar. They are also influential.

Some firms hardly dare change the wallpaper without consulting a guru," observed *The Economist* in 1994.[169]

Warren Bennis provides a telling comparison: "My mentor, Doug McGregor (who Tom acknowledges as having written one of the most seminal books on management, *The Human Side of Enterprise*), sold 30,000 copies of his book in its peak year, 1965. I remember some of the McGraw-Hill 'suits' coming to my MIT office sometime around then, bursting with pleasure at the numbers. I have no idea about the total sales of Tom's books, but it would be safe to say that there must be millions of copies in print."[170]

Bennis is right: Peters has sold a great many books. Around six million copies of *In Search of Excellence* for a start. His other books have failed to match that number – *A Passion for Excellence* sold significantly less than *In Search of Excellence* even though it topped the bestseller lists; Peters' sales rose again with *Thriving on Chaos*, and then diminished with *Liberation Management*, which only sold around 500,000. (Of course, to anyone else, sales in the hundreds of thousands would be a triumph.) In total, a fair estimate of Peters' total book sales would be around 10 million worldwide. Peters himself confesses to having little idea about the total figures. "I don't know how many copies the books have sold. At one point I remember *In Search of Excellence* had sold 1.4 million in hardback and 2.2 million in paperback, but that was insane. If a book was really not selling well it would weigh on my mind. But, *In Search of Excellence* was a phenomenon; it was like being Neil Armstrong. It won't happen again, and it certainly won't happen to *me* again."

In the guru world, success matters – and the first stepping stone is a place on the bestseller lists. Heaven and earth are moved to ensure that this is achieved. Recent years have seen exposés of the imaginative means used by some authors and their consultancy firm employees to ensure that their books reach the bestseller lists. (Actually, their tactics weren't that imaginative – they simply bought an awful lot of copies in as many different book stores as they could find.) Indeed, I was told by more than one person that *In Search of Excellence* was the first management book to be artificially lifted into the bestseller lists – I have found no evidence that this is the case, and it is an accusation McKinsey rapidly denies. "We develop ideas to develop people, not to sell books. For us a book is a book, we're not going to buy truckloads of copies like some of those gurus do," says McKinsey's Bill Matassoni.

Elevation to the bestseller lists has brought business and management publishing into the mainstream – though, as we have seen, it has not necessarily improved managerial or business performance. As I write, *The Dilbert Principle,* Scott Adams' spoof on the absurdity of corporate life is the *New York Times* non-fiction bestseller. Everyone – including the conductor of the Boston Symphony Orchestra, Fran Tarkenton, and the ex- Minnesota Vikings quarterback – is attempting to board the bandwagon. Even academics are letting their hair down – or, at least, letting their publishers select titles for their books. Harvard's John Kao has written *Jamming,* in which John Coltrane meets the corporation. And, academic publishers are discovering marketing – Harvard Business School Press has doubled its marketing budgets over the past four years; McGraw-Hill published 110 business titles in 1996, compared with 25 in 1991.[171]

This flurry of sometimes indecent activity can partially be attributed to Peters. "I find it intriguing that Tom has, indirectly, influenced both publishers and management authors – academics and commercial professionals – as well as managers about the significance of management," says Warren Bennis. "For lack of a better word, he has vivified the field, made it a significant study of human behavior. He has also made the writing of management books a heavy industry. Inevitably, this has also created a glut of schlock and gelatinous, gooey, and wrong-headed 'how-to-do' guide books, about which the less said the better. Anyway, he who catches the first wave inevitably attracts others to try, even, on occasions, with great success. Anyway, we can't blame Tom for the epigones who try to follow in his steps."[172]

No executive office is complete without a neatly arranged row of management bestsellers. They are as much a fixture as the family portrait and, cynics might say, as much practical use. Research by the Management Training Partnership found that three quarters of human resource directors buy at least four management books a year. But, only one in five is actually read.

"Perhaps five million people have bought copies of *In Search of*

Excellence, including its fifteen translations, since its publication in mid-October 1982," reflected Peters in *A Passion for Excellence.* "If history is any guide, two or three million probably opened the book. Four or five hundred thousand read as much as four or five chapters. A hundred thousand or so read it cover to cover. Twenty-five thousand took notes. Five thousand took detailed notes."[173]

The truth is that executives aren't great readers. They buy books but don't read them. In fact in the US alone they buy $750 million-worth of business books every year. This curious and expensive habit is fueled by pressure of time. Even the *Harvard Business Review* publishes précised versions of its articles, just in case you can't find the time to consume the full 4000-word version. But there is more to it than that. For tired and harried executives, books are a balm for their worries – twenty buck placebos.

They may not be hard drugs, but placebos are habit forming. As the books gather dust, executives absorb the latest big ideas at seminars and conferences. There can hardly be a manager in the Western world who has not been to an event promoting a particular individual's view of how they should be managing their business. Then there are the consultants with their theories and formulae; the business schools with their resident experts advocating particular tools and techniques. There is no escape from the maelstrom of bright ideas. Thanks to Tom Peters, the guru business has arrived, and everyone wants a fix.

Elvis Peters

Tom Peters created an industry. Few others can claim to have done so – Henry Ford, Steve Jobs, perhaps, or Walt Disney. The trouble for Peters is that it is not necessarily an industry he would have wanted to create. The world of bullshit *ubber alles* is not rocket science. Nor is it patently useful to civilization. "The first management guru" is not the epitaph he wants.

The industry Peters created has a bad press. Indeed, hardly a week goes by without another article, report, or book lambasting management theorists as a group of publicity-seeking megaloma-niacs who make far too much money and whose ideas are usually little more than common sense. There is some truth in all these accusations. The gurus tend to come from much the same backgrounds and often say much the same things.

The passage to guru status usually involves a progression from an American business school (preferably Harvard), to articles in a leading American business journal (*Harvard Business Review* or *Strategy & Business*), and then to work with a big name consulting company (McKinsey, BCG, Bain, or Booz.Allen and Hamilton). From there it is a long trek – via PR companies, publishers, publicists, marketing advisers – and it involves a lot of handshak-ing, travel, and some measure of sycophancy.

To find the wellspring of the guru journey, you might as well start at birth. It certainly helps to be American. Some gurus have taken this requirement very seriously. Igor Ansoff, the father of strategic management, was born in Vladivostock to a Russian mother and an American diplomat father; Peter Drucker was born in Austria; Ted Levitt, the marketing guru, was born in Germany –

all moved to America. Those that aren't American can be Americanized – Japan's only guru, Kenichi Ohmae, is known as "Ken." European gurus are few and far between – the only current representative on the management equivalent of Mount Rushmore is Charles Handy, author of *The Age of Unreason* and *The Empty Raincoat.*

Given this standard route to fame and fortune, it is hardly surprising that the media asks sometimes difficult questions. "The case against management theory has four legs: first, that it is constitutionally incapable of self-criticism; second, its terminology usually confuses rather than educates; third, that it rarely rises above basic common sense; and, four, that it is faddish and bedeviled by contradictions that would not be allowed in more rigorous disciplines," say John Micklethwait and Adrian Wooldridge in *Witch Doctors.*[174] (They go on to identify Peters as "the most influential guru of the past two decades – not just because of what he has said but also because of the way in which he has said it.")

Micklethwait and Wooldridge are right. Management thinking is still a haphazard science (it may even be more art than science). It is easy to forget that, as sciences go, it is also in its infancy. Management thinking is a creature of the twentieth century. Look at the literature. The first 50 years of the century saw a handful of influential and useful management texts – works by the like of Chester Barnard, Mary Parker Follett, Taylor, and Henri Fayol. Between 1950 and 1982, from McGregor to Mintzberg, there was a steady but unspectacular increase in numbers. Then it took off. (And, if it didn't take off *because* of *In Search of Excellence*, it certainly did so at exactly the same time. "The book was a watershed. It was after the book that the multi-billion dollar industry of gurudom sprung up. It didn't exist then," says *Inc.*'s Bo Burlingham.)

Look also at academia. Compared with most other disciplines, management has only just arrived on the scene. Its recognition as a discipline and profession is undoubtedly a modern phenomenon. Only in the twentieth century has management come of age, gaining respectability and credence. Even now, the study of management is still in a fledgling state. In Europe, France's

INSEAD offered an MBA for the first time in 1959. It was not until 1965 that the UK's first two public business schools (at Manchester and London) were opened. Cambridge and Oxford Universities, have only embraced management in the past decade. Elsewhere, however, management has been seriously studied (at least in academic terms) for a longer period. In the US, Chicago University's business school was founded in 1898; Amos Tuck at Dartmouth College, New Hampshire – founded in 1900 – was the first graduate school of management in the world; and Harvard offered its first MBA as long ago as 1908, and established its graduate business school in 1919. Of course, these statistics pale into insignificance when set against the centuries spent educating lawyers, clerics, soldiers, teachers, and doctors in formal, recognized institutions.

Young disciplines are apt to be hijacked, taken off in new, unexpected directions. They are pliable, sometimes uncontrollable. Tom Peters has taken management thinking along unexpected corridors, some of which have been marked "No exit."

Despite his MBA, his gilt-edged education at the best universities America could offer, and his time at McKinsey, Tom Peters created an industry not through his academic credentials, nor through the diligence of his research or even the originality of his ideas. Peters created an industry through his performances, the sheer weight of his personality. And, some would say, herein lies the problem. "Peters is selling instant potions. It is Wild West stuff, but his impact is immense," says consultant George Binney. "From being a respectable McKinsey consultant, Peters has become an unbelievable, out and out showman. He is like a pop star."

Propelled to fame, and no little fortune, by the success of *In Search of Excellence*, Peters traveled the world giving seminars and speeches. He lectured, pontificated, told stories, insulted, and hectored audience after audience. During the 1980s and into the 1990s, he swept through the States, Europe, and far beyond, and then back again. Hardly a country in the world has been spared one of his whirlwind performances. "Tom Peters is probably the most famous management guru in the world, and certainly one of the richest. His ability to command lecture fees of up to $50,000 owes much to his stagecraft. Striding urgently back and forth, bellowing and bantering, he nearly achieves the difficult feat of making management seem exciting," noted *The Economist* with its customary sardonic wit.[175] To Peters, unquestionably, management is exciting – or should be. "I have always particularly admired Tom's moral outrage," says Harvard's Wickham Skinner. "So many consultants and business school professors don't have that personal fervor which attracted me to the study of management."

Peters is more than a guru: he is a rock star. Management is exciting and, yes, this is dry ice. "He is no austere spiritual teacher, but rather an evangelist who passes among his flock," reported *The Economist.* "He becomes intimately involved with their problems, shouting 'you too can be saved'." On the platform at his seminars (which are really rallies), he does not spout theories or present data but instead tells stories, usually parables about companies just like yours which saw the light and were saved."[176]

Peters was the first guru of a new breed. Igor Ansoff never recounted parables. Henry Mintzberg never sported his shorts on book covers. Peter Drucker never said "Wow!" We can, perhaps, be thankful. Peters was Billy Graham after the dull regime of Sunday school (though donations to Peters are destined for the coffers of the Tom Peters Group rather than a more hallowed organization). He was Elvis after a succession of Bill Haleys.

Some have success thrust upon them and drown. Others have success thrust upon them, wallow in the greasepaint and await an encore. Watch Peters in action. He is a combination of TV evangelist and your favorite shrink. One minute he is encouraging and comforting; next he is bewailing your very existence. "The fact that he jumps up and down and shouts when he lectures turns some people off. Fortunately, it also turns many managers on – many who need it," observes Harold Leavitt (who holds the distinction of being one of the first people to be upstaged by Peters).[177] A Tom Peters seminar is a good show.

On stage, Peters takes an annual report and waves it around. "Look at the picture of the board of directors. There it is with their names neatly printed underneath. Now look at the rest of the annual report. It's full of pictures of other people who work for the company. Look at it. Great pictures but not a name underneath. Doesn't anyone else have a name?" Such colorful flourishes are archetypal Peters – thumbing his nose at authority, making an obvious, but overlooked, point.

Over the years since *In Search of Excellence* Peters has carefully honed his technique, though the fundamentals remain unchanged. "His delivery style was the same in 1982, though he was talking to a small group of 35 or 40 people rather than the huge audiences he now attracts," says Penn State's Albert Vicere. "He paced, ranted, and raved, telling stories and parables. At the time it was a new style and people loved it. They particularly liked the stories because the only success stories you read or heard were about Japanese companies. Peters stories were about US companies. Though they weren't household names – companies like Stew Leonard's. It was a great motivational talk."

The Peters of the late nineties is a little louder, perhaps, more strident. "Tom kicks ass. He is a brand. He exists as books, videos, seminars. There is a Tom Peters experience which sometimes makes people uncomfortable. The people in the videos and seminars are squirming, like kids watching a magic show. Tom is very good at persuading people to sit near the front but two rows back. If they feel reassured, the seminar's doing nothing," says Imagination's Ralph Ardill. "Tom is a great improviser. He can work with a conference of thousands or a room of four, and his message is the same but improvised to fit the audience. There is an energy in the improvisation – something which good politicians are also adept at. It is wonderful to see the penny drop. They go with the hope that it won't be too painful."

Peters works the audience, and works them hard. He is more early Elvis than the Las Vegas sequined version. There is a relentless and unquenchable energy to his performances as he works himself into a frenzy of energy and opinion. In 1988, after attending a particularly lively Peters seminar, a doctor from Sutter Health in Sacramento left a message at Peters' office declaring that, at 46, he was a "walking heart attack in the making" and offered a complimentary treadmill fitness test. (In response, Peters went for a ten minute walk and has carried on taking a daily walk ever since.)

"Frankly, there are times when I do not know how he can generate so much energy for a session," says James Brian Quinn of Dartmouth College. "Even after a long travel schedule, he can radiate energy in a manner that few can approach. He is much more than a showman, although he is a consummate performer."[178]

Like any natural performer, Peters knows exactly what he is doing. "There is a duality in his personality and in his presentations. The points he makes are grounded in theory but presented in a folksy way," says Lennart Arvedson. "Tom treats his craft very seriously. It is never just a matter of giving a presentation. He tries to get a response from the people he is working with. This is particularly obvious when he works with non-US groups, when he can't use American vernacular. He will come at a single point from any number of directions until he can see the penny drop. It's an impressive act to watch."

Peters works at his technique. He is perpetually shuffling his current batch of slides to fit them to the audience. Taxi journeys in Peters' company are as likely to see him sorting out 35mm slides as admiring the sights. When Peters first hit the road he had an 80-slide carousel which he aimed to change completely every 90 days. And, he did. If it doesn't work, doesn't strike home, it is discarded. "People develop their 45-minute pat speeches which don't change. My speech changes because its important to my success."

To Peters, performance is an art. At times, a blunt art: "I do pretty good seminars because I know when to fuck with people's minds. You can take them to the brink and pull them back." And he does, time and time again.

"It's like being an artist. Why does someone perform *Phantom of the Opera* 600 times?," says Jan Lapidoth, formerly with SAS. "You get a kick from seminars. You are acknowledged. The audience admires you, they come up to you in the break and want to talk to you. And while you are up there you control the stage. It is well directed. The audience can question your ideas but not your right to stand there. They've paid a lot of money to be there. When you finish, you are on a high."

Lapidoth has shared a platform with Peters, to recount his

experiences at SAS, and stood in for him as a last-minute replacement when Peters canceled a seminar at Credit Suisse in Zurich because of sickness in his family. "It was in a chalet in the mountains above Zurich on Midsummer's Eve," Lapidoth recalls. "Initially I said no because Midsummer's Eve in Sweden is like Thanksgiving in the States. You have to be at home and eat your herring and drink your aqua vit. But I accepted on condition that I was home by the evening. I was picked up by helicopter in Zurich and taken up into the mountains, and then collected when the seminar was over. I must have been OK because I still get a Christmas card from the organizers."

Rock stars take liberties. They push pianos through windows and work hard at acting outrageously, but they have one saving grace – their music. If you love the Rolling Stones, you don't see a band of wrinkled substance abusers with a catalog of exotic lovers – you feel connected. Through the dry ice, the excesses, the recognition and the money, rock stars connect.

On stage, Peters makes those connections. "You can get away with murder, as long as it is done with genuine affection. I feel a common cause with people in my audiences," he says. "If you feel that it's tough-love parenting, wake up, for crying out loud. There is genuine affection. I feel we are in the same boat."

Of course, Peters and his audience are not in the same boat at all. The rock star in the leopard-skin leotard is the not the guy in row 535. Peters, the presenter, is earning tens of thousands of dollars for a day-long seminar. Members of his audience often earn less in a year than he does in a day. Yet they sit there, preoccupied with their own problems. Even though they aren't in the same world as he is, Peters feels they are. His gift is to make them believe it.

On stage, Peters is in his element. (It still makes him nervous – "I get flush and breathless before *any* speech, to this day."[179]) He believes in his job. He lives it. He revels in the atmosphere. He drinks it up (and occasionally appears to be spitting it back out). He has a reverence for what he does and where he does it. He likes the mystery of dealing with an audience, manipulating people. "If I'm scheduled to speak to 17 or 1700 people in Miami or Timbuktu, I like to sneak down to the slumbering meeting room at 1 a.m. or so the night before. I can sense the spirit of the group that will assemble eight hours later. It invariably primes me to go back and do a few last preparations. In fact, such stealthy visits to deserted spaces frequently have led to total revision of my remarks."[180]

And, undoubtedly, though he may not sport a leotard, he likes being the center of attention. "He comes alive on stage," says Jayne Pearl, former TPG employee, going on to contrast his stage persona with his off-stage personality. "He likes his solitude. He doesn't want to go out for dinner with the conference organizers or do cocktails. He is painfully shy and is totally at a loss with small-talk. He is uncomfortable."

Warren Bennis, a long-time friend of Peters, provides another perspective: "At the podium and in his books I find him warm and open and engaging and accessible. In person, he manifests these same characteristics but with a more subtle hue. I've often wondered what people like Tom and other gurus talk about when they're not talking to an audience. My impression is that Tom holds an interior dialog with himself. Curiously, he is a private man. And I admire him for that."[181]

Peters argues that the private man and the stage persona are not incompatible. "Shy people tend to be garrulous. I have read anecdotal literature which says large numbers of people who end up acting on stage or performing in public are getting over their inability to communicate in private," he says. "All of life, be it giving a seminar, being a chief executive officer or reporting, is acting. If you are intent on convincing somebody of something, there is an element of showmanship. And showmanship has both seedy and legitimate connotations."[182]

Being in front of an audience gives Peters a buzz. Self-effacing and shy Peters may be off stage, but certainly not while he treads the boards. "Tom has the capacity to energize a whole room full of people. It comes from his persona. He can transmit his enthusiasm," says ex-McKinsey colleague, Jim Balloun. It is a performance, and Peters is a performer. He is emotional in an arena where emotion is usually reined in and hidden. "Has anyone succeeded at anything they didn't *love*? Is there any room for *un*emotional behavior in business?' asks Peters.[183]

One of the few countries where Peters struggles to connect with his audience is Germany, the land of his ancestors, where high energy, emotion, and fun-seeking behavior is certainly not top of the boardroom agenda. Max Worcester of *Frankfurter Allgemeine Zeitung* has seen Peters struggle in front of a German audience. "Tom is used to speaking to audiences of 600 or 700 in packed auditoriums. Put him in front of a US, UK, Dutch, or Scandinavian audience and they are enthralled. In Germany he ran up against a wall and it got to him. He couldn't understand how he could captivate a room full of CEOs and then fail to captivate a single German," says Worcester. "In Germany business is very serious. You don't go to work to have fun. There is no reaction to wow and that sort of thing. That intrigued Tom. I told him he was doing nothing wrong; it was just that his attitude was not their attitude."

Germans aren't the only ones who don't get it. With the guru as rock star, performance is all; delivery takes precedence over footnotes. It is loud, colorful, and controversial. Not surprisingly it has its critics. "There is a degree of narcissism. Gurus boost their self-esteem talking in front of audiences. They get a buzz, safe in the knowledge that if things go wrong when managers try out their ideas they bear no responsibility," says psychologist Robert Sharrock of consultants YSC.

Traditional academics are dismissive. They can accept that Peters has ideas (but don't like the fact that he changes them so brazenly). They can accept his delivery, frantic as it is. But his love of the adulation is more thorny territory. To academics, ideas, research, and tenure count. Success is not measured in encores but in published papers in obscure journals.

Peters is the antithesis of academic dryness and studious moderation. His seminars aren't delivered in the language of Stanford lecture theaters, but in the vernacular of business people. He is wildly enthusiastic and, even if you disagree with everything he says, it is still usually worth the entrance fee.

Some say this reduces management theory to the lowest common denominator. "Peters set the guru model. A lot of the gurus are pretty thin with one theory after another. Management has been trivialized as a result," says McKinsey's Bill Matassoni.

London Business School's Gay Haskins, who organized Peters' conferences in Europe for The Economist Conference Unit, observes that "You don't need to know a lot about management to get Tom's messages."

Other former colleagues of Peters are among the skeptics who contend that the medium has overtaken the message. "Taken to the extreme, it's just theater, and that's not sufficient to deal with some problems," says Richard Pascale. "The thing that's hardest to get across with US audiences is that we're not caught up in game. You pitch the message at a simplistic level, and it's an assumption that the customer won't buy unless it's simple."[184] Pascale first met Peters at Stanford: "I knew Peters when he was an MBA student. He was energetic, a live wire. He had zeal, but I wouldn't have predicted what he has become." But what *has* he become? "I wouldn't like to get drawn into that," replies Pascale.

Bob Waterman is among those who studiously avoid the rock star approach. Since *In Search of Excellence,* Waterman has pursued a quieter path, spending his time interspersing a little consulting with painting watercolors and writing well-received books. Waterman has little time for Peters' presentational excesses. "Tom has found he can make lots of money thumping the podium and sweating a lot. He talks about things changing so quickly we must accept chaos in our organizations. But if you look back at each decade, everybody thought business was changing at a much greater speed than during the previous decade," said Waterman in a 1996 interview. "I know Tom thinks you need to invent phraseology which will make people think, but audiences can get numb to that kind of thing."[185]

Those Who Pay Homage

Peters' audiences seem anything but numb. His tirades, insults, and critiques of their every move and thought are accepted and enjoyed. "Peters has perfected a technique which combines insight and insult in just the right proportions to slay his audiences," observed the London *Sunday Times*.[186]

And they *are* slayed. *The Economist*, in an examination of gurus, gave marks for influence, originality, intellectual coherence, and devotion of followers. It is curiously difficult to imagine Drucker, Ohmae, or Porter encouraging devotion from their adherents. Devotion is Peters' territory.

	Peters	Drucker	Porter	Ohmae
Influence	3	5	4	2
Originality	2	5	3	4
Intellectual coherence	2	3	3	3
Devotion of followers	5	2	3	2

Devotees swoon, or get as near to swooning as middle-aged men or women in indifferent leisure wear are likely to get. Jayne Pearl, who worked closely with Peters on his weekly columns and edited the TPG newsletter, remembers his impact. "You know when Tom walks into a room. There's a buzz. All eyes are on him. He has a presence which is compelling and exciting. It was wonderful being just outside that bright spotlight," she says. "People carried his books like the bible. They were highlighted in different colors. They were well-thumbed and dog-eared through re-reading. There were fanatics who hung on every syllable. It was amazing to watch. It was like a religious cult and I bought into it." Another former Peters employee, Paul Cohen, says: "I was ill-prepared for the reverence with which people thought of Tom. It was like being an emissary from the Pope. I hadn't realized what a big deal it was." From the catholic supremacists of McKinsey and Company, it seems Peters made the obvious career move. The dry ice may well have been the right colored smoke emerging from the Vatican.

One magazine described Peters' adherents as "sensible, but-toned-down managers seeking inspiration."[187] It is bemusing to watch the managers who pay $1000 or more to see Peters in action. (As I write, a Peters seminar is charging £720 – over $1000 – per seat.) They are Peters' audience, his customers, the buyers of his books, the viewers of his videos, his fans. And yet, at times, he treats them with extraordinary disdain. "The average seminar participant I work with comes dressed in a drab suit, uses drab language – and noticeably quivers when I suggest that the most likely path to career salvation for the beleaguered and endangered middle manager is to try to get fired," Peters noted in one of his articles.[188] In *Liberation Management* he wrote: "Am I a middle-management basher? Yes. Are most of the people who attend my seminars middle managers? Yes. Why do they come? Beats me. Middle management, as we have known it since the railroads invented it right after the Civil War, is dead. Therefore, middle managers, as we have known them, are cooked geese. "[189] And this is the tempered, considered, written version.

So, why *do* executives attend? Only a minority are true Peters zealots. The majority may be cooked geese, but they are also hard working, ambitious executives who want to learn more about their craft and the dilemmas they encounter. But, what persuades them that Peters – or any other guru, come to that – has the answers?

Peters explains it this way: "We are the only society in the world that believes it can keep on getting better and better. So we keep on getting suckered in by people like Ben Franklin and Emerson and me."[190] This is not one of Peters' more modest observations.

It may explain his success in North America, but what about the rest of the world where the inevitability of improvement is regarded more skeptically? Why should a manager in Oslo, Auckland, or Prague believe in Tom Peters? What is the apparently global need he taps into?

All executives have an unquenchable desire for instant solutions which tackle every managerial problem in one fell swoop. While they may acknowledge that many guru-generated ideas have a short shelf-life or prove practically impossible, managers continue to board the bandwagons when they arrive. They appear incurably fashion-conscious. Some turn into fashion victims: *The One Minute Manager* has been bought by millions. Would barristers buy *The One Minute Advocate*? We all know the answer.

"I see it as a wonderful show, a great performance which reaches many managers. But I fear it encourages people to seek out instant solutions," says consultant and author George Binney. "It encourages managers to learn the latest jargon and not to use their own intuition and experience to work through their own problems. Managers are impeded by the fact that they have to speak the jargon – and each organization has a slightly different version. The positive part is that it encourages managers to look outside their business, to raise their sights." Binney believes the continuing propensity for managers to leap onto the nearest available bandwagon results in a lack of direction. Executives are in touch with the gurus, but woefully out of touch with reality. Fashion-conscious organizations end up attempting to implement every bright idea their senior executives have recently come across – Binney found one company with 19 initiatives underway simultaneously.

It seems that managers are in need of security and reassurance. "People who read management books often want the safety of a proven formula or need a precedent before they act," says psychologist Robert Sharrock. "They like techniques which rationalize their jobs. The trouble is that, for all the techniques at their disposal, managers generally act at a very intuitive level." Managers may have absorbed the latest thinking on core competencies, but are more likely to base a decision on prejudice or personal opinion rather than a neat theory. Peters taps into this.

He is the king of the anti-rationalists. People matter and, unfortunately, they are frequently indecisive, inadequate, and incompetent. As Robert Waterman said, people – and managers – do a lot of dumb things.

Strangely, the global managerial search for security and reassurance leads managers to read books and listen to gurus whose message is anything but reassuring. Peters goes to great lengths to make people feel uncomfortable. He wants them to shift uneasily in their seats. He wants the sweat to rise on their brows as they contemplate their redundancy in the modern corporation. The currency of Peters, or Richard Pascale or Charles Handy, is insecurity and uncertainty. There is, perhaps, the reassurance that the gurus are identifying trends, feelings and fears which managers are already experiencing, but it is usually scant recompense for a sweat-drenched shirt and an uncomfortable feeling at the pit of your stomach that you are as dispensable as a piece of office furniture. *Inc.*'s Bo Burlingham, who has often witnessed Peters at work, says: "At his seminars there were a lot of managers who were going through things that made them think they were crazy. Tom got up and said you're not crazy but what's going on is crazy. It was reassuring." Paradoxically, the more extreme the message, the more reassuring it could be.

It is notable that the influence of the gurus appears to become less and less the further up the corporate ladder you look. The CEOs who get to the top do not slavishly follow an individual thinker. They tend to be confident in their own methods and are skeptical of gurus. They are their own men and women. (Most don't even read business books. Worryingly, they often prefer military history.)

Lower down in the corporate hierarchy things are different. Aspiring managers cast around for recipes for success and ideas which can distinguish them from the crowd. They feel pressure to keep up to date with the latest thinking and fashions. "People want to know what is going on and what others are talking about. The last thing you want is to be out of touch," says Ray Wild, principal of the UK's Henley Management College. "It is a question of credibility but if it gives managers confidence there is nothing wrong with that."

More cynically, gurus fuel the art of one-upmanship. If your son or daughter discovers that you have never heard of the latest pop sensation they are incredulous and inevitably bemoan your advanced age. Managers behave very similarly when they discover a colleague knows nothing of the latest addition to the managerial vocabulary. Jargon is an essential tool in the guru's armory. Managers are addicted to jargon and gurus exploit their craving. Jargon is the art of one-upmanship. Managers like to know what "reengineering" means before their colleagues. As the inventor of the latest buzz-word the guru can travel the world unraveling its true meaning to enraptured audiences. Tom Peters has perfected the art of jargon. He does not follow the technological or biologically-inspired route – his jargon comes in the form of snappy phrases which everyone understands (such as "stick to the knitting," "managing by wandering around" which appeared in *In Search of Excellence*). But understanding such phrases is not the same as making them happen.

More broadly, the guru industry benefits from managers remaining slightly reticent and ill-at-ease with the worth of their profession. (This is something which Tom Peters has heightened.) Managers feel a need to explain themselves in a way that lawyers or doctors do not. They are professionals, but where is the kudos? After all, young children do not express strong urges to become chief executives – and those that do are more likely to be taken to child psychologists than to witness their first production line in operation. Managers frequently explain themselves with their business cards and their job titles. They explain themselves through their company cars and a stunning variety of executive perks. And they seek legitimacy through the acquisition of knowledge.

The books gathering dust on their shelves are not merely decorative. They are statements. The executives with *Liberation Management* hovering unread above their desks are acknowledging their willingness to think, to acquire new skills, to make a difference.

Managers crave a clear set of guidelines on the skills and knowledge required to become a manager. If theirs is a profession, they would like professional qualifications. There is a perennial and largely futile debate about the mythical "chartered manager" – as if a single qualification could equip an executive to manage a steel producer in Illinois, a chain of shoe stores in Spain, or a wine importing business in New Zealand. Peters has derided the professionalization process. In the past, the quest for knowledge – new tools, techniques, and ideas – was part of the process of professionalization. It is now the route to survival. No surprise, then, that business book publishing is thriving.

It is little wonder, also, that for some, gurus are simply motivational. Forget the daunting complexity of the detail, become inspired by the evangelical presence. Peters is the most notable member of this inspirational wing of gurus. David Hearn, managing director of direct marketing agency, Anderson Hearn Keene, attended a Peters seminar. "It was inspiring and you return to work believing that you can change things. The inspiration, in itself, is a good thing. It gives you another new perspective even if you don't do everything they say. The bottom line is that the gurus make money, but usually not from running a business."

Attending a Peters seminar convinces managers that they can do things. It shows them that they can make a difference. "True, he is willing to rant to get his point over; but he has persuaded more managers to reflect on what they are doing than almost anyone else alive," says Stanford's Harold Leavitt.[191] He cajoles them into action. The trouble is that after the initial excitement, the willingness to act becomes dissipated in the fogs of corporate ennui and politics.

Does It Work?

Do the gurus make managing easier, more efficient, or more enjoyable? Feeling good is one thing; doing good for the corporation is quite another. Do gurus really have all the answers – or any answers which bear examination in the reality of the factory floor? Does Tom Peters have the answer to anything?

The first charge laid at the door of gurus is that they are unlikely to come up with the answers precisely because their knowledge of the factory floor is limited. How can a globetrotting multimillionaire have any grasp of reality? George Bush didn't know what a grocery scanner was and no doubt the gurus are equally ignorant of reality.

Arguments about whether Tom Peters or a manager in a Michigan factory know more of reality are largely futile. At his seminars, executives are always liable to ask if Peters has ever had a real job. His reply usually begins politely. "I've got a real job. This is it." Then he bridles with indignation going on to describe his years waiting on tables. To Peters accusations of never having existed in the real world are met with a firm rebuff: "In fact, I have been there: I've bagged groceries, counted nickels from slot machines (even gotten money-counter's hand rash), waited on endless tables, washed mountains of dishes, looked up catalog prices in an architect's office. Hey, I inspected sewers one summer in Anne Arundel County, Maryland! I defined 'low man on the totem pole' in most of these instances and had my share of creeps for bosses."[192]

Gurus are almost always consultants or academics. The list of worthwhile books written by executives is short (Sloan's *My Years with General Motors*, Ricardo Semler's *Maverick!*, Robert Town-send's *Up the Organisation*). "There are two kinds of people in this world. Those who talk about it and those who do it," says Peters. "Executives make lousy observers of what they do. An effective executive is instinctive, intuitive, reactive and not particularly reflective."[193] The advantage of not being an executive is clear. If gurus are actually managing, they are duty bound to put their ideas into practice. If they are consultants or academics, they can sit back as other people grapple with the true implications of their ideas. When they hit problems gurus can shrug their shoulders and tell the managers they have missed some vital nuance. As we have seen, Peters' writings and sermons are not easily translated back into the workplace – even in his own company.

While managers gripe that Peters and the other gurus know nothing of reality, academics complain that there is too much reality in Peters' work and not enough theory. This is an accusation which actually has more substance (though the case is weakened because it is usually put by academics, whose grounding in reality is as firm as a sapling in a hurricane). Peters knows what a grocery scanner is and is liable to indulge in a ritual celebration of the effect of technology on customer service. "There is a lot to learn from everyday life," he says. In recent years he has built entire arguments around visits to restaurants and regards reality – or his reality, at least – as a fertile source of material. "Ideas about corporate renewal come from spring barn cleaning in Vermont. Routine trips to the grocery store provide more 'data' on customer service than reading the trade journals. Watching kids at play offers inspirations about self-organization," he observed in one of his columns.[194] Academics tend to regard barn cleaning as a source of nothing other than a bad back.

Whatever Peters' work experience, it takes a certain amount of arrogance to stand up and offer your views on anything, let alone something as idiosyncratic as management. Breathtaking arrogance bedevils the guru industry. Their publicity material invari-ably proclaims that answers to the world's problems are at hand – if you pay the seminar fee.

Experience suggests that such promises are largely groundless. Look at the failure of many TQM programs. Look at the faltering progress of reengineering. Peters has championed customer service for years, yet service excellence is still as elusive as footprints on the moon.

Research at the Massachusetts Institute of Technology suggests that management fads follow a regular life cycle. This starts with academic discovery. The new idea is then formulated into a technique and published in an academic publication. It is then more widely promoted as a means of increasing productivity, reducing costs, or whatever is currently exercising managerial minds. Consultants then pick the idea up and treat it as the universal panacea. After practical attempts fail to deliver the promised impressive results, there is the realization of how difficult it is to convert the bright idea into sustainable practice. Finally, there follows committed exploitation by a small number of companies. (It is little wonder that Peters' business partner, Bob Le Duc, admits that they were fearful of becoming yet another managerial fad.)

Once again, among the fiercest critics of this merry-go-round of ideas is Richard Pascale. "It's like the practice of medicine in the Middle Ages. A leech under the armpit and one to the groin, with no understanding of bacteria, viruses, or how the body worked. There were lots of prescriptions by the physicians of the Middle Ages, but cures were largely the product of random chance. A parallel holds today. Lots of remedies but very few successful examples of authentic transformation. Organizations churn through one technique after another and at best get incremental improvement on top of business as usual. At worst, these efforts waste resources and evoke cynicism and resignation."

New leeches, old ailments. "The questions are the same, but the answers from the gurus change," says Derek Pritchard of Hay Management Consultants. "It is difficult to tell whether they are the initiators of change or simply commentators on trends. But, often they are providing ready-made answers to complex questions when in reality there isn't a ready-made answer. Managers cannot take what the gurus say in isolation, but need to distil and interpret the ideas, opinions, and trends observed by the gurus."

The critics are now hovering around reengineering. Hailed as the latest in a long line of corporate saviors when it was delivered at the beginning of the nineties, reengineering has followed the well-trodden route through cynicism towards resignation. It is now in the final death-throes of the MIT life cycle. The answer has become the problem. And, according to the critics, the problem was that reengineering provided too ready an answer in the first place. "The trouble with reengineering, and why it won't stand the test of time, is that it is too situation specific," says Ray Wild. "If something is seen as an easy solution, it has a detrimental effect. If it develops dependency, it is bad for business. But it is a poor manager who sees it in that way."

Professor Wild regards the guru business as "part of management development and education" and points to its potential benefits: "If a manager reads books or attends a seminar and as a result better understands the complexity of his or her business, that is good. Indeed, anything that prompts managers to do the right thing for the right reason must be good. Often, gurus are offering sanitized, popularized versions of what has been round for a while. Hopefully, it encourages managers to stop and think. They must then decide if what the guru is suggesting is appropriate."

Frequently it is this final element which is missing. Instead of seeking out approaches which are appropriate to their businesses, managers appear in perpetual search of the holy grail of management. It is not that these various ideas – whether reengineering, empowerment, or TQM – are poor concepts. Many do work, but not if they are set in tablets of corporate stone. They have to be open to flexible interpretations, and used when needed rather than as all-encompassing "solutions." Becoming the slavish disciple of a particular managerial luminary is likely to end in commercial disaster no matter whether it is Tom Peters, Steven Covey, or Michael Porter.

The companies which have succeeded in making reengineering work, for example, appear to be those which have adopted a pragmatic approach rather than those which have tried to implement it wholesale. They have taken ideas and experiences from a variety of inspirations. Reading a book or attending a conference might help ideas to gel or offer a few ways forward, but it is down to managers to work out the best combination. It is akin to being presented with a recipe book and, having bought the prescribed ingredients, then preparing, combining and cooking them as you think best.

Even so, managers realize that ideas and the people who generate them have, occasionally, sparked revolution. If the time is right, the audience receptive, and the concepts practical, ideas do count. Managers can't afford to miss the opportunity when, and if, it arises. Look at the post-war resurgence of Japanese industry. Its growth was based on the precept of quality – built on the ideas and research of two Americans, W. Edwards Deming and Joseph Juran. While the duo were listened to in Japan, their ideas were all but ignored in the West until the 1980s. By then it was almost too late. The Japanese converted theory into practice and became a huge industrial power thanks, in part, to their highly effective implementation of the ideas of Deming and Juran.

So, what should the role of gurus be? Should they be masters of simplification and accessibility, but little else? Or, should they be pioneers of theory, leaving managers and organizations to wrestle with the practicalities?

"The term guru is too broad. People like Porter and Handy aren't offering solutions, but ideas," says Ray Wild. "The test of ideas is how long they last. Some, like TQM and JIT, have become absorbed into conventional thinking." It is ideas, not solutions, which stand the test of time and make the leap from dust-gathering book to factory floor. All-embracing solutions to a manager's problems may sound good as you put the book down, but are unlikely to make waves next day in the office.

If they are to contribute anything, gurus should be thought-provokers, pathfinders shedding new light on difficult problems. They should make people think by being radical, and sometimes provocative, rather than being prescriptive. Here, at least, Peters unquestionably fits the bill. He is willfully provocative.

Amid the hard sell, the bandwagons, the quick-fixes, and organizational placebos, it is true to say that little is original. But, without management gurus, managers would lose a rich source of inspiration, information, and controversy. Without the patchy framework of theory, opinion, and examples of best practice provided by the gurus, managers would be even more isolated and many would learn that, as Van Morrison observed: "No guru, no teacher, no method."

Delighting in Inconsistency

It is not just that gurus come up with ideas that don't actually work. The most common complaint against management thinkers is a simple one: they are inconsistent, willing to change their views and arguments as events unfold leaving executives to pick up the pieces.

"Few people are easier to ridicule than management gurus," noted *The Economist*. "Irrepressible self-publicists and slavish fashion-merchants, they make a splendid living out of recycling other people's ideas ('chaos management'), coining euphemisms ('downsizing'), and laboring the obvious ('managing by wandering around' or 'the customer is king'). Their books draw heavily on particular case studies – often out-of-date ones that have a nasty knack of collapsing later. And their ideas change quickly."[195]

Tom Peters' ideas change more quickly than most. Tom Peters is inconsistent and, what's more, he is brazen about it. "My six books could be by six different authors. I have no patience with consistency, so I regard this as a good thing. I consider inconsistency as a compliment," he says.

That Peters has been inconsistent is unquestionable. *In Search of Excellence* implicitly venerated large companies; the entire focus of his work in the 1990s has been on the potential of smaller business units. While *In Search of Excellence* virtually ignored structure, it was elevated to the top of Peters' agenda a decade later. And so on.

Peters' rebuttal of accusations of shifting his ideas rests on two foundations. First, the basic values are the same though the emphasis may change. "I went back and looked through the opening chapters of *In Search of Excellence* and, though a lot of other things have shifted, a lot remains the same. For 20 years everything I have said is consistent with what people I admire – such as Mintzberg, March, Weick, and Quinn – have been saying. Their work reaches conclusions which are antithetical to the world of Michael Porter. I deny the charge of inconsistency because the base of the case remains the same." He points to one of *In Search of Excellence*'s eight points – a bias for action – as something which has endured throughout his work. "It could be called atheoretical but it is deeply logical and consistent with the work of people I admire. You can't think your way out of a box, you've got to act."

Second, changing times shift the emphasis. On this, others agree. "Many people have criticized Tom Peters because every three years he is proclaiming something that contradicts his earlier work. In view of how business is going today, I would regard this as a compliment. I've known people who have said the same things for 25 years. This is more amazing to me than people who change their minds every three to four years," says Dutch management thinker Fons Trompenaars.[196] "He has contradicted himself spectacularly over the past decade; but then the business world has changed spectacularly too," noted *The Economist*.[197] Buckman Laboratories' Robert Buckman suggests that the true fault lies elsewhere: "I would fault anyone who doesn't change. I have a problem with people who think things are cast in stone. My job changes every day. I have to adapt to succeed."

The criticism of inconsistency is similar to examinations of the performance of the companies featured in *In Search of Excellence*. It is, I believe, a flawed debate. When *Three Men in a Boat* becomes *Deliverance,* thinkers or commentators who do not shift with the times are dead in the water.

Hard Cash; Hard Sell

The guru world is more than ideas and a show. It is a business. Even rock stars eye their accountants with respect – or fear. Turn off the lights and the adrenaline, wipe off the greasepaint, and the lure is money, the currency of ideas. OK, there is power and influence. It is no doubt highly satisfying when a word you invented enters the managerial vocabulary or when companies throughout the world start using your amazing new managerial tool. But, away from the hype and hyperbole, gurus are human. They have families, houses, a liking for the good things in life. They are as fixated by material and financial gain as the next man or woman. They trade in ideas, but that is simply the currency of our age.

Perhaps the most cynical view of the business comes from reengineering guru Michael Hammer: "The demand is for what I call respectable entertainment. You want somebody you can tout as a guru, who can kill some time, arouse the customers."[198]

Tom Peters is a rich man. He has property in California and a farm in Vermont. He has his own company, a steady supply of book royalties, and a large income from his continuing seminars. How much Peters charges for a seminar is a matter of perennial debate in newspapers throughout the world. Even in comparatively poor countries, Peters has raked in the dollars – in Ecuador he charged $50,000 for a one-day seminar. His current quoted fee (at the beginning of 1997) is $65,000 in the US (although this often has a percentage of gross clause) and $95,000 elsewhere. During 1996 he delivered a total of 75 seminars and has another 75 planned for 1997. "I'm not planning to cut it down," he says.

The money, Peters admits, is enormous. You don't have to be a mathematical genius to make that particular calculation. "I cash the checks but it's nutty when people in India are making 25 cents an hour. There is something obscene about $100,000 a day," says Peters. "I'm comfortable with it when I'm rational. When I'm in India, I'm uncomfortable. I am not a bad economist and I understand the market logic, the fee structure. In the US there are 10 or 11,000 trade associations and all have annual meetings with three or four speakers. Looking at the economics it isn't that strange. The US has set the market. It is good simple economics. Every year produces another hero – Schwarzkopf, Ford, Kissinger, Thatcher, Powell. That sets the top of the market and we glide in between them. Every time there's a war it puts the price up. It's like the spot market for speeches. You can explain it all the way down. The bread and butter are seminars for the general public."

In the mid-1980s, as his price escalated, Peters competed for the top dollars. He wanted to be the best paid of the bunch. "When I was competitive I used to be pissed off that Kissinger earned more than me. Then I started laughing at myself. There's some research which found that everyone's desired net worth is usually twice their current net worth. I am competitive to the core. I am competing with myself – what I have to prove. I go talk to a few hundred people over a seven hour seminar. New challenges, new places. I am not a perfectionist but I am intellectually curious."

Peters' direct competitors are a select few. "While exact figures are difficult to work out, the best estimate for the major suppliers of executive education is that there are probably only 50 people in the world who are 'global superstars'," say Robert Fulmer and Albert Vicere of Penn State. "Many are riding the crest of a very successful book and are able to charge prices that range from $20,000–50,000 per session for 100 or more days per year, working throughout the world. Tom Peters, Ken Blanchard, Steve Covey, and Mike Hammer probably fall into this category. Others, such as Ram Charan or Maurice Saias, bill an incredible amount of days each year. A few, including John Kotter of the Harvard Business School and Peter Senge of MIT, charge extremely high rates in order to limit the number of days they spend on the road. Most academic institutions limit the amount of time that professors are able to spend away from campus. High demand and limited availability can result in daily billing rates of $20,000 plus for the *crème de la crème* of individual faculty suppliers."[199]

The number of global superstars remains largely static, with a handful being added and subtracted each year. Among the recent additions are Gary Hamel, C.K. Prahalad, and Sumantra Ghoshal. I have been told that Hamel, after the success of *Competing for the Future,* recently received around $150,000 for two days' work. Beneath them are a host of aspiring gurus eager to compete.

It is, suffice to say, a good business to be in. Using Vicere and Fulmer's figures you can estimate the total value of the guru whirl. Any such calculation would tend to be an underestimate of the real figure, but, if you take the mid-range of each group, the total value of the market is some $953 million.

Little wonder, then, that big names are marketed. It is in the marketing that the guru business is at its zaniest. Today's gurus are prone to gimmickry. *Financial Times* columnist Lucy Kellaway is skeptical: "Why is it that management gurus feel the need to grow their hair, wear kipper ties or have their pictures taken half-undressed? Perhaps the sad truth is that most people will not buy books about organizational structures unless a zany personality is thrown in too."[200] Tom Peters has actually done all three of these things, with varying degrees of regret.

Today's star names are marketed with an enthusiasm once reserved for bath soap. Their ideas and their products are sold, and sold hard. "You can now write a fairly good book and be projected to fame. The book is quickly followed by the video and then the satellite TV seminar. Few have staying power. But Peters has proved that he is not a one-hit wonder," says Albert Vicere. Michael Porter, *éminence grise* of the world of competitiveness, refers to the Michael Porter brand. There is life beyond the individual. And the individual human being is sometimes forgotten – someone asked Peters "What happened to Tom Waterman?"

The new incarnation of the guru is media-friendly and adept at the hard sell. Take Steven Covey, author of the amazingly successful *Seven Habits of Highly Effective People.* The book has sold over five million copies since 1989, in 28 languages, in 35 countries. Covey now employees 700 people at the Covey Leadership Center which has annual revenues of $70 million. "He has sold himself with a brashness that makes the over-excited Tom Peters look like a shrinking violet," observed *The Economist*.[201]

Partly by default, partly through good timing, Peters created an industry which is becoming ever larger, ever more brash. At the same time, there is little evidence that the managers of the world have become more adept or more efficient. Depending on your beliefs this is either proof that the guru industry is a fraud or evidence that management is so complex and ridden with uncertainty that it is becoming increasingly harder. I believe the latter is probably nearer the truth. And, while the practice of management becomes ever harder, the desire for all-embracing solutions is likely to continue to expand exponentially.

Individual suppliers of executive education/leadership development

Classification	World total	Daily rates	Days per year
Global superstars	50	$10,000+	100+
Global stars	250	$5–10,000	75+
Major leaguers	1000–1500	$2500–5000	50+
Professionals	2500–5000	$1000–2500	50
Semi-pro	5000–25,000	under $1000	10+

Source: Fulmer, Robert M. & Fulmer, Albert A., *Crafting Competitiveness*, Capstone, Oxford, 1996.

The Guru Business

Guru	Claim to fame	Daily fee ($)
Anthony Robbins	Author and personal development guru	75,000 +
Steven Covey	Author of *The Seven Habits of Highly Effective People*	50,000–75,000
Michael Hammer	Author of *Reengineering the Corporation*	30,000–50,000
Michael Treacy	Author of *The Discipline of Market Leaders*	30,000–50,000
Ken Blanchard	Author of *The One Minute Manager* and many others	20,000–50,000
Zig Ziglar	Author of *Over the Top*, sales and motivation expert	20,000–50,000
Philip Crosby	Quality guru and author of *Quality is Free*	20,000–30,000
Albert Casey	Ex-CEO American Airlines, now author and academic	10,000–20,000
James Kouzes	Author of *The Leadership Challenge* and CEO of TPG/Learning Systems	10,000–20,000
Roger Axtell	Author and expert on doing business in different cultures	5000–10,000
Charles Garfield	Author of *Peak Performance*	5000–10,000
Oren Harari	Senior consultant at TPG and author	5000–10,000
Richard Schonberger	Author of *Building a Chain of Customers*	5000–10,000

Source: Leading Authorities Inc., *The Guide to America's Best Speakers and Entertainment 1996*.

SEVEN

THE CHAOTIC
REVOLUTION

*❝ Every middle manager
should spring out of the
gate each morning as a
dedicated, proactive
boundary basher ❞*

Tom Peters[202]

Welcome to the Revolution

By the mid-1980s, Tom Peters was known throughout the executive world. His two books had sold in huge numbers. His fees for seminars had reached astronomical levels. A succession of videos and tapes, in addition to his seminars, kept the expectant market satiated.

In 1987, Peters' *Thriving on Chaos* was published. With a flourish of bravado, it opened with the proclamation: "There are no excellent companies."[203] (This is probably the most quoted single line from Peters' work – used variously as proof of his inconsistency, as evidence that he learned from his mistakes, or as an indictment of his tendency to write in slogans.) It was his first guru book – and the first he wrote without the tempering presence of a co-author.

The roots of *Thriving on Chaos* stretched back to the second TPG Skunk Camp in December 1984. While the first Skunk Camp had been a celebration and something of an indulgence, the next was a profit-making event and was less successful. "The first Skunk Camp was at the time we were ready to go forward with *A Passion for Excellence* and it was great. We had a lot of famous people there, people like Rene McPherson," recalls Peters. "Then we had the first for-profit Skunk Camp where Bob Le Duc and I received a merciless beating. Suddenly we didn't get the ratings we expected. We realized we were having to justify our material. People wanted to know what to do with it."

Bob Le Duc, not surprisingly, has vivid memories of the second

Skunk Camp: "There was a strong message during the seminar that we were preaching to the choir. They said we believe what you're saying, but tell us how to do it. Tom came back on the evening before the last day and we talked about it. Tom then produced on a single piece of paper a list of seven things to implement – he called it 'The so-you-want-a-fucking-list list'."

The list was expanded and torn apart throughout 1985. Every Skunk Camp added to the dialog so that eventually Peters and Le Duc ended up with around 50 of what they labeled the "Skunk Camp Promises." Le Duc then organized the list into four categories. Peters added a fifth. (The five were: creating total customer responsiveness; pursuing fast-paced innovation; achieving flexibility by empowering people; learning to love change; and building systems for a world turned upside down.) Eventually, the promises were developed into a 60-page booklet which was handed out at seminars. The booklet didn't have any supporting examples, but was just a basic list of things to do to turn excellence into reality. *Thriving on Chaos* is really a 500-page version of this 60-page document.

As such, the roots of *Thriving on Chaos* stretch back very clearly even to *In Search of Excellence* – it is basically a lengthy riposte aimed at all those critics who suggested that Peters' theories could not be turned into reality. Each chapter ends with a short list of suggested action points. "*Thriving on Chaos* was the final, engineering-like, tidying up," says Peters. "It was organized in a hyper-organized engineering fashion." For Bob Le Duc, *Thriving on Chaos* was the real nuts and bolts book after the vignettes of *A Passion for Excellence*.

It is probably just as well that Peters left the world of engineering. *Thriving on Chaos* is true to its title. It is badly organized with an ornate numbering system for the chapters which defies explanation. But, once again, Peters' timing was immaculate. *Thriving on Chaos* appeared on Black Monday as Wall Street fell 20 percent. Times *were* chaotic and the book's title promised an escape route – in the same way as *In Search of Excellence* tempted readers to believe in excellence. *Thriving on Chaos* eventually spent 60 weeks on the *New York Times* bestseller lists.

The book's subtitle, "Handbook for a management revolution," was equally inspired. Managers, and Peters perhaps, are drawn to the idea of being revolutionary though, in reality, they are more George Washington than Che Guevara – revolutionary by self-proclamation rather than through violent rebellion against the status quo. "Though the word 'revolution' . . . appeared in the subtitle of *Thriving on Chaos*, in retrospect I don't think it was a revolutionary book," concluded Peters in *Liberation Management*.[204] Adding the word "handbook" to the subtitle was also a wise move as it suggests that the books actually delivers a way out, a means of negotiating the unnegotiable. Peters now bemoans the fact that "linear people love *Thriving on Chaos*," which is ironic given its deliberately nonlinear title.

In *Thriving on Chaos*, Peters was searching for the meaning and nature of the revolution he anticipated. "Revolution: it's a word business people have trouble with, and justifiably so. But our competitive situation is dire. The time for 10 percent staff cuts and 20 percent quality improvements is past. Such changes are not good enough," he wrote.[205] After the folksy, fluffy, and anecdotal *A Passion for Excellence*, Peters preached a hard-hitting message: corporate apocalypse was near.

The echoes of *In Search of Excellence* were loud – it, too, had bemoaned corporate inadequacies, blindness to widespread deficiencies, and mapped something of an escape route. *Thriving on Chaos* painted a picture of a broader and more dramatic malaise and suggested many of the same escape routes. But, while *In Search of Excellence* was painted in fairly genteel water colors, Peters painted *Thriving on Chaos* in his brighter, seminar oils.

Thriving on Chaos magnified the debate ignited by *In Search of Excellence*. In *In Search of Excellence* Peters and Waterman presented the alternatives in black and white. They described corporate battles between good and evil. The evil empire was ruled by rationalists; the counter to this was the enlightened world of MBWA and actually giving people responsibility. *Thriving on Chaos* presented a more balanced view of good and evil. In the end the conclusion was that to thrive on chaos, paradoxically, there had to be a balance. All evil will fail; all good will fail though for very different reasons. The revolution was no *coup d'état* but a precarious balancing act. And, as Peters repeatedly pointed out, the high wire was continually being raised.

It was not only that *Thriving on Chaos* covered many of the same issues as *In Search of Excellence*. It was also a public recognition of how much had changed in the business environment and in Peters' life and thinking during the intervening five years. The Peters of 1987 had learned from his mistakes – and the mistakes of those excellent companies of 1982. With *Thriving on Chaos* he sought to impress on the world that failure could be as valuable as success. "There's little that is more important to tomorrow's managers than failure," wrote Peters.[206]

In *A Passion for Excellence*, Peters' voice was convivial, a kind of latter-day Burl Ives – "Let's sit around and I'll tell you some great stories." In *Thriving on Chaos* there was a tone of urgency, desperation. The solutions proffered by Peters in *Thriving on Chaos* were drastic and, he argued, time was short. What went before was written off. "If the word 'excellence' is to be applicable in the future, it requires wholesale redefinition. Perhaps: 'Excellent firms don't believe in excellence – only in constant improvement and constant change.' That is, excellent firms of tomorrow will cherish impermanence – and thrive on chaos."[207] – but Peters was unsure about the future shape of organizations and of management. Despite its grand title, *Thriving on Chaos* was a timid step towards the future rather than a great leap forwards.

The book often failed to get to the point. The message was not distilled down. Instead, in Peters' hands the message became dissipated, lost in the book's convoluted structure and enthusiasm for bullet points and lists. *Thriving on Chaos* identified no fewer than 45 precepts for managers to follow. The similarity between some of them served to confuse rather than clarify. While number four encouraged readers to "Achieve total customer responsiveness," number seven advocated that managers "Listen to customers," and number ten recommended that they become "customer-obsessed."[208] To make sense of chaos, Peters settled for overkill.

At the same time, in an attempt to provide much needed clarity, the engineer in Peters returned to the fore. It was as if the machine had been dismantled in front of him and he was seeking a means of putting the pieces back together again – knowing that it could not be reconstructed into what it was. The arch anti-rationalist began to return to his rationalist roots. "I have become a fanatic about quantifying – but a new sort of quantifying," Peters wrote. "I insist upon quantifying the soft stuff – quality, service, customer linkups, innovation, organizational structure, people involvement, and even how much time you spend breaking down inappropriate interfunctional barriers. We must move from lip-service to the ideas of *In Search of Excellence*, *A Passion for Excellence*, and 1000 other books just as good or better, to setting challenging goals for implementation."[209]

Thriving on Chaos even included equations. "Quality is important, to be sure. So is absolute response time. And price. But at least as important as any of these is keeping your word. In fact, I've boiled it down to a simple formula:

$$CP = D/E$$

Customer perception (*CP*) equals delivery (*D*) divided by expectation (*E*). Maximizing *CP* is essential in the squishy, real world, where perception of the intangibles is really everything."[210] Later in the book, Peters noted: "The business equation is simple: Profit equals revenue minus cost. Or maybe it's slightly more complicated: Long-term profit equals revenue from continuously happy customer relationships minus cost."[211]

And herein lay the problem with *Thriving on Chaos*: the soft world of "squishy . . . happy customer relationships" rested uneasily with the hard world of equations and talk of "profit equals revenue minus cost." Peters' point was that the two needed to be combined in any successful business. The trouble was that, at the end of *Thriving on Chaos*, there remained the conviction that polar opposites can never attract. The manager in the "squishy, real world" automatically prefers something hard, solid, and rational to make sense of life.

Even so, *Thriving on Chaos* marked a departure from what had gone before. The past was not discarded, but it was reappraised in less than glowing terms. The Peters of 1987 regarded his 1982 self as too timid by far. "My co-authors and I downplayed the importance of structure in *In Search of Excellence* and *A Passion for*

Excellence. We were terribly mistaken. Good intentions and brilliant proposals will be dead-ended, delayed, and sabotaged, massaged to death, or revised beyond recognition or usefulness by the over-layered structures at most large and all too many smaller firms."[212] Too many layers; too much hierarchy. Peters took off the kid-gloves. Managers had not only been beguiled by the growth of management as a discipline, but had feathered their nests by creating more and more layers of management. There were too many managers and too many inefficient managers addicted to the past rather than obsessed with the future.

Setting the Change Agenda

For all the limitations of *Thriving on Chaos*, the book again demonstrated the ability of Peters' antennae to pick up emerging trends and issues. *Thriving on Chaos* anticipated what quickly became labeled "change management." "To meet the demands of the fast-changing competitive scene, we must simply learn to love change as much as we have hated it in the past," Peters wrote.[213]

Once again it is difficult to remember the time when the management of change wasn't a cliché. Now, ten years on from *Thriving on Chaos*, change management programs fill the prospectuses of business schools. By 1990 the word "change" was a fixture on book covers – and even in some boardrooms.

Thriving on Chaos to some extent set the emerging agenda. It did so in a disorganized, shambolic sort of way, but it did nevertheless start up another bandwagon. "No skill is more important than the corporate capacity to change *per se*. The company's most urgent task, then, is to learn to welcome – beg for, demand – innovation from everyone. This is the prerequisite for basic capability-building of any sort, and for subsequent continuous improvement," wrote Peters.[214] The phrase "continuous improvement" has since become yet another in a long line of vacuous corporate slogans – "If you aren't reorganizing, pretty substantially, once every six to twelve months, you're probably out of step with the times," wrote Peters.[215]

Central to Peters' odyssey in *Thriving on Chaos* was his uncovering of a new world of corporate paradoxes. The book's title was the central paradox – chaos can be understood and managed; you can succeed even in an environment of permanent unpredictability. It was necessary to be free-wheeling *and* structured. The unquantifiable needed to be quantified.

Before long, paradoxes were everywhere. The British thinker, Charles Handy was among those who seized on the paradoxical new forms of management and business which Peters went some way to mapping out in *Thriving on Chaos*. It is interesting that the title of Handy's 1994 book, *The Empty Raincoat*, was changed for the American market. It became *The Age of Paradox*. Americans, so the publishers thought, would be uncomfortable with a title derived from a sculpture in Minneapolis and at ease with the notion of a business world beset by paradoxes. Europeans, it was decided, were at home with sculptures and uneasy with paradox.

Paradoxes represented a sea change in management thinking. Previously, thinkers had settled for opposites – Theory X and Theory Y; centralization and decentralization; control and chaos; simplicity and complexity; the good and evil of *In Search of Excellence*.

Thriving on Chaos examined a bewildering new world in which once mutually exclusive ideas and approaches were combined. Itself riddled with paradoxes, it did not make it any easier for executives to come to terms with or to manage them. With all the bullet points in the world, the contradictions were still there, as unfathomable and unbridgeable as ever. Indeed, skeptics suggest that books charting the paradoxical nature of the executive world are simply avoiding the issue. If you can't reach a definitive or rational conclusion, dress your ideas up as far-reaching paradoxes. In some cases this is unquestionably the case. In *Thriving on Chaos*, however, Peters was desperately searching for answers. Instead, he found that circular reasoning rather than linear logic was the new order of the day.

Paradoxes have continued to form a central plank of many management books. Take, *Leaning into the Future* by George Binney and Colin Williams, two British academics and consultants. "*Leaning into the Future*," they say, "is a potent and practical way of working with change which combines apparent opposites:

leading *and* learning; being forthright *and* listening; giving direction *and* allowing autonomy."[216]

In *Thriving on Chaos*, Peters suggested that, discomfiting though they may be, paradoxes are the only available and reasonable explanation of the issues and challenges facing executives now and in the future. Paradoxes are not a convenient shorthand, but valid explanations in a world without answers.

The world of paradoxes was not the only new area explored in *Thriving on Chaos*. If *In Search of Excellence* introduced a new language for management, *Thriving on Chaos* introduced new metaphors for management. Since *Thriving on Chaos*, the imagery of management writing has undergone a creative renaissance.

With attention focusing on the nature of the questions rather than the pithiness of the answers, managers found themselves in the uncomfortable world of chaos and complexity theory. There was much talk of fractals and cognitive dissonance; uncertainty and ambiguity were the new realities. Organizational metaphors metamorphosed. The organization was once talked of in mechanical terms. After *Thriving on Chaos* it was variously described through natural and scientific metaphors as an ameba or a random pattern. The old images of machines and cogs were cast aside.

Peters argued that most business organizations exhibit a mix of complexity and chaos. Corporate systems were not static but creative and constantly moving. Yet again, the uncovering of this new world of confusion, chaos, and paradox produced few definitive answers. However, two themes emerged. First, linear models of the world based on Newton's idea that action leads to reaction are insufficient to handle some kinds of circumstances – namely, complexity and uncertainty. Second, many business problems contain elements which are inherently unpredictable.

Metaphors, imagery, stories, and anecdotes became a central core of organizational life to Peters. "People, including managers, do not live by pie charts alone – or by bar graphs or three inch statistical appendices to 300-page reports. People live, reason, and are moved by symbols and stories," he wrote.[217] "There are those who object that a manager such as I describe is paying too much attention to style, not enough to substance. This is nonsense.

Because the fact is, there is no perceived substance without symbols. Trust and credibility come through everyone's observation of the manager's symbolic integrity, not his or her policy documents."[218]

To hard-boiled rationalists this was anathema. They regarded chaos theory as mere metaphorical color which sounded clever but didn't actually help get the job done. Peters' point was that symbols, metaphors, and the like were the only practical means of understanding the new business world. Ralph Stacey, author of *Complexity and Creativity*, says: "Complexity is an effective metaphor and practically useful. Everything's a metaphor. It's not possible to make sense of anything apart from through a paradigm. It is a different way of making sense of human systems and so it is more important than another recipe or technique. Some people are quite hostile because acceptance of complexity undermines their way of thinking. To others it is a release."

Where this left aspiring or practicing managers remains a matter of lively conjecture. They are, according to different commentators, fearful of the uncertainty now surrounding them or upbeat, set on making themselves indispensable in the managerial marketplace. In reality, there is no stereotypical situation or attitude. Instead, there is a bewildering array of options, tools, techniques, new ideas, and old ideas. Either/or questions have become either/and imponderables. The free-wheeling pragmatism offered by some offers all the answers and yet none at all. There is a thin line between order and chaos.

The world mapped out in *Thriving on Chaos* was undoubtedly uncertain. The challenge laid down by Peters was enormous: cast off your previous thinking and embrace a new world of constant change. In reality, corporate reactions to Peters' new world of paradoxes were limited in imagination. In the decade since its publication, the corporate motto has been: if in doubt, downsize. It is clear cut, belonging to the world of incompatible extremes rather than paradoxes. It was an easy answer and the one taken by corporations throughout the world.

Thriving on Chaos made the case for downsizing as bluntly and categorically as any book has. "The organizational structures of US firms continue to feature bloated management ranks, with reductions of 50 to 80 percent still required at many firms," wrote Peters.[219] (There is, in typical Peters fashion, no explanation of where the figures came from.) "We are being strangled by bloated staffs, made up of carping experts and filling too many layers on the organization chart. Today's structures were designed for controlling turn of the century mass production operations under stable conditions, with primitive technologies. They have become perverse, action-destroying devices, completely at odds with current competitive needs."[220] Peters determined that five layers of hierarchy was the most any organization required – and that three layers (supervisor, department head, and unit boss) was sufficient for any single unit.

The knee-jerk reaction from the corporate world was to downsize. This appeased stockholders, but not Peters. The trouble was that while managerial numbers were reduced and spans of control widened, actual layers of hierarchy often remained in place. Peters preached flexibility: "Today's successful business leaders will be those who are most flexible of mind. An ability to embrace new ideas, routinely challenge old ones, and live with paradox will be the effective leader's premier trait. Further, the challenge is for a lifetime. New truths will not emerge easily. Leaders will have to guide the ship while simultaneously putting everything up for grabs, which is itself a fundamental paradox."[221] But, the reality was that age-old inflexibility remained largely intact. Peters was adamant, and ever more vehement, that this had to change.

EIGHT

LIBERATING MANAGEMENT

" My objective in general . . . Is to Irritate "

Tom Peters[222]

The Cuttings Service

Tom Peters is a voracious reader. His office has stacks of business and management books – although one of his colleagues reckons that Peters stopped reading business books for "information" years ago. He turns them, marks them, and remembers them. His taste goes further than just business blockbusters: he reads novels, too, and prefers to talk about his latest novelist discovery rather than the perils of strategic management. Give him Roddy Doyle rather than Igor Ansoff any day. Peters calculates that around 90 percent of his reading is fiction. He also rifles through magazines for interesting snippets, which he adds to his mountainous stockpiles. Lennart Arvedson says: "He is extremely well read and keeps reading prolifically across the social sciences. He gobbles up newspapers and magazines. The way he remembers details from material and uses it is amazing. His mind is something else."

While some people remember obscure baseball stats, Peters recalls quotes and figures from journals no-one else has read, or probably even heard of. "He has the original garbage-can mind," says Sven Atterhed. "If you want to get a message across you tell a story. Tom uses metaphors and stories to capture people's imagination. He has always been dependent on his stories."

Somehow, along the way, Peters brings it all together. One-line comments on ergonomics from obscure specialist journals are welded into discussions on emerging organizational forms. His morass of slides becomes an argument. "Tom's real contributions come from the fact that he surveys the world so widely, and has an extraordinarily creative mind that associates dissimilar ideas and creates a new synthesis," says James Brian Quinn of Dartmouth College's Amos Tuck School. "Tom's approach to research is not the classic 'hypothesis-posing and testing' approach. Instead, he tends to operate in a 'discovery' and 'pattern developing' mode. These are perfectly valid methodologies for doing research, although they are not widely recognized or accepted in 'graduate school academic' circles. Tom's purpose is to observe and to help. He is much more interested in changing practice and having high impact that he is in kowtowing to academic niceties."[223]

This point is echoed by Stanford's Harold Leavitt: "Substantively I am in complete sympathy with Tom's writings – at least most of the time. He moves out three sigmas beyond where 'respectable' academics are willing to go, and his evangelical ways turn off more conservative folk. But his direction is absolutely right and his influence on managers has been enormous."[224]

Peters welds, synthesizes, blends, and mixes. "When I'm writing I think whether people who've influenced me would throw tomatoes at it or not. To some extent I am a translator who is good at finding interesting examples which make it relevant to people," he explains. It is a method which is questioned by some. Why doesn't he find his own examples? Isn't that what research is really all about? Dan Carroll, who wrote the damning *Harvard Business Review* article on *In Search of Excellence*, has grown no fonder of Peters' methodology and writing style. "I've read Tom's other books and they don't get any better. It's a shame," says Carroll. "He is a very bright man and should go back to his academic roots and do the research he is capable of rather than running a magazine cuttings service."

But, Peters goes on collecting, assembling a massive collage of disparate material. It *is* a cutting service, but an idiosyncratic, wide-ranging one. "He read everything from physics to spy novels and then molded it all together," says Jayne Pearl. Others who have witnessed Peters' hoarding of material are staggered by his capacity for information. Consultant, Don Laurie traveled around with Peters for a week. "The most interesting thing was how he learned. He was making a lot of speeches. They were innovative and it sounded as if he was always in and out of companies. The reality was that he got up at four o'clock in the morning and read and wrote. Most of what he learned he got from his reading.

Getting on a plane he always had a pile of books and magazines, and was always ripping things out."

Peters has an important advantage over mere mortals: he doesn't need a lot of sleep. He gets out of bed at four or five in the morning and gets down to reading and writing. "Tom does have one serious defect. He is so damn energetic and indefatigable that when I am around him I am in fear that I will catch St Vitus's dance!' says Herb Kelleher of Southwest Airlines, who is no couch potato himself.[225]

For someone whose exercise consists of walking for half an hour a day and little else, Peters has incredible stamina. McKinsey's Bill Matassoni remembers having lunch with Peters and a *BusinessWeek* reporter at a famous restaurant in LA. Jack Lemmon and Liza Minnelli were there. "Tom was regaling this guy from *BusinessWeek* with his research and then remembered we had a flight to catch. We got in the limo and then on our way to the airport realized we were going to be late," says Matassoni. "We decided to go back and went to an Italian restaurant in Beverly Hills where we had pasta and some bottles of red wine. We then caught the red eye to get to New York. I thought I'd get some sleep as soon as I got on the plane. All the way Tom read and kept waking me up to show me something interesting. He slept three or four hours a night."

Peters makes no pretense about his methodology. He shrugs his shoulders at Dan Carroll's criticism of his mountain of press cuttings. "The clipping service thing is correct and I'm proud of it," he says. "The biggest influence on my professional life was Gene Webb who believed the highest form of research was re-translating other people's research. The classic example is the research of 3M in *In Search of Excellence* where we found research which had been done at Harvard but which had lain fallow." Peters sees it as his job to disinter useful research from the caverns of business school knowledge. If it's good and makes his point, why not use it? "I'll come across a revealing quote in a business periodical or get a fascinating question at a seminar or talk to someone sitting next to me on a plane," says Peters. "While still on the plane, in the latter case, I often end up phoning my office in Palo Alto and directly ordering up a new 35 mm slide.

Forty-eight hours later, in Dusseldorf or Detroit, I'm using the slide in a seminar for 600 people. Elaborating on the underlying story. Sometimes it falls flat. (Goodbye slide. Goodbye story.) Sometimes it begins to grow legs."[226]

Peters believes there is a great deal of academic snobbery at work. "People see the press as the source of all evil, but I've got a lot of respect for them. It's absolutely fabulous to have working for me – as researchers – magazines such as *Fortune, Business Week, Forbes*, and *Inc.*," he says. "If someone writes something which is fascinating I would be a fool not to use it to buttress my argument. If you can buttress it by referring to five different sources all the better." He is particularly proud of the section on F.A. Hayek's work in *Liberation Management* in which he gives a reporter-style précis of the economist's theories.

The Peters research method has largely remained the same since *In Search of Excellence*. "Tom did no real research. He did secondary research, there was nothing primary about it. He was a voracious secondary researcher who popularized and synthesized a lot of thinking," says Bill Matassoni. "In his apartment in San Francisco he had a dresser. Every drawer was full of articles he had cut out and he seemed to know where everything was." Peters' preoccupation has always been with information rather than fashion.

Peters is an obsessive accumulator, so much so that Lennart Arvedson observes that "Tom's presentations were almost like a distraction, something he did while he was doing the real work of gathering material." He is constantly on the look out for pithy remarks, words of wisdom to slip into his books. He gave a talk in Sweden in August 1982 and Lord Sieff shared the platform. Later a quote from Sieff appeared in *A Passion for Excellence* – not from Sieff's circulated text but an *ad lib* remark which Peters had noted down verbatim.

Peters' one-man cuttings service is a means of reassurance. It may not be academic, but he needs the reassurance of other thinkers plowing the same or similar furrows. If a dozen academics are saying similar things – even in completely different areas – Peters sees the link and builds from it.

Yet, Peters retains a fascination with the ways and wiles of academia. After all, he has been to two of America's top academic institutions – Cornell and Stanford. "There is a fair hunk of me who is still an academic and when I went on sabbatical from McKinsey I gave serious thought to teaching at Stanford. I did teach there for two years as a lecturer," he says. "Being a dean was a job I thought about. But that's just fundraising. The one job I wanted was to be President of Stanford University, despite the failings associated with universities. I have an enormous respect for research."

Oddly, given this background, the public perception of Peters is that he is as non-academic as it is possible to be. "He is very serious about establishing academic and intellectual credentials as well as his influence in the business world. It is important to him that he gets respect from academics. Of course, that is where he has the least credibility," says Paul Cohen. This is undoubtedly true. Peters' books are more likely to be derided by business school professors than placed on their reading lists.

Academics blanch at the thought of using Peters' works because his books do not lay down a new theory and then explain the research behind it. There are no appendices, no tables with complex variables. Collecting cuttings is not what academics call research. (Interestingly, *In Search of Excellence* did feature what academics would call research – but, having explained what the research involved, Peters and Waterman then filled the rest of the book with discursive text as likely to feature comments overheard in a bar as mentions of standard deviation from the research model.)

Managers, of course, tend not to have a high regard for academics. To them, making things work is everything. Theory is nothing without practice. (The academic rejoinder is that there is nothing as practical as a sound theory.) Max Worcester of *Frankfurter Allgemeine Zeitung* dismisses the theorists: "You don't have to have an academic fall back. Management is a life science. The theory is in the practice. There really aren't many theories as to how you should run companies."

Peters is robustly defensive about accusations of a lack of substantive theory in his books and seminars, but defensive nevertheless. "I am not atheoretical, absolutely not," he bridles, irritated by the accusation. "I see my work as academically well-grounded. My economics, marketing, sociology, and psychology backgrounds are sound. My hero is Henry Mintzberg." Of course, Tom Peters is no Henry Mintzberg, whose books are the apotheosis of academic credibility; and vice versa.

Somewhat surprisingly, Mintzberg himself believes there are some similarities and echoes the comments of others admiring Peters' capacity to absorb material. "In a sense we have a similar kind of view of the world – managers have to get off their high horses and get on with the specifics. Tom offers a bridge between the academic and non-academic worlds," says Mintzberg. "You could accuse him of a lot of hype but he does do his homework. I am amazed how much Tom reads. He is incredibly well read."

Peters' thirst for literature is not just a mad scramble for ideas and examples of best practice. There is more to it. He is fascinated with being a writer. (Dan Carroll, the critic of *In Search of Excellence* says: "Tom has a facility as a writer. Sometimes he is clever to a fault. I would tell him never to use the word 'arguably' again!") When pushed, Peters categorizes himself as a writer, but then quickly pulls back: "I am not a writer. I have too much respect for great writing to call myself that. In my field, I think I am a good writer, but that is not the same thing as being a writer." Academics are prone to dismiss Peters as a "reporter." To them this is an insult; to Peters it is an accolade.

Peters the Columnist

In 1985, Tom Peters met up with Leonard Koppett, who was then editor of the *Peninsula Times Tribune*. Peters asked his advice about writing a weekly syndicated column – he had long admired the columnist George Gilder, one of the most commonly cited sources of material in *In Search of Excellence*. Koppett warned: "Some week you'll find you just don't have anything left to say."[227] Undeterred, Peters pursued the idea. Eventually, his column was taken by 110 newspapers in the US as well as in Korea, the Gulf States, Europe, India, and Latin America.

"It was not a lucrative use of time – $3000 to $4000 a month," says Peters. "But I enjoyed it and it gave me discipline. When I came across an interesting story I could write it down. The columns became the file cabinet of my thoughts." This, at least, was an improvement on a dresser.

The Tom Peters column ran until 1995. That's a lot of column inches. Along the way, Peters the corporate man transformed himself into a gun-toting, quote-wielding, snapper at corporate heels. No subject was too small. No irritation unimportant. "My objective in general, and in this column in particular, is to irritate."[228]

"Some of his columns were jewels; very poignant observations compressed into a small space," says Lennart Arvedson. Others were not, as Peters cast about, expressing opinions on virtually everything. He derided ties: "Ties bind, constrain. A man with a tie is mentally constipated. I hate ties. I hate suits. I hate when I give in and wear them. Why do I do it? Beats me."[229] He scorned board meetings: "I hate sitting in on big-company board meetings.

The setting is somber. The people are somber (even after a good quarter). Proposals that come forth have been staffed and re-staffed until every iota of energy has been drained from them. Presenters wear undertaker suits, speak in undertaker tones. Each wooden word has obviously been rehearsed, and then rehearsed again. I often wonder if boardroom denizens would bleed if cut by a razor."[230] And he even contemplated the managerial lessons from cooking: "A couple of hours in a hot kitchen can teach you as much about business and management as the latest books on reengineering or total quality management."[231] In one of his more controversial columns in 1992, he called for the legalization of marijuana.[232]

Peters the columnist was eminently readable and personable. In a column entitled "Hey-heggggggggggggggggggggggg!" he observed: "I have to admit that my past decade's importuning about delighting customers has mostly come to naught. OK, I'm a modern-day Don Quixote when it comes to service. Yes, I've got an attitude problem. And, it's not doing my hypertension a bit of good."[233] The Peters column was a mass of sound-bites, celebrations of the mundane, and not so mundane, delivered in a convivial style. The biggest mail bag Peters received from those hundreds of articles was for a column singing the praises of thank-you notes, not a subject given much thought by academics. "Though verbosity is my stock in trade (I routinely give eight-hour seminars), I did run on fumes a few times. But then I'd dig back through my week – and something like the thank-you note idea would emerge. I learned that the worst columns were when I was thinking too hard."[234]

The column became his main platform; people would go there for their fix of Tom Peters. Even the seemingly innocuous columns got a response. For Peters the column provided a blessed release. Columnists are expected to be opinionated. "The column got to the point where it took a day to write. I'm a ten- to twelve-draft person. What was neat about the column was that since it had no particular message I could write anything I wanted. It generated 75 percent of my correspondence and became the love of my life. The reason I could do it was that there were no rules." But there were, of course, two very important rules: the column had to be delivered on time and be the right length. Amazingly, given his schedule and prolixity, Peters stuck to them.

The column provided a mound of material (50,000 words a year), as well as a regular supply of ideas and insights. By 1990 all this was accumulating as surely as $5 in Warren Buffet's investment account.

The Route to Liberation

In the late 1980s, as the world pored over his knockabout columns, Peters rediscovered the works of the economist Hayek and business historian Alfred Chandler. On vacation, he eschewed the attractions of Harold Robbins to read them back-to-back. This reading – combined with the robust journalese of his columns – was to form the cornerstone of Peters' massive 1992 book, *Liberation Management*.

The roots of this fascination can be traced back to a 30-minute CNN debate after *A Passion for Excellence* featuring Peters, his co-author Nancy Austin, and Robert Reich, later to become US Secretary for Labor. Reich gave Peters a lesson. "Bob didn't beat me up. He beat me. He talked about industrial policy and went back into history to make his points. I realized I was under-read in business history," says Peters. With typical gusto, he sought to remedy his problem. During a month-long vacation in France in 1985, he started writing a book on trade policy bringing in his heavyweight reading of social and economic history along the way. The book was never finished though much of it was slipped into Peters' columns of the time. "Though the book didn't see the light of day it influenced everything. I read the history of the industrial revolution. It was a license to steal, but I threw it away because I knew I didn't know my basics and didn't want to invest an additional two years in acquiring that knowledge," says Peters.

His intensive reading determined the initial direction of what was to become *Liberation Management*, though the book's working title was *Beyond Hierarchy*. The book is a perfect example of the Peters approach to gathering material. "*Liberation Management* was the first time since *In Search of Excellence* I had really gone on the road to research things," says Peters – while he personally visited and did interviews at over 20 companies, he was backed by a team of researchers. "I did some preliminary research for *Liberation Management* in spring 1989," says Paul Cohen. "Tom's books were written through an interesting process involving freelance reporters. I did a number of site visits and phone interviews." If a company caught Peters' roving eye, a researcher was despatched to find out more. The TPG newsletter, *On Achieving Excellence*, then used the stories or they were adapted for his column before Peters selected the most appropriate and shunted them into the book's emerging framework.

What is interesting about this approach is that Peters and his researchers often went into the companies with largely preconceived ideas of what they were looking for and wanted to find. The research was to some extent a self-fulfilling prophecy. "Tom always saw what he wanted to see and heard what he wanted to hear. If it didn't fit his paradigm it was overlooked. But, those who look for the nuances are left on the sidelines," reflects McKinsey's Bill Matassoni.

Take the experiences of two companies eventually featured in *Liberation Management*. Imagination, a London-based creative consultancy, was one organization which Peters grew particularly fond of. It and its chief executive, Gary Withers, were continually mentioned in his columns and featured in *Liberation Management*. Imagination is unquestionably an interesting and vibrant company. It arranges launches for new models for Ford, creates "events" with lots of lasers and fireworks, and is involved in everything from design to brand development.

Imagination fitted Peters' thinking perfectly. "In his mind there was already a company like Imagination which had ripped out hierarchy and was intent on breaking barriers," says Imagination's marketing director, Ralph Ardill. "He heard about us and was curious, though he had figured out what we were before he got here. We were the corporate validation of his theory and he was the management endorsement of what we were doing."

Peters spent a couple of days with Imagination. "He was relieved and surprised that a place like this did exist. We're in the wow business," says Ardill. "What he wrote was accurate and served his purpose but it was too utopian. We're not utopia but we have integrity. We keep it simple and everyone can explain what we do and why. Tom overpromises a little. No organization is that perfect. We make mistakes and not enough of that came across. For us it was an important point. It was like when a child prodigy finally realizes that they have to grow up. We have since grown up."

Another company visited personally by Peters was the FI Group, based a few miles north west of London. Again, the visit was short and succinct. "He came out to visit us at our headquarters in Hemel Hempstead around nine months before *Liberation Management* was published," recalls chief executive Hilary Cropper. "My first impressions were that he was naturally dynamic and personable. He listened very well and we had a healthy debate over a couple of hours. He thought that we were innovative. What he wrote was very lucid and accurate. It captured what we were doing."

To critics of Peters, such research methods are viewed with suspicion. Academics routinely spend weeks and months inside companies extracting information and interviews from all and sundry. Peters was not interested in such detail. He was more passionate about catching the atmosphere, the flavor of the place and the people. To some this is superficial. Peters would counter that all the time in the world spent with a company does not allow you to become part of it, to truly understand. A cornucopia of flavors, to him, is preferable to a single strong taste.

In any case, do managers really want complex theories whose implementation is likely to be even more complex? Asea Brown Boveri CEO, Percy Barnevik, is one of those who thinks not. "I have always favored a hands-on, case-based approach to analyzing management rather than theorizing. Ideas and strategies are important, of course, but execution is the real challenge," says Barnevik. "That's why I appreciate Tom Peters' approach. He looks for cases to benchmark against, explains them well, and makes a clear point. He thinks like a manager, not an academic. He puts a strong focus on networking, which has always been a key part of our approach at ABB, where we strive to bring out the synergies and scale effects that come from being multicultural and global."[235]

To Barnevik, Peters' approach was notable for its willingness to embrace the company's reality rather than seeking to imbue it with his own theories. "He is flexible in his views and looks at companies with an open mind. Although he has never been a big fan of the matrix organization, for example, he still recognized that we could manage to get a competitive advantage from it," says Barnevik. "So you could say he walks the talk when he preaches the virtues of flexibility and is then willing to open up his views to ideas that go against his own conventional wisdom."[236]

Tom Peters wanted to make *Liberation Management* exciting, to capture the excitement he saw in the organizations he visited. In this quest, a lot of material was discarded as too dull. "The nice thing about thin skin is that small remarks go to the center," says Peters. "Kathy Dale-Molle was doing some research for *Liberation Management* on a company and she said it was boring. I realized she was right and redirected the entire research." *Liberation Management*, Peters determined, was not going to be another tedious business book. It was going to be much more.

At a seminar in September 1991 Peters, for the first time, exposed a group of executives to the full thrust of what was to become *Liberation Management*. The 80 people present came from as far away as Malaysia, Brazil, and New Zealand. They received a shock. *Liberation Management* was as far removed from *In Search of Excellence* as New Zealand was from Palo Alto.

The miracle was that Peters could condense the mountain of material into a manageable seminar. In writing *Liberation Management* Peters became totally turned on by the cases. He felt he was truly treading new ground and couldn't contain himself. After the 850-word length restrictions of his weekly columns, words spewed from him on to the paper.

The original manuscript for *Liberation Management* was 1962 pages long and was only reduced to a manageable size after savage cuts. "I submitted a very long book manuscript to my publisher. A few weeks later my editor arrived at my doorstep, suitcase in hand. She proceeded to loom (she also worked). Cowed by her presence, I ended up slashing my own dear manuscript, five years in the making, by 50 percent in the next three weeks," says Peters.[237]

The editor, Corona Machemer, had worked on *A Passion for Excellence* and was working on *Thriving on Chaos*, but then moved to Alfred A. Knopf, still part of Random House. Peters followed partly out of professional admiration but also out of literary snobbery – the idea of being published by Knopf, with all its literary heritage, fired his enthusiasm and flattered the writer within him. "The idea of me being published by Knopf was mind-boggling."

During *Liberation Management*, Peters was probably under the most intense pressure of his career. First, there were deadlines. *Liberation Management* was, he says, at least three years late. The pressure from Random House was discreet but no publisher likes late deliveries.

There was also personal pressure. Peters wanted *Liberation Management* to be a great book and one which was truly innovative in its thinking and style. In *Thriving on Chaos* he had proclaimed the past was dead, but had failed to map out the future with any great passion. In *Liberation Management* he discovered the future and the passion to accompany it. Intellectually, too, *Liberation Management* was demanding. "Writing this book has been agony. I've finally shaken off the vestiges of years of traditional thinking," he wrote.[238]

These heightened personal and professional expectations came at a time when Peters' optimism had become increasingly tempered by experience. "He became depressed because he was dealing with a lot of big companies in a hopeless state. He was gloomy about the future and was spending his time talking to audiences he insulted," says *Inc.*'s Bo Burlingham. (In 1989 Peters wrote an article for *Inc.* entitled "Doubting Thomas" charting his utter dismay with the biggest and brightest's failure to respond to major economic discontinuity.) "During the late eighties, Tom became soured," says Burlingham. "His business was a mess and he thought that by that point he wouldn't have had to work for a living. He was trapped by his own fame and success and was drinking heavily. There was a lot depending on him and there was a lot of pressure for him to deliver *Liberation Management* which was a nightmare for him to write."

Despite all this, *Liberation Management*, says Peters, "is the only book I enjoyed writing. I was and am more pleased with *Liberation Management* than anything else I've ever written." He now thinks that more could have been done to make it more accessible. "For *Liberation Management* I should have had an editor who was a son of a bitch, not a friend. It received the best and worst reviews I have ever got." Indeed, most editors rub their hands at the very sight of *Liberation Management*. It is a book which justifies their profession. "I would have loved to have got my hands on *Liberation Management* before publication. It needed surgery," says Jayne Pearl.

Liberation Management was undoubtedly a self-indulgent book which could safely have been 40 percent shorter. Yet, it is a gold mine. (Journalists use it continually as a source of quotes and stories.) The trouble with gold mines, of course, is extracting the gold. "*Liberation Management* is too long. There is a lot of stuff which doesn't need to be said but there is a lot of good stuff. It is like the famous quote about advertising – only half of it works, the trouble is you don't know which half," says Max Worcester of *Frankfurter Allgemeine Zeitung*.

The final published version of *Liberation Management* was 834 pages long. Peters took solace in the massive length of Michael Porter's *Competitive Advantage of Nations*, published in 1990: "I figured I was safe because I was 25 pages shorter than Porter. I loved the *Liberation Management* stuff, though perhaps it was self-indulgent, and certainly the fucker was too long. If I had to go back I wouldn't change it."

Writing in Hypertext

Large, rambling, and gushingly anecdotal, *Liberation Management* is a sprawling compendium of Tom Peters' thinking on management in what he labeled the "nanosecond nineties." It was a change in direction which Peters explains in mixed metaphors: "I've moved from the hyperorganized *In Search of Excellence* with its McKinsey logic to the very scatter-shot *A Passion for Excellence* to the hyperorganized *Thriving on Chaos* then the mightily disorganized *Liberation Management*. Think of an accordion. It tightened up with *In Search of Excellence,* loosened up and then became anal-retentive with *Thriving on Chaos* and then completely loosened with *Liberation Management*."

While Peters' anal metaphor is open to misinterpretation, *Liberation Management* is unquestionably a big book (and along the way Peters also gained 20 pounds during its writing). It is also loose, very loose. "Mr Peters has not extended his passion for downsizing to his own prose," tartly observed *The Economist*.[239] "In such a thicket the reader quickly gets lost, so entangled in the undergrowth that each fresh anecdote detracts from others rather than adding to them. A man who wants firms to 'think small' and to be accessible has ended up writing an inaccessible book."[240]

But it is not only the size of the book which makes it daunting. In *Liberation Management,* Tom Peters unleashed a new voice on his largely unsuspecting audience. Readers had to scamper for their dictionaries as Peters' writing style evolved in front of them to become an unlikely combination of Hunter S. Thompson, a *Marvel* comic and a thesaurus. It was not an obvious marriage, involving an awful lot of exclamation marks, exhortations, and lists of adjectives. "I like the word 'ephemeral' almost as much as 'fashion' or 'fickle'. In fact, I'm fond of speaking of 'the four ephemerals:' ephemeral 'organizations'. . . . joined in ephemeral combinations . . . producing ephemeral products . . . for ephemeral markets . . . FAST," wrote Peters.[241] One idiosyncratic commentator compared *Liberation Management* to George Eliot's *Middlemarch* (Peters wrote back saying how flattered he was). *Liberation Management* is certainly as long as *Middlemarch* – other similarities are slightly harder to find.

Brash, colloquial, and largely unreadable (in linear fashion at least), *Liberation Management* is an expansive mass of a book filled with diversions, detritus, and delight. More of a reference book than a straight business book, it is perhaps best read as a lucky dip of pithy quotes and enlightening anecdotes. "*Liberation Management* was a massive collection of case studies loosely managed," says *Liberation Management* researcher Paul Cohen. "It attempted to get everything Tom has ever thought in one book. It has been misconceived. It is really a kind of eclectic reference book."

Liberation Management was, observed Karl Weick, written in "hypertext' and offered a serious challenge to the reader. "To go through the book is to live through the nineties and feel the need for each of us to make some sense of what is happening."[242] The language is colorful – "middle managers, as we have known them, are cooked geese;" "the definition of every product and service is hanging. Going soft, softer, softest. Going fickle, ephemeral, fashion" – and, at times, impenetrable as Peters' passion overwhelms his prose. "*Liberation Management* is a hodgepodge, but it is hard-hitting," says Peters. "I was thinking through thorny problems. I thought I did a brilliant job explaining things like Hayek in layman's language. It is basic reporting on research, reporting on theoretical stuff. I don't apologize for it."

Liberation Management brought Peters the reporter to the fore. "Though one might accuse Tom Peters of being more journalist than management scholar, *Liberation Management* previewed many of the themes that would come to occupy management thinkers in the 1990s," said Gary Hamel. "One might wish, though, that the ratio of insight to data were a bit higher, and that there were a few less case studies and a bit more conceptual structure. Nevertheless, the book remains a good, though over-long, introduction to new age management philosophy."[243]

Whatever its literary merits, *Liberation Management* was impor-tant to Tom Peters, and marked a critical development in his career. It was the first of his books since *In Search of Excellence* to feature in-depth examinations of individual companies and *Lib-eration Management*'s central message reflects a substantial change of emphasis from that of Peters' earlier works. Ten years on from *In Search of Excellence*, Peters argued that his previous work was marred by paying too little attention to the perennially vexed question of organizational structure.

With *Liberation Management*, Peters set something of a record by apologizing again for his previous books. "If you've done all the close-to-the-customer things that I begged you to do in my first three books . . . I'm not sure you'll be any 'closer' five years from now than you are today."[244] The world of the nineties was a different place and, in *Liberation Management*, Peters examined just how different it was.

The New Organization

"Tomorrow's effective 'organization' will be conjured up anew each day," wrote Peters.[245] And, in *Liberation Management*, Tom Peters started anew. It could be read as a remake of how *In Search of Excellence* might have been. Peters went in search of organizational structures which worked successfully and then set out to describe them as accurately and as vividly as he could. Whether he managed to achieve this is open to debate. What cannot be disputed, however, is that *Liberation Management* ignited a debate.

In *In Search of Excellence* structural questions were generally peripheral, perhaps because companies were doing very little that was structurally innovative in the late 1970s and early 1980s. By 1990 they were, and Peters' priorities shifted. "Organization structure comes first in this book; customers last. And that is quite a switch from *In Search of Excellence*, *A Passion for Excellence* and *Thriving on Chaos* ('structure' issues accounted for about 2 percent of those books, but they take up over 50 percent of this one)," Peters wrote.[246]

As Peters acknowledged, when he and Waterman wrote *In Search of Excellence* they were still under the influence of Alfred Chandler's credo that structure followed strategy. In *Liberation Management*, Peters turned this on its head.

Chandler's premise was drawn from his research into major US corporations between 1850 and 1920. He argued that a firm's structure is dictated by its chosen strategy: "Unless structure follows strategy, inefficiency results." First, a company should establish a strategy and then seek to create the structure appropriate to achieving it. Chandler defined strategy as "the determination of the long-term goals and objectives of an enterprise, and the adoption of courses of action and the allocation of resources necessary for carrying out these goals."[247]

Chandler observed that organizational structures in companies such as DuPont, Sears Roebuck, General Motors, and Standard Oil were driven by the changing demands and pressures of the marketplace. He traced the market-driven proliferation of product lines in DuPont and General Motors and concluded that this proliferation led to a shift from a functional, monolithic organizational form to a more loosely coupled divisional structure. Chandler's conclusion that structure follows strategy had largely been accepted as a fact of corporate life.

"I think he got it exactly wrong," counters Peters with typical forthrightness. "For it is the structure of the organization that determines, over time, the choices that it makes about the markets it attacks."[248] To the Tom Peters of the early 1990s, structure was not all, but it was certainly all important.

To strategists, Peters' opinions were akin to a red rag to an already confused bull. "Those who dispute Chandler's thesis that structure follows strategy miss the point," wrote Gary Hamel. "Of course strategy and structure are inextricably intertwined. Chandler's point was that new challenges give rise to new structures. The challenges of size and complexity, coupled with advances in communications and techniques of management control produced divisionalization and decentralization. These same forces, several generations on, are now driving us towards new structural solutions – the 'federated organization,' the multicompany coalition, and the virtual company. Few historians are prescient. Chandler was."[249]

In *Liberation Management*, Peters did not tackle structure in the traditional hierarchical and functional sense. Indeed, his exemplars of the new organizational structure were notable for their apparent lack of structure. And herein lay Peters' point. Companies such as CNN, ABB, and Body Shop thrive through having highly flexible structures, able to change to meet the business needs of the moment. Free-flowing, impossible to pin down, unchartable, simple yet complex – to Peters, these were the paradoxical structures of the future.

ABB was one of the organizations most vociferously celebrated in *Liberation Management*. It embodied everything Peters was looking for in the corporation of the nineties and, in its redoubtable leader, Percy Barnevik, Peters found a kindred spirit – and one who was turning some of Peters' ideas into reality. Their first shared belief was in the importance of communication. In an organization as huge and complex as ABB, Barnevik had identified it as a key skill – and a source of competitive advantage. "One of Tom's big strengths is his ability to communicate," says Barnevik. "He is unusually skilled in getting his message across. In a company like ABB, communication is essential to getting everyone pulling in the same direction. You need to give people clear messages with information that they can use in their work, not vague or high-flying generalities. So I appreciate Tom's strength in this area. Some people may feel that Tom is a little extreme in the way he communicates his messages. But to come across strongly with a clear message, you can't have too many nuances, too much on the one hand but then again on the other hand. I find Tom's language refreshing and eye-opening and we have used it internally to stir people up."[250]

The strongest common cause between Barnevik and Peters was an obsessive loathing of hierarchy. Barnevik had demolished ABB's hierarchy. Peters applauded. "Tom is also anti-hierarchy and anti-headquarters, another theme that is close to my heart. Hierarchies just get in the way of business, cutting off managers from their customers, insulating them from the market and creating slow bureaucracies," says Barnevik.[251]

This was music to Peters' ears. Only with such vibrant structures would companies be able to deliver the customer service championed by Peters in his previous books, and only through such dynamic organizational forms would companies be able to survive. Not that Peters forgot customer service. "How customers perceive their relationship with your company determines whether or not you'll have a customer for life. That's almost obvious, if almost always ignored."[252]

Key to the new corporate structures envisaged by Peters were networks with customers, with suppliers, and, indeed, anyone else who could help the business deliver. "Old ideas about size must be scuttled. 'New big,' which can be very big indeed, is 'network big.' That is, size measured by market power, say, is a function of the firm's extended family of fleeting and semi-permanent cohorts, not so much a matter of what it owns and directly controls," he wrote.[253]

And, networks must move quickly. The book's central refrain is that of fashion: "We're all in Milan's *haute couture* business and Hollywood's movie business," wrote Peters. "This book is animated by a single word: fashion. Life cycles of computers and microprocessors have shrunk from years to months."[254] The new model organization moves fast and continually does so, seeking out new areas which make it unique in its markets.

Clearly, this requires quite different managerial skills than those traditionally needed by managers. Indeed, Peters admitted that the new organizational forms he depicted are "troublesome to conceive – and a downright pain to manage." The new skills are now familiar. Peters bade farewell to command and control, ushering in a new era characterized by "curiosity, initiative, and the exercise of imagination." It was, he argued, a step into the unknown for most organizations but also a return to first principles: "For the last 100 years or so . . . we've assumed that there is one place where expertise should reside: with 'expert' staffs at division, group, sector, or corporate. And another, very different, place where the (mere) work gets done. The new organization regimen puts expertise back, close to the action – as it was in craft-oriented, pre-Industrial Revolution days . . . We are not, then, ignoring 'expertise' at all. We are simply shifting its locus, expanding its reach, giving it new respect – and acknowledging that everyone must be an expert in a fast-paced, fashionized world."[255] The language was often ugly and unwieldy, but the point was passionately put. Though Tom Peters couldn't write like George Eliot, he beat her on raw emotion.

Ironically, one of the new organizations which Peters extolled in *Liberation Management* was McKinsey & Co. Even when Peters worked with the company, over a decade before *Liberation Management*, its *modus operandi* was based on project teams. As Peters observed in *Liberation Management*, McKinsey's team system was ahead of its time. It is only in recent years that the corporate world has woken up to the potential of team working, McKinsey had been making it work for decades, aiming simply to bring the best minds to bear on a problem. The McKinsey expert on the Asian pharmaceutical industry may be based in Singapore, but would likely be drafted on to a European project if his or her knowledge was needed. The teams are led by a partner who takes care of managing the client and bears the final responsibility. Typically, the rest of the team is made up of an engagement manager, associates and, sometimes, a business analyst.

McKinsey's use of teams caught Peters' eye, as did its undying faith in knowledge. The latter was picked up by Peters as a key competitive weapon for the future. McKinsey had foreseen this and committed itself to building its own knowledge – it now spends $50–100 million a year on knowledge building and claims to spend more on research than Harvard, Wharton, and Stanford combined. "Fashioning a business that's perpetually reinvented into a highly profitable, billion-dollar-plus, global enterprise is possible for only one reason: McKinsey *is* its talent. And unlike the average industrial firm, even in 1992, it understands that and acts accordingly," wrote Peters. "My point is not to extol McKinsey (where I hung out for seven years), but to consider it and other professional service firms as the ultimate 'knowledge players.' Wise car makers, transformer manufacturers, and chemical concerns must start mimicking the likes of McKinsey . . . Junior and senior staff at McKinsey spend loads of time on all aspects of nurturing talent, from recruiting to on-the-job development to courting alumni. Such effort is not seen as a distraction, but as the essence of the business."[256]

Returning to McKinsey, Peters talked to Bill Matassoni, who had done much to promote *In Search of Excellence*. McKinsey's reaction was, says Peters, generally positive. "McKinsey was never an institution, it was a collection of friends I developed over the years. Over *Liberation Management*, McKinsey people were nicer than I expected. We now have a positive relationship. McKinsey has got over its bitterness. I was good for them in some ways and vice versa."

In picking up on knowledge as a vital corporate resource, Peters was hardly original. The terminology of the knowledge worker had been around for a long time – since Peter Drucker's 1969 classic, *The Age of Discontinuity*. Where Peters *was* original was in exploring the full organizational ramifications of the rise of knowledge as the new capital of the working world.

The scale of the challenge, he argued was, more significant than many commentators acknowledged. Employing numbers of highly skilled, professional, knowledge workers keen to exploit their "employability" offered different challenges from those faced by managers 20 years ago. Yet again Peters' antennae were attuned. In the US, despite the downsizing epidemic, the numbers of managerial and professional workers has *increased* by 37 percent since the beginning of the 1980s. And, by the year 2000, it is estimated that the UK will have 10 million people who could be termed knowledge workers compared with 7 million manual workers.

Soon after *Liberation Management*, knowledge became a constant topic at managerial conferences and within books. Job titles included the magical "k" word often in the hope that it would rub off on the organization. The Swedish company, Skandia, even has a "director of intellectual capital." To Peters, the rise of knowledge as a source of competitive advantage put the final nail in the coffin of the corporate monoliths of *In Search of Excellence*.

Knowledge wasn't the only topic which Peters picked up on and welded into *Liberation Management*. The changing shape of organizations had been picked up by various writers in the preceding years. William Davidow and Michael Malone had explored *The Virtual Organization*. Speed had become an issue thanks to George Stalk and Thomas Hout of the Boston Consulting Group and their book *Competing Against Time*. The impact of technology on organizational structures had been explored by Harvard's Shoshana Zuboff in *The Age of the Smart Machine*. Rosabeth Moss Kanter had espoused the need for genuine empowerment in her book *When Giants Learn to Dance*. Peters took all of this and added the spice of life. His case study of CNN, for example, is one of the best pieces written on the company. It is genuinely vibrant and exciting. He accurately captures the fever pitch excitement of global news gathering.

Despite its frenzied writing style and inaccessible structure, *Liberation Management* has proved influential. As Peters says: "Business book after book is working over the companies in *Liberation Management*. It changed the dialog a little bit. People hadn't looked at those companies. If I had to stake my claim on one book it would be *Liberation Management*."

Indeed, no book is now complete without a fresh interpretation of ABB's remarkable performance under Percy Barnevik; GE's Jack Welch is feted and analyzed; CNN is examined and heads are shaken. At least when IBM was the premier corporate model you knew where you stood – Peters and Waterman certainly thought they did in *In Search of Excellence*. Now we have ABB, which has a structure that works exceptionally well but which few seem to understand (even if they work for ABB); GE, which appears to have been reinvented through the drive and imagination of a single individual (and one who has, against all the prevailing wisdom, spent decades with a single employer); and companies like CNN, which seem to be run like a High School without the discipline.

What is remarkable is that the same sources of inspiration are pored over time and time again with differing conclusions. Managers yearn for clear, unequivocal messages, but that is no longer what they receive. They are saturated with reports and books on creating the global organization but are still asking: what does it mean? When it comes to the huge international corporations detailed in case study after case study, our knowledge is extensive but highly fragmented.

Many of the companies covered in *Liberation Management* have become benchmarks of how to manage in the 1990s; Peters sees this as a vindication of the book. Companies are beginning to move to the *Liberation Management* rhythm. Traditional structures are being reappraised. The skills of management are shifting from hard to soft. Management has not exactly been liberated, but it has changed. Peters celebrated in characteristic manner – by ordering a new slide which read: Jack Welch 1 Tom Peters 0. "It was at the time Welch was unloading all his work-out stuff," says Peters. "The slide was the overarching logic of *Liberation Management*. Some McKinsey person said Peters was vindicated: Jack

Welch now sounds like Tom Peters." He did, but this probably says more about Tom Peters' ability to move with the times than it does about Jack Welch.

Discovering the World

Liberation Management was the first book from Peters to look beyond the US. During its research, Peters finally discovered the world. Given that he had served in Vietnam and traveled the world many times over, this was long overdue.

All of his previous books had been resolutely centered on the United States. (Peters wasn't the only one: Rosabeth Moss Kanter's *The Change Masters* relied solely on US examples; Robert Waterman has remained similarly American centered – his 1994 book was titled *What America Does Right*, though it was called *The Frontiers of Excellence* elsewhere in the world.) The research for *In Search of Excellence* had been in part commissioned by the German company Siemens, but the European companies were excised from the final selection of excellent companies. *A Passion for Excellence* carried on from there and *Thriving on Chaos* provided only a few examples from Europe and beyond. In contrast, *Liberation Management* overflowed with international examples. The new exemplars of the corporate world were companies such as the UK's Body Shop, the Swiss/Swedish Asea Brown Boveri, Brazil's Semco, and a host of smaller German businesses.

"As late as 1982, America's world view was that the sun rises over the East of America and sets over California. If you were born in 1942 it's not surprising that you have an Ameri-centric view of the world," says Peters. Often criticized for his studiously American view of the world, Peters holds his hands up. "Despite two tours in Vietnam, a stint as a US Navy midshipman on a British warship, and eight years' membership in a thoroughly international firm . . . McKinsey, I'm no internationalist – not by the standards of my Japanese, German, Swedish, and British friends. I go 'there' (wherever) a lot. But I don't stick with it and penetrate the surface. I blame a lot of that on my schooling and, frankly, my age; if you're in your late 40s, you grew up when America dominated the world. Why bother with outsiders? We aren't helped by our mother tongue either. Since much of the world speaks at least a little English, we don't have to work that hard when we do travel. "[257]

Though Peters prides himself on his curiosity, it seems he is curious up to a line somewhere around passport control. This appears at odds with his fundamental beliefs in asking questions and being people-oriented. "I think there are basic human values to do with organizing and managing people which are pretty universal. Intellectually, I believe in the global village," he says. "I have lived in Silicon Valley for virtually all my adult life. It is a cultural melting pot probably unmatched anywhere else in the world."

Even so, until the early 1990s, Peters remained a well-traveled middle-aged American rather than a confirmed internationalist, despite the international success of *In Search of Excellence* and his subsequent truly international career. "After *In Search of Excellence* I did a video training package which was incredibly successful. Air India said it was the first Hindu-based training program and I am a lapsed Presbyterian," says Peters. The book tapped into universal subjects – wherever Peters now goes, people tell him how awful the service is there – but managed to restrict its analyses to American companies.

This is largely a reflection of traditional prejudices. "American management was – and is – preeminent whether it is good, bad, or indifferent," says Lennart Arvedson, a Swede. Indeed, the entire history of management thinking – short as it is – is centered on America. American role models dominated through the 1950s, 1960s, and 1970s. It was simply a question of which part of the country they came from.

At the beginning of the century, managerial thinking was geographically located on the East coast of the United States, whether it was Chester Barnard (New Jersey), Mary Parker Follett

(Boston), or Frederick Taylor (Philadelphia). Peter Drucker's introduction to management theorizing was in New York.

Then the emphasis moved westwards to the great Ford plant at Highland Park. For half a century, managerial thinkers toyed with the ramifications of the new industrial reality. But they pondered from the safe havens of learning. Over the past two decades there has been a geographical shift from Detroit to Silicon Valley. Harvard may remain the benchmark, but it is places like the Santa Fe Institute which appear to be the future. Peter Drucker now lives in California.

Tom Peters has confessed to struggling with his seminars outside the US. "Though I worked with the English in McKinsey, it took me until the nineties to feel good when giving a seminar in London. Now I understand more of the nuances. I can tease the audience more. Outside the US and London I have never walked into a seminar without thinking: what am I doing here . . . I don't know shit?" He still regards working with a group of foreign executives as 20 times more demanding than working with his native audience. In the US his seminars are full of baseball parlance and Americanisms. Elsewhere, he has to watch the vernacular. When he works with American audiences, he can easily see when the pennies drop. In Europe he didn't know when this happened and often had to try different angles and approaches.

"The European context scared Tom a lot. We're back to the idea of preparation and feeling safe," says Michael Pieschewski. "What I saw all the time was that when he was talking about the US he felt safe and he relied on things he had read and studied, people he'd talked to. In Europe he realized that what happens in the UK is not applicable in Sweden or France. He couldn't take general views. The whole technique of his presentations is provocative. He is not saying 'maybe.' He is not reasoning. He is coming out with strong statements. When you see him at his best you see someone who has read and prepared a lot. He doesn't really improvise. He doesn't like to be caught unprepared. That is part of his personality." Performing in Europe was like being on a trapeze without the safety net.

Tom Peters' route to discovering life outside corporate America was in part uncovered by his work with the Tom Peters Group.

The European side of the company meant that Peters spent more time in Europe, and that brought him into contact with Lennart Arvedson of TPG Europe "who conned me into becoming an internationalist," Peters jokes. The five-year hiatus between *Thriving on Chaos* and *Liberation Management* saw Peters spending around seven weeks a year in Europe. "I felt an internationalist to an extent I hadn't before." Peters was introduced by Arvedson to a wide range of new friends and contacts

Soon after the fall of the Berlin Wall, Peters visited Germany. On New Year's Eve, 1989, the fast developing Euro-phile was among the crowds celebrating freedom at the newly opened Brandenburg Gate in Berlin. Later, in fall 1991, Peters gave a presentation in Dresden. Max Worcester translated as Peters spoke to an audience of East German students. He warned them against making the same mistakes as the West had made.

His German experience provided a wealth of material for *Liberation Management*. Key to his discovery of Europe was Peters' work on the German phenomenon of *mittelstands*. This came about through Frankfurt-based Worcester. "I was becoming a little annoyed that Tom thought that America was the only place companies could be successful," says Worcester. "I organized a series of meetings with people from mid-sized companies in Germany. We met for a weekend in a pub near Munich with six people around a table. I chaired the meeting and Tom took a back seat. He wrote and wrote for the two days only occasionally asking questions. He then made a film about the subject and wrote about it extensively."

The mittelstands are, Peters discovered, the driving force behind the German economy – indeed, 96 percent of German GDP comes from small and medium-sized companies. They became, in his eyes, the new exemplars, the models for the future. The man reared on big US corporations, found that smaller European enterprises were a new world. They struck a chord with the entire message of *Liberation Management*. "I think he got it right. He understood the *mittelstands*," says Worcester. "An economy built around lots and lots of minnows rather than a few dinosaurs is infinitely better."

The globalization of Peters was yet another sign of his

prescience. Once again he tapped into an emerging trend before it had really taken off. In this case, the big idea was globalization, and, yet again, it appears blindingly obvious in hindsight. By the early 1990s globalization had risen to the top of the business agenda. From a theoretical perspective the important works were by Harvard's Ted Levitt, and Sumantra Ghoshal and Christopher Bartlett's 1989 book, *Managing Across Borders*. Bartlett and Ghoshal argued that global competition was forcing many firms to shift to a new organizational model, which they called the transnational. This firm combined local responsiveness with global efficiency and the ability to transfer know-how – better, cheaper, and faster.

Now Peters looks to Europe, and increasingly to Asia, for inspiration. Others have followed suit. Rosabeth Moss Kanter has also globalized herself – her most recent book was entitled *World Class*. And the views the business thinkers have of the world are not only more global, but more objective. The unquestioning praise of Japanese management in the 1980s is unlikely to be repeated. Japan is now passé. Contemporary research is directed at Singapore (which now has a higher GDP per person than the United States) and the Tiger economies of Asia.

The *Liberation Management* research opened Peters' eyes to this new world of opportunity. But, rather than providing answers, it provided yet more questions. "I am surprised at my success outside the US. I don't know what's going on in Singapore or Thailand, but people read the books and go to the seminars. The catch-22 is that the more sensitive you become to cultural differences the more you realize how difficult it is to understand your own culture." Quite a catch.

Wow?

In the wake of a decidedly mixed reception to *Liberation Management*, Peters decided to move on to more of the same. Instead of turning down the already deafening volume, he cranked it up. His work has grown more strident, more down-to-earth, more folksy, more vernacular. He has become even more crusading and opinionated. Some argue that this strain has always been evident in his work: "Tom has always been polemic. There are shades of that in *In Search of Excellence*," observes Henry Mintzberg. Others shake their heads in disbelief as they are told that "The world is wackier than ever," "Crazy times call for crazy organizations," or that anything other than beer is "yeasty."

Yet, maybe Peters' flow of ideas has dried up. The books which followed *Liberation Management* have largely gone over much the same ground, using many of the same examples in a different way. (Peters, the reporter, is perhaps honing another journalistic skill – re-cycling material. "Tom is a brilliant packager. He is very good at drawing on the same material in different ways. Depending on who he is addressing, he can put different spins on the same stuff," notes Paul Cohen.)

Liberation Management took a lot out of Peters intellectually, emotionally, and physically. It was the book he invested the most time and the most of himself in. To some extent it left him spent, although, after *Liberation Management*, he still had two largely untapped areas of new material: his columns – only some of which had found their way into *Liberation Management* – and his seminars. These became increasingly barnstorming as Peters turned on the oral version of *Liberation Management*'s hypertext.

Peters decided he wanted to turn his seminars into a book and quickly, by his standards, came up with a manuscript. He then met with his agent and publisher and decided to do a series of paperback originals. *The Pursuit of Wow!* and *The Tom Peters Seminar* were the result. "The seminar book was exactly what it said it was. People asked for the slides. Post-*Liberation Management,* the seminar had evolved. It was tightened up," says Peters. "I was not writing a book, I simply had three or four days in my schedule. I sat in California with my slide projector and I re-gave the presentation from the slides. There was no thought about what it could become. I was smarting from the criticism of *Liberation Management*'s length. In the end *The Tom Peters Seminar* is to *Liberation Management* what *Thriving on Chaos* was to *In Search of Excellence.*"

While *The Tom Peters Seminar* basically presents a Peters seminar from early 1994, *The Pursuit of Wow!* is the book of Peters' columns. By 1994 he had amassed 450 and wanted to put them out together in a book. As Peters organized the columns into something readable and marketable, he dictated his seminar. Along the way he tinkered and edited, unable to totally revisit old material without revising it – in the end only 20 percent of *The Pursuit of Wow!* was actually column material.

Coincidentally, Peters came across Donna Carpenter of a company called Word Works. Carpenter wrote Peters saying she would like to work with him and the two met in Amherst, MA, before Peters gave a speech to the University of Massachusetts. Peters thought he would give Carpenter a try. The link up with Word Works marked something of a change in direction for Peters. Word Works specializes in ghost-writing business and management books. (Though not so in Peters' case – "I'm impervious to charges that I didn't write the books," he says.) The acknowledgments pages of business bestsellers show that Word Works has been involved in a large number of them over the past ten years. The names of the company's writers do not appear on the cover but Word Works is usually credited inside. Among those who thank Word Works for turning their ideas or manuscripts into readable English are Champy and Hammer, Treacy and Wiersma.

The typical Word Works author is an experienced speaker with a chronic inability to convert a brilliant seminar into prose or no time available to do so. Word Works outlines the potential chapters and then asks the "author" to give a presentation following the proposed structure. This maintains the person's voice. Drafts are then produced. The process usually involves dozens of drafts – 40 is not uncommon – though the drafts Peters hands over are usually only the fourth or fifth version. After anything from 90 days to 18 months, the bestseller is on the street.

For Word Works, Peters represented a different sort of challenge. He could write (like George Eliot on acid, but no matter) and his sales were still enormous. But the concept of the paperback originals was new ground for him. "The idea was kind of disposable books, something which was user-friendly. Tom said he had a manuscript," says Donna Carpenter, who had seen the editorial possibilities offered by *Liberation Management* but knew it was decidedly not user-friendly. "*Liberation Management* has lot of books inside one book – it could have been four different books it's so full of ideas. It is much easier to edit someone who has a lot of material, shaping and pruning it. From that point of view, Tom is the dream person."

The attraction for Peters of working with Word Works is summed up by *Inc.*'s Bo Burlingham: "After *Liberation Management* he didn't want to do any more books. Donna Carpenter said she would make it easy for him."

There was also the realization that *Liberation Management* had been marred by comparatively gentle editing – if cutting hundreds of pages can be called gentle. While it demanded a machete, it only received a gentle pruning. Word Works offered a more severe alternative. Their machetes were sharp. "Tom was extraordinarily responsive to changes. We made suggestions and notes on the script and returned it to him and he would respond. He likes being pushed and is not prickly at all. He likes the back and forth, the criticism," says Carpenter.

The two books to emerge through the Word Works process are as far removed from the serious world of *In Search of Excellence* as Peters is from Robert Waterman. "They are shallow and an anticlimax," says Max Worcester of *Frankfurter Allgemeine Zeitung*, reflecting a general view. While *Liberation Management* smacked of indulgence, *The Pursuit of Wow!* and *The Tom Peters Seminar* smacked of cashing in on the last vestiges of popularity. Reviewing *The Pursuit of Wow!* in *Fortune*, Andrew E. Seward noted that it was "Laced with *bon mots*, but many points are simply soothing bromides for upset managerial stomachs . . . this volume is really just a sort of *Reader's Digest* for the new management order."[258] Seward was particularly scathing of Peters' obsession with his farm in Vermont. "This is business-visionary-meets-gentleman-farmer stuff, and it ain't pretty," he wrote. There is some truth in this. *The Pursuit of Wow!* includes a picture of Peters' office on his farm as well as eulogies to Vermont farmers ("The average 'hick' in my neck of the woods is a crafty, multiskilled networker/trader/entrepreneur.").

While *Liberation Management* seriously considered the emergent organizational structures, its two bedfellows elevated fun and vibrancy to key issues. Peters appears on the cover of *The Tom Peters Seminar* bare legged, sporting orange shorts and a jacket and tie. (It is to be hoped that Marvin Bower never saw a copy.) "What has kept me awake at nights since writing *Liberation Management* in 1992 is the growing realization of how stale, dull, and boring most organizations are. And yet even our new theories of management steadfastly ignore the issues of creativity and zest. In fact, more than a few of today's theories actually imply strangling creativity and suppressing zest at a time when they've become the prime creators of economic value."[259]

What is notable in the two books is Peters' rediscovery of the world of design. The engineer returned. Word Works decided that Peters' slides looked dull so they brought in a designer, Ken Silvia, who had worked on *Inc.* "We wrote the last two drafts of *Seminar* and all of *Wow!* literally there with Ken in front of a huge terminal. It was on-line editing. We had the pages on the screen and there was a real sense of the importance of design. It was a kick. There was a whole different feel. Donna, Ken, and I thought we were inventing something," says Peters.

Part of the fun in *The Pursuit of Wow!* was a series of discussions with business people in which life and the universe were put to rights. "The idea of the question and answer sessions was for Tom to talk to potential buyers of the book and users of the material. I think they worked," says Donna Carpenter.

The discussions reveal more of Tom Peters than give insight into how to run a business. One of the round-table discussions, held during a single morning at the Museum of Science in Boston, featured entrepreneurs. The entrepreneurs had been rounded up by Peters' public relations firm. Bill Davis, CEO of Holland Mark Martin, was there. "He was very casual and exuded a great deal of confidence. To be honest, I think when our session began I was a bit awed by the man. Over the course of the next few hours my opinion of him changed. The first thing I noticed was that he was more comfortable talking than listening. Put another way, he spent a lot of time telling us what he thought," recalls Davis. "I think it was intended as a free-flowing session. I didn't get the impression that we were following a script of any sort. Sometime near the end of the session I remember forming the opinion that his 'gift' is assimilating other people's ideas, and then repackaging and merchandising them. Somewhere in the process, they come across as his own ideas."[260]

Another entrepreneur, Ben Cole, believes the end-result was misleading. "It was an open-ended discussion. It was very interesting but not seminal. I liked *The Pursuit of Wow!* but the fact that it's called 'Wow' gives the wrong impression. The meeting we had was not about wow. People think of themselves more seriously than that. It's no piece of cake. There are no simple solutions. It is about persistence and character."

Yet, fun had taken over. *The Pursuit of Wow!* and *The Tom Peters Seminar* are a world away from *In Search of Excellence*. While *In Search of Excellence* introduced a new language for management, in these two books the language ran wild. Peters has continued in much the same vein. A current slide of his reads:

Excellence!

Pretzel Crumb-less-ness

+

WOW!

It is little wonder that these books have led to suggestions that Peters is heading rapidly up an intellectual dead end. (Peters himself argues that the books were enjoyabale to write and that the medium was right for the times. More are planned.) The two softback originals were attractive books which added painfully little to the fund of ideas – that didn't prevent them selling moderately well, with sales way into six figures. However, what they said had already been said (mostly by Peters in *Liberation Management*). It is difficult to find anyone with a good word to say about them. Even Peters' strongest adherents appear dubious. While Peters preaches that more of the same is no longer good enough, *The Pursuit of Wow!* and *The Tom Peters Seminar* were more of the same, and not good enough.

NINE

UNCLE TOM'S CABIN

" In the end, one will be remembered for, at most, a couple of significant accomplishments"

Tom Peters[261]

December 1996, London

As Tom Peters enters the conference center, eyes turn. I am by his side but am ignored. The conference organizers from TPG Partners walk quickly over clutching their folders and their mobile phones. Their smiles would blind the unsuspecting. They freeze a little as they pass my way – when I last spoke to them they were studiously unhelpful and made no mention of the conference. The over-zealous protectors have now been transformed into beaming acolytes. Handshakes are exchanged. A journalist emerges from the side and catches Peters' attention. They exchange greetings. "I was supposed to see you at seven this morning," says the journalist. "Shit, sorry I knew there was something. I had it written down. Can we make some time at lunch?" The conference organizers exchange concerned glances, but keep on smiling. "You've got the FT for 15 minutes," says one. But Peters remains keen to accommodate, to be liked, to fit everything and everyone in. "Lunchtime then," he says, and heads off down a corridor into the bowels of the building.

Peters and the two conference organizers find the room – a kind of cross between a dressing room and a meeting room. There are comfortable chairs, a TV, a table and the constant whirr of air conditioning. It is not a room you would like to be in for very long.

Peters sits down, pours himself a glass of water and pulls his horn-rimmed glasses out. He is focused and has forgotten I am there. The organizers run through the people attending. Companies are sponsoring the event and bringing along their customers. As the organizers talk – "He wrote you a letter a few months back;" "You remember, she came last year" – Peters takes notes in his laborious left-handed writing. He checks on the pronunciation of a place name and wonders if he is over-dressed. He is in a suit with a pale blue striped shirt. The clothes he intended to wear – more casual – were muddied on a walk at the weekend. There is a story about a child buying one of his book's at an airport for his executive father. Peters roars with laughter and closes his pad.

While Peters has been checking on who they are, the audience has filed in to the massive auditorium to pick up their bright red "survival kits." The kits are a sign of what Peters has become – psychologists could make a lot of the contents. Inside are children's sweets, a stress ball, a child's sugary fruit drink, notepad, pen, and a copy of The Pursuit of Wow!

The stage is expansive and on either side are huge draped banners with pictures of Peters. The words Delight, Passion, Wow, Creative, Innovation, are splashed on the sides of the banners. The audience sits in corporate groups. One of the organizers approaches the podium and begins a nervous introduction. "Tom is in the middle of his usual relaxed few days in Europe – Amsterdam, Frankfurt, and London . . ." He finishes and Peters bounds on to the stage. He takes the man's hand and, in the manner of a politician, puts his spare hand on top. He gives the thumbs up sign. Then he is presented with a football shirt worn by a group of managers in the audience. Peters puts the shirt on (immediately winning over at least one part of the audience) and begins.

His opening is quiet, perhaps he is nervous. "I don't want to waste any time, we've a lot to get through today." He walks down the aisles with his zapper in his hand. He turns and presses. Slide one. There doesn't appear to be a plan. He talks around the slide on screen and zaps to the next.

He moves on to a joke about all the people at his seminars wearing lime green polyester golf trousers. He has been telling it for a few years and the audience love it, even though they have probably heard it before. Within two or three minutes he warms to his task. His words begin to flow. "You'd have to be an idiot not to realize that what we've been through is anything other than a prelude to what's next." He pauses. "How many of you have been to Asia in the last year?" A scattering of hands go up. Peters bellows. "Not enough. If you haven't been, you're not in touch with what is going on in the economy. Period." He puts his hands in his pockets, looks to the floor, and strides to the front of the audience. Next slide. "The nerds have won!" he proclaims.

Fickle Fame

Fifteen years on from *In Search of Excellence*, Tom Peters is still famous. He is still traveling, pontificating, talking. His energy levels remain off the normal human scale. His seminars are still packed to the rafters. Companies want to hear him. He still makes a lot of money. "He may have had his 15 minutes but he is still a global superstar in management education," says consultant and author Randall White.

Tom Peters' 15 minutes of fame weren't without their personal and emotional downside. He is now married for the fourth time. He has been through therapy (but then again he has lived in California for most of his adult life). The media have celebrated him and murdered him. He has received more barbs than most. Peters' 15 minutes have stretched into 15 years.

"It was a weird experience. The ultimate American experience. From being a black suited management consultant to having a double page spread in *People* magazine," he says. "Success can administer a beating and I really got beaten up by the *In Search of Excellence* experience. A lot of it in retrospect was very painful. It took me six years to get over it – though you never really get over anything. I am now coming out of my shell. It was a bewildering experience, a ridiculously distorting process. I'm glad it happened, but I would sooner be dropped into the ocean with a rock attached to me than go through it all again."

Most people's lives lack a defining moment. Instead, the moments blur into something life-changing; evolution rather than dramatic revolution. Fame can be sad: witness former sports heroes on the seminar circuit reliving old glories, or writers who have struck gold with their first novel struggling through one poor-selling sequel after another. But, only the famous can bewail the effects of fame on their lives. The rest can only guess at what it is like to have people hanging on your every word, or the media knocking at the door.

The effect of all this on Tom Peters is difficult to gauge. I have spent time with him, been out for dinner, gone to early morning meetings to fit into his crazy schedule, driven to the dry cleaners with him. He is candid, willing to venture opinions, keen to talk. He is easy to like. He is charismatic, but he gives little away. "I'm afraid Tom isn't having as much fun as he once did. I think he's not as open with people as he was except for those very close to him," says his former business partner, Bob Le Duc. "It is not surprising that this whirlwind of fame has taken its personal toll, though he has stood up to it reasonably well. I think he loved it and hated it. I'm glad I didn't go through it."

Perhaps the inevitable result of fame is that you withdraw into yourself, you erect barriers, create a veneer. It is the art of self-preservation, an art Tom Peters has had to learn. He is personable, but somehow not personal. In all the time I spent with him, he never asked a question about me or about the project I was involved in. He was happy to talk and give me his time, but didn't want to know any more. There was no small talk, no establishing of ground rules, no curiosity. There appeared to be some kind of unexplained contract of trust. It was unusual and a little disconcerting, but refreshing too – better that the veneer of friendship many others insist on creating or the insincere bullshit you usually have to put up with. Most people want to know what you intend to write, where and when it will appear, what kind of questions you are going to ask. Surely, I thought, he would want to know who else I was planning to talk to or more about the publishers of the book? His lack of interest was revealing. It was child-like – taking things as they are without questioning, wanting to be liked, intuitively placing trust.

This may be part of the survival instinct the famous develop. With all the distractions – the media clamoring, the hangers on, the clients, the publishers – how do you cut out the crap to stay focused on what you are actually doing? Tom Peters does so by closing out the peripheral worlds.

The man remains aloof to survive. Somewhere along his rollercoaster ride, corporate man became the corporate skunk, an all-round business luminary, with a syndicated column, boisterous seminars, and regular TV appearances. The same man became undeniably different, shaped by public demand. "I am curious about Tom's inner voyage. He has traveled another journey; one he hasn't yet written about," says Sven Atterhed.

And yet, to those who know him, Peters remains much the same. "For the life of me I can't remember exactly when I met Tom; would have been early eighties. In any case, it was before *In Search of Excellence* and before he was famous. What I do remember vividly was that he seemed to be the incarnation of his ideas: audacious, spunky, unafraid, passionate, imaginative, and, most of all, generous. Very generous: always crediting other peoples' work and citing them, and, more importantly, generous with his ideas," says Warren Bennis. "Two Yiddish words summarize Tom for me: *chutzpah* and *mensch*. I don't know exactly how to define them. Chutzpah [is] that quality of boldness and insouciance that animates his work. The second is somewhat harder to define, but, like pornography, you know it when you see it. It's got to do with bigness of spirit and decency. A person of consequence."[262]

Despite such eulogies, Peters is uncomfortable. "I'm aging and fretting about my own legacy," Peters wrote in 1995.[263] He uses a quote from William James in his seminars: "The deepest principle in human nature is the craving to be appreciated." Peters is probably right to fret. Rarely has one person divided business opinion so obviously. Debate about a person's particular contribution to a field of knowledge usually begins after their death. Peters enjoys no such privilege.

Daniel Carroll, his long-time arch-critic, continues to argue that Peters has sold himself short. "He is making a lot of money. Perhaps that has become more important. I believe he is capable of doing significant research on executive behavior in a more profound way. He has access to a lot of people and organizations which academics do not," he says. "I've seen Tom since [my review of *In Search of Excellence*]. He is a good man. You can't dislike someone who is a liberal and likes Mozart."

The charge against Peters is that although he has raised awareness, he has done so in a superficial way. He has pandered to the masses. Though his messages are hard, they are overly adorned with empty phrase-making – "yesterday's behemoths are out of step with tomorrow's madcap marketplace"[264] – and with insufficient attention to the details of implementation. Managers know they need to keep abreast of the latest thinking, but what they would like is a one-page fax with the latest phrase. Peters' critics suggest that the one-page fax is exactly what Peters is delivering.

There isn't much middle ground in people's reactions to Peters. His friends are bubbling with enthusiasm; his enemies seething with indignation. Herb Kelleher of Southwest Airlines is a long-time supporter. "Tom, to my mind, is a seminal, sage and vatic thinker who, like Einstein, is continually open, learning, growing and changing. No one, in my opinion, has had a greater impact on the way people in the US today manage and think about management," says Kelleher. "He is truly a liberator in overthrowing the traditional mechanistic, bureaucratic, hierarchical, purely quantitative approach to management. He has shown how to unleash the power, potential, and spirit of people in order to achieve true excellence as a matter of substance, not merely form."[265]

Former McKinsey consultant Andrew Campbell recalls: "He was always full of enthusiasm, all arms and legs. His books are the same: gloriously enthusiastic and sane. He will go down as a monumental influence on the second half of the twentieth century."

The plaudits go on. "There is no question that his work has had an extraordinarily high impact. He has helped create a high awareness among an entire generation of management in the US about shortcomings in flexibility, customer orientation, innovation, and action as opposed to mere analysis," says James Brian Quinn. "Tom was and could be a superb academic, if he chose to be. He is an outstanding lecturer and consultant. His most profound impacts have been in moving managers away from their rigid analytical techniques and toward structured, but more human-oriented organizational and managerial solutions. Tom's impact has been international, not just in the US. Because he is dealing with real people and real problems, he is constantly fresh. I have never heard Tom make two presentations in a row that sounded like each other. He adapts to his audience and challenges that audience in ways that very few people can."[266]

Like any human being, Tom Peters delights in the plaudits. But he knows that there can only be one real measure of his success or failure. Peters would like to be appraised against his ideas. "We are all abstractionists," he says. In the late 1990s, ideas are valuable currency, both personally and organizationally. "I'm a reasonably good student of the epistemology of ideas and it has to get into the language to some extent, Quality is now in the language. If you're talking about really big ideas then it'll take 20, 30, or 40 years to have an impact," he says. "Be patient" is his message – the jury is out.

The mistake, as he sees it, is regarding popularity as the measure of his success. And yet, no-one has courted popularity more assiduously. Peters may say uncomfortable things, but he is a crowd pleaser whose impact is measured by the ringing endorsement of applause. Once again there is a split. The introspective Peters wants to be measured against the impact and longevity of his ideas. The extrovert courts the short-term satisfaction of applause.

Adulation obstructs introspection. Asked to appraise his contribution, some suggest he is more of a motivational writer and speaker than a scholar. And then, there is the applause. His popularity speaks for itself. Yet popularity explains nothing.

Tom Peters still believes there is something to prove. Why else carry on? "He overworks, but he doesn't see it that way. I fear he will die young, but then I live a quieter life. He's loud, boisterous, articulate, informal, and brilliant," says Harold Leavitt.[267] Yet, Peters is unsure about what he has achieved and even more unsure as to why. "The big question is not how he became what he has, but why him?" said an envious consultant. It is a question Peters has probably asked himself many times: "Why me?"

Leaping Into the Unknown

The answer to the question "why me" provides the source of much of his discomfort. Peters' transformation from unknown consultant to famous guru could be attributed entirely to luck. His timing has always proved impeccable. With *In Search of Excellence* he certainly got lucky – and admits as much. But his luck has continued to the extent where you begin to question whether it is luck at all.

Peters' antennae to management trends and issues provide the key to his success. *In Search of Excellence* touched a nerve because the timing was right. *Thriving on Chaos* did much the same and *Liberation Management* anticipated many of the corporate preoccupations of the nineties. If it is a run of luck, it is a long one.

Peters' skill is intuitive. He can get under the skin of an organization without really thinking what he is doing. "He has the most remarkable lens which enables him to see things on his terms," says Don Laurie. "I thought I knew a lot about customers. After a while with Tom he, said 'You've almost got it.' He was right. His great strength is his remarkable ability to see everything through the eyes of the customer." Peters cuts away the peripherals and gets down to the core.

Once again, this makes him uncomfortable. An engineer by training, he wants to make sense of things, discover patterns. In a business sense he achieves this. He picks things up and makes them fit, even if the pattern is ever more random. The problem is he does not know *how* he does it, and, in the end, he wants to know. He wants to understand.

People who have a gift are usually very poor at analyzing what that gift is and how it works. Ask Michael Jordan how he manages to hang in the air longer than anyone else and it is unlikely he could tell you. (Ask him why he couldn't hack it as a baseball player and he will tell you exactly why.) Peters is no exception. Trying to make sense of "a gift," an intuitive knack of picking up shreds of evidence, is an impossible task and one more likely to lead you to question your sanity than provide sane explanations.

Of course, Peters is not alone. Management and leadership (and life) have always relied on the inexplicable, the feeling that a decision is right or wrong, an instinctive judgment of someone's personality or likely next move. "Once I have a feeling for the choices, I have no problems with the decisions," says IBM chief, Lou Gerstner.[268] Or take this description of Michael Eisner by Barry Diller, formerly Eisner's boss at ABC and Paramount: "Michael looks like Goofy, and he often acts like Goofy, and he's definitely in the body of Goofy! But he's got one of the most smartly spirited minds that I've ever come across. You can see the electrical charges moving from one point to another in his brain. Spectacular instincts. Of course, he's not always right, and when it comes to that he has a somewhat tractionless memory."[269]

The world of Gerstner and Eisner is also that of Tom Peters. It is the world of spectacular instincts. Such instincts are meaningless unless they are backed by an unwavering commitment that, one way or another, you are right. Following your antennae is a leap into the unknown. If you don't have commitment to something – or someone – it is a leap into a vacuum. The sensible advice is don't jump. It takes belief or arrogance to back your intuition. Peters – like anyone on a public platform – requires the foundation of belief to survive and the arrogance to say it out loud.

"Too many consultants are superficial about the big things and detailed on the little things. Tom is superficial on the small things but very solid on the big things," says Wickham Skinner. "The really outstanding thing about Tom is that he has an emotional fervor that centers around the ultimate moral responsibility of top managers for the success of their enterprise as well as the thousands of people dependent on them.

"We used to teach seminars together and we felt the same way. Too many CEOs had become imperial fiefdoms in their own comforts, status and cashing in on the benefits of their position. They had lost a sense of responsibility for the enormous powers that they had. Tom was fervent, like a good minister. He was in a rage that people could be so lazy and almost corrupt in not living up to the trust placed in them. It centered around a failure to question and search and dig into the central problems of their companies."

Peters believes that power is a privilege and the privilege can only be earned by treating people humanely. In Vietnam he saw for himself the moral redundancy of a strategy based on counting bodybags. During his time at Stanford, he fell under the influence of Gene Webb's brand of libertarian intellectual rigor. At McKinsey he slowly realized the deficiencies of management by dictatorship and bureaucracy. In the years since, the strand that runs through his work is outrage with the systems which constrain human potential ("Workers in the United Sates – and even more so in England – have been treated like dog food for the past 150 years. In fact, such treatment forms the bedrock logic of the Industrial Revolution: Forget craft. Specialize jobs to the point any idiot can perform them"[270]) and those who run them ("Bosses are clearly the chief source of our troubles . . . I attack bosses for a living!"[271]).

In a 1995 BBC television program on, of all things, religion, Peters indulged in a rare burst of self-analysis, which surprised even himself. (On religion, Peters says: "I would like to think there is something out there but it is not a major part of my life."[272] He professed that his career was a reaction against the McNamarian-rational-bodycount approach to life and work. "The dignity of human beings is what religions have in common and that is a world away from the sterile McNamarian style of management. The human condition has at least as many commonalities as differences."

Is Peters a man with a mission? Though he possesses missionary zeal, that does not necessarily mean his life is driven by a single obsession. In fact, there is a lack of obsession in his work. He is willing to be taken by the moment and steered in new directions. If his slides don't work, he throws them away.

When the opportunity arose for him to move beyond the confines of the managerial world, he shied away. In the late eighties he considered moving into politics. A congressional seat opened up in his Californian district representing both Stanford and Silicon Valley. "We had a long-term Congressman who left to run for Senate. Both Republican and Democrat nominations were up for grabs. I started to talk about it with some friends and then they began taking it seriously. My name recognition was high so I could have had a great shot but wimped out. I pulled out late. I decided I was too old to be a freshman," says Peters. There are numerous other reasons Peters puts forward for his refusal to move into politics. The thought of being one of 435 members did not appeal; business people do not thrive in politics; the relentless traveling to and from DC was a daunting prospect; and he did not relish the loss of privacy. The Republicans won.

Prior to this Peters was active in the Dukakis Presidential campaign – when the betting was that another guru, Rosabeth Moss Kanter, would get a cabinet position. After Bill Clinton's first Presidential victory a caller on a phone-in to the KRON radio station in San Francisco suggested Peters for Secretary of Labor – "I was highly amused," he says. He was subsequently "somewhat involved" in Vice-President Gore's "Reinventing government" initiative during the first Clinton administration.

Despite such political involvement, Peters has not taken the bait. He would be an adept speech maker and campaigner, but politics is high profile, low impact. "I'm a blowhard in public and a wimp in private. I tend to compromise too much in private," says Peters in explanation of his unwillingness to test the political waters. Perhaps the best way of interpreting this is that Peters didn't feel the need to narrow down his basic beliefs. He is more comfortable with a broad-ranging, loosely defined mission than a politically limited one and believes what he does now can have a greater impact.

In his autobiography, *Adventures of a Bystander*, Peter Drucker writes: "The single-minded ones, the monomaniacs, are the only true achievers. The rest, the ones like me, may have more fun; but they fritter themselves away. The monomaniacs carry out a 'mission;' the rest of us have 'interests.' Whenever anything is being accomplished, it is being done . . . by a monomaniac with a mission."

Though he admits that he has "always been rather singularly focused," Tom Peters is no monomaniac. "I'm one of those pathetic souls who doesn't have stamp collecting or gardening to retire to. Reading is my only real hobby. I envy people with interests. I would like to be totally taken with a passion." It is ironic that a man who appears so passionate on stage should crave an all-consuming passion (though he does collect baseball caps).

Without a narrowly defined mission, Peters has moved with the times and been condemned for doing so. "I've been beaten up by journalists about my mission. My mission is to amuse myself. This year I am involved in starting a textile company." To the world at large this is interpreted as the height of arrogance. Few would admit to a mission solely to amuse themselves.

Elsewhere, Peters has ascribed his continuing quest as one driven by curiosity. Indeed, he would steal Warren Bennis' chosen epitaph: "He was curious to the end."[273] "Being curious to the end is the ultimate religious act," he says.

Curiosity, the great act of questioning, is what Peters learned from Gene Webb. "My obsession is stirring the human imagination," he says. "Today's marketplace calls for zesty responses from bankers, metal-benders, and software creators alike. Yet most of our companies seem to be purposefully designed to stamp out curiosity and imagination."[274]

To the Tom Peters of the late 1990s, curiosity is all. It is only through curiosity that you learn anything. "Tom is a great reporter of where success is as the world changes. He puts a spin on it so people listen," says Robert Buckman. "He carries on because he learns something. All of us who care about whether things move forward is looking for a better idea. He cares if things move forward. It is nothing to do with wealth. He was like that when he was poor and he's like that now he's rich. That's just the way he is, a fountain of ideas."

What is unique about Tom Peters is that the apparently

indiscriminate fountain has followed prescribed channels. The journey of Tom Peters from corporate man to corporate skunk mirrors the development of management over the past 20 years. Peters has gone with the flow as the nature of management has changed. It is just that he has sometimes been ahead of the pack. "Tom is clearly a unique character, so I'm not sure any institution he may build will carry on beyond him. In this age of impermanence, though, so what?" says Stanford's Harold Leavitt. "His ideas will last, if for no other reason than that they are consonant with the flow of managerial history. Tom's thoughts just move a little faster and his charisma injects them into many managers."[275]

Peters is adept at picking up a scent and then following it. His philosophy is summed up by Jack Welch's comment on the GE way: "Here at head office, we don't go very deep into much of anything, but we have a smell of everything. Our job is capital allocation – intellectual and financial. Smell, feel, touch, listen, then allocate. Make bets, with people and dollars. And make mistakes."[276] (Welch, too, has favorable things to say about Peters: "Obviously I, like most in the business community, have been enormously impressed by Tom's work. His justifiable irreverence really did put the profession of business in its proper perspective."[277])

Peters follows his senses. Few other management thinkers have been willing to change course or shift perspectives so easily or dramatically. They are left behind – fitting their passion or theory into a new environment where it simply does not fit. The only one who has somehow kept abreast of the relentless flow is Peter Drucker. Drucker changed the language. He made management something to talk about and placed it center stage. "In my secret prideful self, Drucker and me are uncategorizable," says Peters. "We are of the same sort. He and I get fascinated by things. We are enthusiasts who get to play with interesting things. I love being asked to write things by computer and marketing magazines."

Warren Bennis provides a comparison: "What's Tom contribution to management thought? I suppose the most significant contribution is his capacity to articulate in graphic and persuasive terms what it is that organizations and managers must do if they want to create successful human communities (and also make a profit). He put into words what a lot of people had been talking about but never took all that seriously. And he writes with unbridled lucidity. He goosed us all, managers and academics alike.

"His other major contribution is a bit more subtle, but no less important, I think. I can best put it this way: if Peter Drucker invented management, Tom Peters vivified it and yes, popularized it and legitimized it as a worthy endeavor."[278]

Going with the flow has demanded shifts in direction. In Peters' case – partly because of his high public profile – these have been loud and dramatic. He was not the only thinker who in the 1980s turned his attentions away from large to small companies. He wasn't alone, but he was the loudest. Academics throughout the world traveled a similar road but through the quieter corridors of academia rather than in front of large audiences with the press gallery filled.

Things change. What's best now is not best tomorrow. Peters named his boat *The Cromwell* inspired by Cromwell's comment "No one rises so high as he who knows not whither he is going." This is an apt description of the development of Peters' career. Everything changes and, if you move with the times, you have to be prepared to change even if you don't know where you are going.

In Peters' early career, until the *In Search of Excellence* research, management was tangible (or so he and executives were led to believe). And, when it wasn't, managers tried their damnedest to make it so. They produced reports, budgets, strategic plans, memos, directives, rules, and minutes. Peters the MBA student and McKinsey consultant was part of this world. *In Search of Excellence* embraced corporate giants. He belonged.

During the 1980s and 1990s, corporate reality has shifted. Managerial life is no longer so straightforward. Dependable at what? Loyal to whom? The decisions are bigger, the information more complex and the time-scales shorter. Peters has subsumed all of this. "It is not a good time to be a 54-year-old white collar worker in a *Fortune* 200 company," reflects Peters. "People have seen enough bloodshed around them to begin to realize they have to face hard choices. Generation X has a different perspective.

They don't want to work for GE for life. They have a lot more malleability."

There is a sense that, emotionally and intellectually, Peters is now approaching the crunch. He has mapped out the corporate world; charted its deficiencies and excesses; and celebrated its successes. He has shocked and provoked. But what next? Where is the new insight? And, if the medium is the message, how much further can the Tom Peters show go?

Peters has contemplated a sabbatical, but rejected the notion. Once you step off the merry-go-round it is difficult to get back on. He has considered developing his work in television but dislikes the idea of being in a studio every week for a few years.

In an article celebrating the tenth anniversary of *In Search of Excellence,* Peters reflected on what he had learned. He came up with a list of 13 points:

1. Unintended consequences outnumber intended consequences.
2. Certainty is a delusion.
3. Fiction beats non-fiction.
4. Success begets failure.
5. Democracy and markets are untidy, but effective.
6. Try it.
7. Vermont farmers have a lot to teach us.
8. Lighten up.
9. Neckties are diabolical.
10. Smile if it kills you.
11. Each day is a miracle.
12. Beware true believers.
13. Reject simple explanations.[279]

Such a list is characteristic of Peters. It embraces cod spirituality, skepticism, curiosity, opinion, and homely truths. It is as unhelpful as any other list on things to do and not to do. Perhaps the key is number 12: Beware true believers.

Since this list was written, six years have passed. Peters has changed. He has a host of believers. Now, he is in search of belief. In a hotel room in Atlanta after a seminar, he went down to the hotel shop and bought index cards and wrote the 125 things he believed in. Belief is everything. But belief in what?

Some of his audience and some of his friends believe that his fire has gone out. "I think to a degree he has failed his followers. He has not kept up his own development," says Jan Lapidoth, going on to ask: "Why does a king continue to be a king? Why doesn't he abdicate? Perhaps it is because there is no crown prince." Has he gone off the boil? Is he now merely reciting his lines. Watching Peters on stage, it is difficult to believe so. The fire is there, but Peters' beliefs have turned in on themselves. He may not want to write a Covey-style self-help book but, increasingly, he realizes that a lot depends on the self-motivation of individuals to break out. In the end there is the individual.

Tom Peters has discovered that what he believes in is the most elusive thing of all: his own gift, his spectacular instincts. He is an outstanding speaker. Of that, at least, there is no doubt. In the age of technology – an age he pronounces with ever greater enthusiasm – he has mastered the very human art of persuasion. "A shrink spent a year telling me that I have a gift and should use it. I am obviously good at what I do. I am turned on by people but I'm also reclusive. I feel a real personal connection with the people I'm talking to and I have the ability to connect with individuals in large audiences. I have a gift to communicate which is not taught."

But why carry on traveling the world at breakneck speed? What is there to prove? "I do it because I enjoy it, presumably. I find the seminars totally exhilarating. I used to say I didn't like it but it's like the sweet spot on a tennis racket. I get lost in seminars and in editing. Sometimes I edit and just sit still for five or six hours. Though I love the seminars, I hate the logistics. I'm doing 70 or more speeches a year so that's 140 days in an airport. Then again, it's not exactly the worst life in the world."

Tom Peters has realized what he is good at and what he enjoys. "I reckon he is now more optimistic," says *Inc.*'s Bo Burlingham. "He has decided he likes doing his seminars and that's the first time he said he was doing something because he liked doing it. Perhaps he feels more in control. He seems calmer, more settled." The corporate man has come to terms with the corporate skunk.

June 1996, Vermont

Tom Peters has gone back to nature. His home is in the affluent, maple syrup world of Vermont, a place where reclusive novelists hang out counting their royalties or awaiting inspiration; where well-paid corporate executives go for the weekend; and where tourists drive the heritage trail . The nearest airport is Albany, over an hour's drive away. From there it is another 45 minutes on a 16-seater to Boston's international airport. A man who spends so much time on planes lives far from an airport.

As I drive, the roads are quiet. Passing drivers give me a wave. There is a turtle on the highway.

The Peters home is hard to find. You have to be careful you don't take the wrong turn and end up on a dirt track leading nowhere. Eventually I reach a small wooden sign with a number and take the turning. I pass a couple of small places and carry on along a tree-lined road. Then I emerge from the trees and see Peters' farm. The house itself is not enormous, just like the thousands of others I passed on the way through the quiet Vermont towns. It is white and wooden, nothing outstanding. All is quiet.

There is a marvelous view down into the valley and beyond that there is forest. In the field is a spectacular modern sculpture featuring huge pieces of slate dangling from a metal construction. The wind gusts down the valley. Such is its power that it managed to break one of the huge pieces of slate in two. There is a lake with no fish since they were taken by some children.

Peters' office is a few yards down a hill from his home. His office has a kitchen and comfortable chairs. Downstairs there is a bedroom. It hardly feels like an office at all. More of a summer house. There are discarded clothes on the floor and two dogs mooch around. Climbing the wooden stairs, I pass a signed copy of The Beatles' Sergeant Pepper album cover, and enter Peters' bright writing room. There is a huge handmade desk in the middle and beautifully straight jurors' chairs. Along the walls are piles of business books. It is dusty, with a lived in feel and a musty smell of dogs. It is comfortable without being comforting; functional rather than personal. On the wall there is a poster promoting a Peters seminar somewhere in the Far East.

Tom Peters sits in one of the comfortable chairs. He moves his hands as he speaks and looks me in the eye. He stretches his legs, then alters his position again. All the time he is talking. He can turn it on like electricity. He turns it on.

When he is talking, in full flow, he cannot be stopped. He looks slightly irritated when I step into the flow. It is as if I don't really understand. That's what he does and what he does well. Why am I getting in the way? And then there is silence. I talk a little and then he revs back to life. It is like taking time out to draw breath.

The phone rings. He doesn't like phones. It is not so immediate, so personal, so physical. He talks in the same way, pausing only occasionally. He sits down again and stretches. His voice is rhythmical, full of life. He swears like he's just come out of the Navy, but that was over quarter of a century ago. He laughs as he remembers. He tells stories. Later, he turns off. It must be draining investing so much into what you say.

We drive into town. Peters is known around here. He chats in the deli. Convivial, he is a regular guy, plain Tom. Untidy, but he doesn't care. Or doesn't appear to care.

Bibliography

Books by Tom Peters

In Search of Excellence: Lessons from America's Best-run Companies (with Robert H. Waterman Jr.), Harper & Row, New York, 1982.

A Passion for Excellence: The Leadership Difference (with Nancy Austin), HarperCollins, New York, 1985.

Thriving on Chaos: Handbook for a Management Revolution, Alfred A. Knopf, New York, 1987.

Excellence in the Organization (with Robert Townsend), Nightingale-Conant, New York, 1988.

Liberation Management, Alfred A. Knopf, New York, 1992.

The Tom Peters Seminar: Crazy Times Call for Crazy Organizations, Vintage Books, New York, 1994.

The Pursuit of Wow! Every Person's Guide to Topsy-Turvy Times, Vintage Books, New York, 1994.

Related Books

Crainer, Stuart, *The Ultimate Business Library*, Capstone Publishing, Oxford, 1997.

Kleiner, Art, *The Age of Heretics*, Doubleday, New York, 1996.

Micklethwait, John, & Wooldridge, Adrian, *Witch Doctors*, Heinemann, London, 1996.

Pascale, Richard, & Athos, Anthony, *The Art of Japanese Management*, Simon & Schuster, New York, 1981.

Pascale, Richard, *Managing on the Edge*, Viking Books, New York, 1990.

Shapiro, Eileen, *Fad Surfing*, Capstone Publishing, Oxford, 1996.

Vicere, Albert, & Fulmer, Robert, *Crafting Competitiveness*, Capstone Publishing, Oxford, 1996.

Waterman, Robert, *The Frontiers of Excellence*, Nicholas Brealey, London, 1994.

Waterman, Robert, *The Renewal Factor*, Bantam, New York, 1987.

Selected Articles by Tom Peters

"Leadership: sad facts and silver linings," *Harvard Business Review*, November/December 1979. (*McKinsey Quarterly*, Spring 1980.)

"Structure is not organization" (with Robert Waterman and Julien Phillips), *Business Horizons*, June 1980.

"Putting excellence into management," *BusinessWeek*, July 21, 1980.

"Management systems: the language of organizational character and competence," *Organizational Dynamics*, Summer 1980.

"Mastering the language of management systems," *McKinsey Quarterly*, Spring 1981.

"Beyond the rational model" (with Waterman), *McKinsey Quarterly*, Spring 1983.

Foreword to *Transforming the Workplace*, John Nora, O. Raymond Rogers & Robert Stramy, Princeton Research Press, Princeton, New Jersey, 1985.

"The destruction of hierarchy," *Industry Week*, August 15, 1988.

"Tomorrow's companies," *The Economist*, March 4, 1989

"Just say no to US memories," Testimony presented to the Judiciary Committee on Economic and Trade Law, US House of Representatives, September 28, 1989.

"Prometheus barely unbound," *Academy of Management Executive*, Vol. 4, No 4, 1990.

"The boundaries of business: partners – the rhetoric and reality," *Harvard Business Review*, September/October 1991.

"War and humanity," Foreword to the *National Performance Review*, September 15, 1993.

Notes

Apart from the published sources listed below, all of the quotes in this biography of Tom Peters are from interviews conducted by the author.

One: The Birth of Excellence

1. Cannon, Tom, *The Guinness Book of Business Records*, Guinness Publishing, London, 1996, p. 92.
2. "A mess of parables," *The Economist*, December 5, 1992.
3. The Tom Peters Seminar, conference notes, December 1996.
4. Peters, Tom, "The legacies we leave," syndicated column, January 6, 1995.
5. Siegal & Gale/Roper Strach Worldwide, *Report on American Business Executives*, January 1996.
6. Peters, Thomas J. & Waterman, Robert H., *In Search of Excellence*, Harper & Row, New York, 1982, p. 12.
7. Peters, Tom, "Power," syndicated column, July 22, 1994.
8. Waterman declined to be interviewed for this book, explaining: "Tom and I are very close friends and my talking about Tom for publication seems to me to infringe on our relationship and trust built up over the years."
9. Peters, Tom, "Pyramids and pebbles," syndicated column, February 25, 1994.
10. Ibid.
11. Correspondence with author.
12. Kleiner, Art, *The Age of Heretics*, Doubleday, New York, 1996, p. 331.

13. Pascale, Richard, & Athos, Anthony, *The Art of Japanese Management,* Simon & Schuster, New York, 1981, p. xix.
14. Ibid.
15. Peters & Waterman, *In Search of Excellence,* p. 9.
16. Peters, Thomas J., Waterman, Robert H. & Phillips, Julien, "Structure is not organization," *Business Horizons,* June 1980.
17. Correspondence with author.
18. Daniel, Ron, Introduction to Pascale & Athos, *The Art of Japanese Management.*
19. Mills, D. Quinn, *Rebirth of the Corporation,* John Wiley, New York, 1991.
20. Peters & Waterman, *In Search of Excellence,* p. 13.
21. Peters, Tom, "School reform: starting at the beginning," February 1990.
22. Peters, Thomas J., "Putting excellence into management," *Business-Week,* July 21, 1980.
23. Correspondence with author.
24. Peters, "Putting excellence into management."

Two: The Bestseller

25. Quoted in Kleiner, Art, *The Age of Heretics,* Doubleday, New York, 1996.
26. Quoted in Clutterbuck, David, & Crainer, Stuart, *Makers of Management,* Macmillan, London, 1990.
27. Kiechel, Walter, "Management winners," *Fortune,* November 29, 1982.
28. Waterman, Robert, & Young, Lewis, "Speaking of excellence," *McKinsey Quarterly,* Winter 1984.
29. Crainer, Stuart, *The Ultimate Business Library,* Capstone Publishing, Oxford, 1996.
30. Peters, Thomas J. & Waterman, Robert H., *In Search of Excellence,* Harper & Row, New York, 1982, p. xxv.
31. Hayes, Robert, & Abernathy, William, "Managing our way to economic decline," *Harvard Business Review,* July/August 1980.
32. Pascale, Richard, & Athos, Anthony, *The Art of Japanese Management,* Simon & Schuster, New York, 1981.
33. Ibid.
34. Peters & Waterman, *In Search of Excellence,* p. xxiv.

35. Peters, Tom, & Austin, Nancy, *A Passion for Excellence,* Harper-Collins, New York, 1985, p. xi.
36. Peters & Waterman, *In Search of Excellence,* p. xxii.
37. Ibid., p. 17.
38. Ibid., p. 197.
39. Drucker, Peter F., *Concept of the Corporation,* John Day, New York, 1972.
40. Peters, Tom, "School reform: starting at the beginning," February 1990.
41. Townsend, Robert, *Up the Organization,* Michael Joseph, London, 1970.
42. Peters, Tom, & Townsend, Robert, *Excellence in the Organization,* Nightingale-Conant, Chicago, 1988.
43. Peters & Waterman, *In Search of Excellence,* p. 164.
44. Ibid., p. 324.
45. Peters, Tom, "The (continuing) perils of professional management," syndicated column, December 30, 1994.
46. Peters, Tom, "Pyramids and pebbles," syndicated column, February 25, 1994.
47. Peters & Waterman, *In Search of Excellence,* p. 134.
48. Peters, Tom, "Ten years later," syndicated column, September 3, 1992.
49. Peters & Waterman *In Search of Excellence,* p. 156.
50. Peters & Austin, *A Passion for Excellence,* p. 404.
51. Peters & Waterman, *In Search of Excellence,* p. 252.
52. Ibid., p. 241.
53. Ibid., p. 63.
54. Taylor, Frederick W., *The Principles of Scientific Management,* Harper & Row, New York, 1913.
55. Ford, Henry, *My Life and Work,* Doubleday, Page & Co., New York, 1923.
56. Peters & Waterman, *In Search of Excellence.*
57. Weber, Max, *The Theory of Social and Economic Organisation,* Oxford University Press, New York, 1947.
58. Waterman & Young, "Speaking of excellence."
59. Peters, Tom, *Liberation Management,* Alfred A. Knopf, New York, 1992, p. xxix.
60. Peters & Waterman *In Search of Excellence,* p. xxiv.
61. Ibid., pp. 53–54.
62. Ibid., p. 75.
63. Peters, *Liberation Management,* p. xxxii.

64. Peters, "Ten years later."

65. Peters & Waterman, *In Search of Excellence*, p. 19.

66. Peters, *Liberation Management*, p. xxix.

67. Carroll, Daniel T., "A disappointing search for excellence," *Harvard Business Review*, November/December 1983.

68. Peters & Waterman, *In Search of Excellence*, p. 19.

69. Peters, "Ten years later."

70. Farnham, Alan, "In search of suckers," *Fortune,* October 14, 1996.

71. Correspondence with author.

72. Farnham, "In search of suckers."

73. Drucker, Peter F., *The Frontiers of Management*, Heinemann, Oxford, 1987, p. 7.

74. Ibid., pp. 11–12.

75. Peters, Tom, *Thriving on Chaos*, Alfred A. Knopf, New York, 1987, p. 241.

76. Peters & Waterman, *In Search of Excellence*, p. 11.

77. Peters, *Liberation Management*, p. 488.

78. Peters & Waterman, *In Search of Excellence*, p. xv.

79. Ibid., p. 201.

80. Ibid., p. 321.

81. Ibid., p. 232.

82. Ibid., p. 12.

83. Ibid., p. 325.

84. Ibid., p. 26.

85. Ibid., p. 57.

86. Ibid., p. 110.

87. Ibid., p. 174.

88. Ibid., p. 106.

Three: Corporate Man

89. Peters, Tom, *Thriving on Chaos*, Alfred A. Knopf, New York, 1987, p. 497.

90. Kleiner, Art, *The Age of Heretics*, Doubleday, New York, 1996.

91. Huey, John, "How McKinsey does it," *Fortune*, November 1, 1993.

92. Peters, Tom, *Liberation Management*, Alfred A. Knopf, New York, 1992, p. 587.

93. Peters, Tom, "House painters and prozac," syndicated column, August 12, 1994.

94. Bevan, Judi, "The management show," *Sunday Telegraph*, June 12, 1994.
95. Peters, Tom, & Austin, Nancy, *A Passion for Excellence*, Harper-Collins, New York, 1985, p. xvii.
96. Peters, *Liberation Management*, p. 642.
97. Peters, Thomas J., & Waterman, Robert H., *In Search of Excellence*, Harper & Row, New York, 1982, p. xi.
98. Bevan, "The management show."
99. Ibid.
100. Ibid.
101. Peters, *Thriving on Chaos*, p. 497.
102. Peters, *Liberation Management*, p.8.
103. Bevan, "The management show."
104. Peters & Austin, *A Passion for Excellence*, p. 326.
105. Peters, Tom, "Who is this boss-person, anyway?" syndicated column, November 25, 1994.
106. Peters, Tom, *The Tom Peters Seminar*, Viking Books, New York, 1994, p. 110.
107. Robinson, Peter, *Snapshots from Hell*, Nicholas Brealey, London, 1995.
108. Correspondence with author.
109. Peters, *Liberation Management*, pp. 755–756.
110. Correspondence with author.
111. Correspondence with author.
112. Correspondence with author.
113. Correspondence with author.
114. Peters, Tom, "Just say no to US Memories," September 25, 1989.
115. Peters, *Liberation Management*, p. 107.
116. Peters, Tom, "Power," syndicated column, July 22, 1994.
117. Peters, *Liberation Management*, p. 628.
118. Huey, John, "How McKinsey does it," *Fortune*, November 1, 1993.
119. Quoted in "The firm walks tall," Francoise Hecht, *Eurobusiness*, February 1995.
120. Huey, "How McKinsey does it."
121. Peters, *Liberation Management*, p. 467.
122. Peters, Tom, "House painters and prozac," syndicated column, August 12, 1994.
123. Huey, "How McKinsey does it"
124. Francoise Hecht, "The firm walks tall."
125. Peters, "House painters and prozac."

126. Peters, Tom, "Pyramids and pebbles," syndicated column, February 25, 1994.
127. Peters, *Liberation Management*, p. 143.
128. Huey, "How McKinsey does it."
129. Peters, "Pyramids and pebbles."
130. Kleiner, *The Age of Heretics*.
131. Huey, "How McKinsey does it."
132. Peters, *Liberation Management*, pp. 755–756.
133. Peters, Tom, "The turnaround champs," syndicated column, March 5, 1993.
134. Quoted in "What investing in people really means," *Business Age*, May 1, 1994.

Four: Peters the Corporation

135. Peters, Thomas J. & Waterman, Robert H., *In Search of Excellence*, Harper & Row, New York, 1982, p. 79.
136. Peters, Tom, *Liberation Management*, Alfred A. Knopf, New York, 1992, p. 199.
137. Peters, Tom, & Austin, Nancy, *A Passion for Excellence,* Harper-Collins, New York, 1985, pp. xii–xiii.
138. Ibid., p. 421.
139. Peters, *Liberation Management*, p. 354.
140. *Business Age*, August 1, 1995
141. Peters, & Austin, *A Passion for Excellence*, p. 106.
142. Ibid., p. 39.
143. Ibid., p. 265.
144. Ibid., p. 4.
145. Ibid., p. 6.
146. Ibid., p. 271.
147. Ibid., p. xix.
148. Ibid., p. 141.
149. Ibid., p. 414.

Five: The Backlash

150. Peters, Tom, "The media as customer," syndicated column, June 17, 1994.
151. Correspondence with author.

152. Peters, Tom, "Lining up to come to America," syndicated column, June 25, 1993.

153. Peters, Tom, "Ten years later," syndicated column, September 3, 1992.

154. Peters, Thomas J. & Waterman, Robert H., *In Search of Excellence*, Harper & Row, New York, 1982, p. 25.

155. Reichheld, Fred, & Silverman, Jeremy, "In search of failure," Essay No. 3, Bain & Co., 1995.

156. Gertz, Dwight, & Baptista, Joao, *Grow to be Great*, Free Press, New York, 1995.

157. Pascale, Richard, *Managing on the Edge*, Viking, New York, 1990.

158. Peters, Tom, "When values become blinders," syndicated article, October 12, 1991.

159. Quoted in Kehoe, Louise, "Blue-eyed boy makes good," *Financial Times,* 12 April 1995.

160. Quoted in Kehoe, Louise, "Change while you are ahead," *Financial Times,* March 18, 1994.

161. Churchill, D.F. & Muzyka, D.F., "Entrpreneurial management: a converging theory for large and small enterprises," INSEAD Corporate Renewal Initiative Working Papers.

162. de Geus, A.P., "Planning as learning," *Harvard Business Review,* March/April 1988.

163. Peters, "Ten years later."

Six: The Guru Gravy Train

164. "In defence of the guru," *The Economist,* February 26, 1994.

165. Drucker, Peter F., *The Practice of Management*, Harper & Row, New York, 1954.

166. "Managing the public sector," *The Economist,* May 20, 1995.

167. Binney, George, & Williams, Colin, *Leaning into the Future,* Nicholas Brealey, London, 1995.

168. Peters, Tom, "A decade's worth of reflections," syndicated column, December 7, 1991.

169. "A continent without gurus," *The Economist,* June 4, 1994.

170. Correspondence with author.

171. White, Joseph B., "Dilbert's principle: business books sell," *The Wall Street Journal,* September 23, 1996.

172. Correspondence with author.

173. Peters, Tom, & Austin, Nancy, *A Passion for Excellence*, HarperCollins, New York, 1985, p. xi.

174. Micklethwait, John, & Wooldridge, Adrian, *Witch Doctors*, Heinemann, London, 1996.

175. "Take me to your leader," *The Economist*, December 25, 1993–January 7, 1994.

176. "A mess of parables," *The Economist*, December 5, 1992.

177. Correspondence with author.

178. Correspondence with author.

179. Peters, Tom, "Presentation secrets," syndicated column, July 12, 1991.

180. Peters, Tom, "I love retail!" syndicated column, February 18, 1994.

181. Correspondence with author.

182. Bevan, Judi, "The management show," *Sunday Telegraph*, June 12, 1994.

183. Peters, Tom, "Hey MBAs, follow your passion," syndicated column, November 23, 1991.

184. Quoted in Trapp, Roger, "Turning doers back into thinkers," *Independent on Sunday*, November 28, 1993.

185. Inman, Phillip, "Method over madness," *Business Age*, March 1996.

186. Baur, Chris, "Management evangelists in showbiz arena," *Sunday Times*, June 19, 1994.

187. "The good guru guide," *Business Age*, November 1, 1995.

188. Peters, Tom, "Hot times call for hot words," syndicated column, December 11, 1992.

189. Peters, Tom, *Liberation Management*, Alfred A. Knopf, New York, 1992, p. 758.

190. Farnham, Alan, "In search of suckers," *Fortune*, October 14, 1996.

191. "Tom Peters: Performance artist," *The Economist*, September 24, 1994.

192. Peters, Tom, "It's up to you," syndicated column, May 24, 1991.

193. Bevan, "The management show."

194. Peters, Tom, "The poetry of business," syndicated column, July 8, 1994.

195. "In defence of the guru," *The Economist*.

196. Correspondence with author.

197. "Tom Peters: Performance artist," *The Economist*.

198. Farnham, "In search of suckers."

199. Fulmer, Robert M. & Vicere, Albert A., *Crafting Competitiveness*, Capstone Publishing, Oxford, 1996.
200. Kellaway, Lucy, "The weird and crazy world of Tom Peters," *Financial Times*, May 23, 1994.
201. "Face value: Confessor to the boardroom," *The Economist*, February, 24 1996.

Seven: The Chaotic Revolution

202. Peters, Tom, *Thriving on Chaos*, Alfred A. Knopf, New York, 1987, p. 369.
203. Ibid., p. 3.
204. Peters, Tom, *Liberation Management*, Alfred A. Knopf, New York, 1992, p. xxix.
205. Peters, *Thriving on Chaos*, p. xi.
206. Ibid., p. 259.
207. Ibid., p. 4.
208. "Take me to your leader," *The Economist*, December 25, 1993–January 7, 1994.
209. Peters, *Thriving on Chaos*, p. 40.
210. Ibid., p. 98.
211. Ibid., p. 185.
212. Ibid., p. 356.
213. Ibid., p. 45.
214. Ibid., p. 275.
215. Ibid., p. 467.
216. Binney, George, & Williams, Colin, *Leaning into the Future*, Nicholas Brealey, London, 1995.
217. Peters, *Thriving on Chaos*, p. 418.
218. Ibid., p. 420.
219. Ibid., p. 352.
220. Ibid., p. 355.
221. Ibid., p. 391.

Eight: Liberating Management

222. Peters, Tom, "Fighting words," syndicated column, December 11, 1994.
223. Correspondence with author.

224. Correspondence with author.

225. Correspondence with author.

226. Peters, Tom, "Innovativeness – protoyping effectiveness," syndicated column, June 1, 1995.

227. Peters, Tom, "Bitten by the (Big R) Renewal bug," syndicated column, February 10, 1995.

228. Peters, "Fighting words."

229. Peters, Tom, "A decade's worth of reflection," syndicated column, December 7, 1991.

230. Peters, Tom, "Hot times call for hot words," syndicated column, December 11, 1992.

231. Peters, Tom, "The way the cookie crumbles," syndicated column, January 27, 1995.

232. Peters, Tom, "The American opportunity," syndicated column, March 27, 1992.

233. Peters, Tom, "Hey-heggggggggggggggggggggggg!, syndicated column, April 3, 1992.

234. Peters, "Bitten by the (Big R) Renewal bug."

235. Correspondence with author.

236. Correspondence with author.

237. Peters, Tom, "The relentless pursuit of the obvious," syndicated column, May 8, 1992.

238. Peters, Tom, *Liberation Management*, Alfred A. Knopf, New York, 1992, p. xxxii.

239. "Tom Peters: Performance artist," *The Economist*, September 24, 1994.

240. "A mess of parables," *The Economist*, December 5, 1992.

241. Peters, Tom, *Liberation Management*, Alfred A. Knopf, New York, p. 18.

242. Letter to Tom Peters, January 2, 1992.

243. Hamel, Gary, Foreword to Crainer, Stuart, *The Ultimate Business Library*, Capstone Publishing, Oxford, 1997.

244. Peters, *Liberation Management*, p. xxx.

245. Ibid., p. 11.

246. Ibid., p. xxx.

247. Chandler, Alfred D., *Strategy and Structure*, MIT Press, Boston, 1962

248. Peters, *Liberation Management*.

249. Quoted in Crainer, *The Ultimate Business Library*.

250. Correspondence with author.

251. Correspondence with author.

252. Peters, *Liberation Management.*
253. Ibid.
254. Ibid., p. xxx.
255. Ibid., p. 445.
256. Peters, Tom, "The age of talent," syndicated column, September 25, 1992.
257. Peters, Tom, "Oh, Canada!" syndicated column, June 6, 1992.
258. Seward, Andrew E., Review of *The Pursuit of Wow!* in *Fortune,* December 26, 1994.
259. Peters, Tom, *The Tom Peters Seminar,* Vintage Books, New York, 1994, p. 5.
260. Correspondence with author.

Nine: Uncle Tom's Cabin

261. Peters, Tom, "Napping your way to fame and fortune," syndicated column, July 25, 1992.
262. Correspondence with author.
263. Peters, Tom, "The legacies we leave," syndicated column, January 6, 1995.
264. Peters, Tom, "Divorce, 1990s style," syndicated column, August 6, 1992.
265. Correspondence with author.
266. Correspondence with author.
267. Correspondence with author.
268. Quoted in Cornwell, R., "The iconoclast at IBM," *Independent on Sunday,* August 1, 1993.
269. Quoted in Huey, J., "Eisner explains everything," *Fortune,* April 17, 1995.
270. Peters, Tom, "Out of the ordinary," syndicated column, July 23, 1993.
271. Peters, Tom, "It's up to you," syndicated column, May 24, 1991.
272. Bevan, Judi, "The management show," *Sunday Telegraph,* June 12, 1994.
273. Peters, Tom, Foreword to Bennis, Warren, *An Invented Life,* Addison-Wesley, Reading, MA, 1993.
274. Peters, Tom, "Spaces with spunk," syndicated column, October 8, 1993.
275. Correspondence with author.

276. Quoted in Jackson, T. & Gowers, A., "Big enough to make mistakes," *Financial Times*, December 21, 1995.

277. Correspondence with author.

278. Correspondence with author.

279. Peters, Tom, "A decade's worth of reflection," syndicated column, February 1, 1991.

Index